BRET EASTON ELLIS

American Psycho, Glamorama,
Lunar Park

Edited by Naomi Mandel

continuum

Continuum International Publishing Group
The Tower Building   80 Maiden Lane
11 York Road   Suite 704
London SE1 7NX   New York, NY 10038

www.continuumbooks.com

© Naomi Mandel 2011

British Library Cataloguing-in-Publication Data
A catalogue record for this book is available from the British Library.

ISBN: 978-0-8264-3562-0 (paperback)
ISBN: 978-0-8264-4648-0 (hardcover)

Library of Congress Cataloging-in-Publication Data
A catalog record for this book is available from the Library of Congress.

Typeset by Newgen Imaging Systems Pvt Ltd, Chennai, India
Printed and bound in India by Replika Press Pvt Ltd

Contents

Series Editor's Introduction

Each study in this series presents ten original essays by recognized subject specialists on the recent fiction of a significant author working in the United States or Canada. The aim of the series is to consider important novels published since 1990 either by established writers or by emerging talents. By setting 1990 as its general boundary, the series indicates its commitment to engaging with genuinely contemporary work, with the result that the series is often able to present the first detailed critical assessment of certain texts.

In respect of authors who have already been recognized as essential to the canon of North American fiction, the series provides experts in their work with the opportunity to consider their latest novels in the dual context of the contemporary era and as part of a long career. For authors who have emerged more recently, the series offers critics the chance to assess the work that has brought authors to prominence, exploring novels that have garnered acclaim both because of their individual merits and because they are exemplary in their creative engagement with a complex period.

Including both American and Canadian authors in the term "North American" is in no sense reductive: studies of Canadian writers in this series do not treat them as effectively American, and assessment of all the chosen authors in terms of their national and regional identity, as well as their race and ethnicity, gender and sexuality, religion and political affiliation is essential in developing an understanding of each author's particular contribution to the representation of contemporary North American society.

The studies in this series make outstanding new contributions to the analysis of current fiction by presenting critical essays chosen for their originality, insight, and skill. Each volume begins with a substantial introduction to the author by the study's editor, which establishes the context for the chapters that will follow through a discussion of essential elements such as the writer's career, characteristic narrative strategies, themes, and preoccupations, making clear the author's importance and the significance of the novels chosen for discussion. The studies are all comprised of three parts, each one presenting three original essays on three key recent works by the author, and every part is introduced by the volume's editor, explaining how the chapters to follow engage with the fiction and respond to existing interpretations. Each individual chapter takes a critical approach that may develop existing perceptions or challenge them, but always expands the ways in which the author's work may be read by offering a fresh approach.

It is a principle of the series that all the studies are written in a style that will be engaging and clear however complex the subject, with the aim of fostering further debate about the work of writers who all exemplify what is most exciting and valuable in contemporary North American fiction.

Sarah Graham

Acknowledgments

I would like to thank each of the contributors to this volume on Bret Easton Ellis for their inspiring and exciting work. It was a true privilege to collaborate with such enthusiastic, committed, and inventive scholars, many of whom I have yet to meet. Each taught me a great deal. Sarah Graham, the Series Editor, gave me the opportunity to edit this collection and remained my stalwart ally throughout the process. Anna Fleming and Colleen Coalter at Continuum Books have been consistently responsive and helpful.

My work on this volume was funded by a University of Rhode Island Career Enhancement Research Grant and supported by Winifred Brownell and Stephen Barber, to whom I owe special thanks. I am grateful to Dana Liljegren from the office of Amanda Urban for the information about translations of Ellis's work. Thanks also to my colleagues Mary Cappello and Jean Walton, who let me read them my "Introduction" on a cold night in Maine, and to Carolyn Betensky, Ryan Trimm, and especially fellow Ellis fan Alain-Philippe Durand. I am grateful to my students at University of Rhode Island for their courageous and imaginative engagement with Ellis's novels. I thank Marco Abel and László B. Sári for their inspiring work on Ellis, and John Hodgkins for his helpful suggestions about *The Informers* and for returning to me his copy of *Lunar Park*.

My mother, Miriam B. Mandel, directly contributed to this volume by sharing her extensive editorial experience and offering excellent advice. My father, Jerome Mandel, and my sister Jessica also sustained me throughout this project, helping me when possible and laughing at me when necessary. I thank my friends and fellow outliers Aaron Stern and Seth Yurdin for their understanding and support. I am grateful to Barry Wall for his wisdom and care. My final and most heartfelt thanks is to Erik Sklar, who missed many movies, fixed countless drinks, ate lots of takeout, and even read *American Psycho* and concluded that it is a very funny book.

Introduction: The Value and Values of Bret Easton Ellis

Naomi Mandel

This collection of critical essays on US novelist Bret Easton Ellis examines the novels of the author's mature period: *American Psycho* (1991), *Glamorama* (1998), and *Lunar Park* (2005). Though his earlier novels established Ellis's reputation as a popular writer and accomplished stylist, this collection treats *American Psycho* as his definitive work. A notable departure from Ellis's previous novels in size, scope, and ambition, *American Psycho* is easily one of the most controversial novels of the twentieth century. Its impact on contemporary literature and culture was seismic. This study pursues the shock waves of this impact into Ellis's subsequent work. The goals of the volume are to examine the alchemy of acclaim and disdain that accrues to this controversial writer, to direct critical attention to the literary and artistic significance of Ellis's recent work, and to confirm the increased scholarly interest in Ellis as evidenced by the prevalence of his novels on University syllabi in the US and abroad and in studies of contemporary literature and postmodernism.

Ellis is an important but underappreciated artist. His novels are greeted with equal portions of condemnation and praise. His books have been translated into 26 languages and are studied and taught throughout the world though he has yet to win a major literary award. But the tide is turning. His name appears with increasing frequency in recent scholarship on violence and representation, literature and ethics, writing and responsibility, globalization and terror. Critics within academia and outside it attest to Ellis's growing significance. Marco Abel, in a scholarly study of violence in film and literature, treats *American Psycho* as an opportunity to articulate crucial philosophical questions about judgment, representation, and critique (*Violent Affect*).

A.O. Scott of the *New York Times* considers *American Psycho* to be "one of the most misunderstood books in all of American literature" and describes *Glamorama* as a book that "in 100 years might be understood as a masterpiece" (qtd. in Tinberg). In an online review of *Lunar Park*, Steven Shaviro describes Ellis as "an extraordinarily *literary* and *writerly* writer," and adds, "few artists of any sort have gone as far as he has in exploring and reflecting upon our current post-literary, multimedia culture" ("Lunar Park"). The contributors to this collection participate in the current critical reevaluation of Ellis, exploring how his work has challenged and transformed contemporary literature in the US and abroad.

Bret Easton Ellis was born in Los Angeles in 1964 and rose to prominence with the critical and commercial success of his first novel *Less Than Zero* (1985). Set in Los Angeles, *Less Than Zero* recounts the lives of cynical, overprivileged young people (most barely out of high school). The novel established Ellis as a representative writer of his generation, alternately described as the Blank Generation or Generation X, and (with authors Tama Janowitz and Jay McInerney) a member of the literary "brat pack"—a group of young, photogenic authors characterized by seemingly infinite media presence, popularity, and marketability. Ellis's second novel, *The Rules of Attraction* (1987), which relocates its portrayal of affluent and jaded young people to a college in New Hampshire where they drink, do drugs, and exchange sexual partners with numbing frequency, was something of a critical and commercial disappointment. It was his third novel *American Psycho* that established Ellis as a central figure in contemporary US literature and culture. Set in Manhattan, *American Psycho* is narrated by Patrick Bateman, whose lifestyle is defined equally by conspicuous consumption and gruesome murders—both the consumption and the murders are rendered in excruciating, and chilling, detail.

The controversy surrounding *American Psycho*'s publication will be described below; for present purposes, what is most significant about the controversy is the extent to which it catapulted Ellis to the center of a media storm and elicited debates about violence, aesthetics, censorship, and ethics that echo to this day. In many ways, Ellis's subsequent work reflects on the implications of the controversy by thematizing, theorizing, and parodying issues as diverse as identity, memory, subjectivity, fame, the media, and knowledge. Thus, *Glamorama* follows the fortunes of Victor Ward, a character from *The Rules of Attraction*, whose relentless pursuit of celebrity in the 1990s takes him from New York to London, Paris, and Milan, while his carefully cultivated public persona is systematically deconstructed by a combination of terrorism, cinema, and fashion. *Lunar Park* centers on a partially fictionalized Bret Easton Ellis, whose wholly fictional suburban family life is threatened when a copycat killer, inspired by *American Psycho*, stalks Ellis and his family. Like *American Psycho*, *Glamorama* and *Lunar Park* have been violently reviled and vehemently acclaimed.

It is this violence and vehemence that make Ellis so intriguing. He has been hailed as timely and significant and dismissed as substanceless and derivative. He commands a cult following and critical attention. His books routinely top the bestsellers lists. His fictional characters live virtually on MySpace pages, websites, and blogs. A *New Yorker* profile of the author noted that a number of Ellis impersonators claim pages on Facebook, and described Ellis's difficulty registering for a Twitter account because several versions of his user name (accompanied by publicity shots) had already been appropriated. In scholarship on postmodernism, globalization, the posthuman, and ethics, Ellis is alternately hailed as an unacknowledged genius and dismissed as a flash in the pan; his works are combed for philosophical insights and evoked as cautionary tales. He is a moralist, an anarchist, a satirist, a bad writer, and a brilliant one. Clearly, this is an author about whom a great many people have plenty to say. For the scholars in this volume, the range of opinions and the intensity with which they are held are opportunities to investigate just what it is about this author that strikes so close to home. We are less interested in determining whether Ellis's books are "good" or "bad" than we are invested in uncovering what these novels, and the debates they occasion, can tell us about such issues as artistic merit, social commentary, publicity, the media, and Ellis himself.

Between Generation X and the Blank Generation

Bret Easton Ellis's first novel *Less Than Zero* was published with little media fanfare but became a runaway commercial success, quickly climbing to the top of the bestsellers lists and propelling its author into the position of celebrity and spokesperson for his generation—all before Ellis had graduated from Bennington College in Vermont. The novel's stripped-down, minimalist, and sparse style has been compared to Ernest Hemingway's, Raymond Carver's, and Joan Didion's; its iconic status has invited comparisons to J.D. Salinger's *The Catcher in the Rye*; its existential bleakness is reminiscent of European classics by Franz Kafka, Jean-Paul Sartre, and Albert Camus. But the novel is best understood in the context of the cultural moment in which it appeared. Alternately claimed as the spokesperson for Generation X and the Blank Generation, Ellis's early work straddles the two and comments on each. Setting the novel in its historical context sheds light on his later work and indicates the direction that the mature novels will take.

"Generation X" (or GenX) refers to people born in the 1960s who reached maturity in the 1980s. Unlike their parents (the baby boom generation) who grew up in the shadow of the Cold War and came of age in the turbulent Sixties, GenXers live in a world marked by the ascendency of the New Right which reached its peak with the election of Ronald Reagan to the US presidency in 1980. They are commonly derided as disaffected slackers, more attuned to the clamor of advertising than to the nuances of art, less likely to evince a strong moral code than to shrug and say "whatever." In his celebratory "Introduction" to *The GenX Reader*, Douglas Rushkoff lists some of the qualities commonly attributed to GenXers: "illiterate, unmotivated, and apathetic couch potatoes [who] have no career goals, no cultural pride, no political ideology, no family values, and no discernable ambitions" (3–4). Rushkoff identifies two central characteristics of Generation X. The first is the centrality of images, particularly from advertising, that function as the main language of the postmodern cultural landscape. GenXers view images not as transparent vehicles for meaning but as complex texts; their much reviled passive spectatorship is but a guise for sophisticated dissection and keen, if detached, analysis. "Exposed to consumerism and public relations strategies since we could open our eyes," writes Rushkoff, "we GenXers see through the clunky attempts to manipulate our opinions and assets . . . When we watch commercials, we ignore the products and instead deconstruct the marketing techniques" (5).

This cynical, ironic, hyper-literate spectatorship contributes to Generation X's much-commented-on disaffection—dropping out, or opting out, of culture and ideology—and leads us to its second characteristic: political and cultural apathy, a lack of commitment to the causes and agendas that characterized the Sixties. "Our parents were rebels of the sexual revolution and Vietnam War veterans, hippies now turned yuppies," writes Martine Delvaux; "we live through talk-shows, sit-coms and email, condoms, and anti-depressants" (171). Peter Sacks describes GenXers as "reacting viscerally to the notion of complexity" and "*proud* of their ignorance" (148–9). Delvaux, more sympathetic, describes GenXers as "engaged in a profound disengagement" (171). This disengagement manifests itself in some cases as apathy, and in others as tacit compliance to an unacceptable status quo: as Kathryn Hume puts it in her discussion of Ellis, McInerney, and Douglas Coupland (all authors associated with Generation X), "American culture is McDonald's and Nike, Microsoft and Armani, cellular phones and the World Wide Web. This is it, we live it, and they do not think we will find anything more worthwhile by looking further, looking backward, or trying to change" (281). For Hume these novelists, and their characters, "hardly celebrate this life, [but] they do not reject it in the name of some other values" (281).

Like the "X" in "Generation X," which simultaneously signals undefinability and negation, the "blank" of "Blank Generation" connotes absence and disaffection. But true to Richard Hell's punk anthem from which it takes its name, "Blank Generation" reverberates with the angst of a counterculture movement; it is informed by an ethos of resistance, however inarticulate or futile. Elisabeth Young and Graham Caveney in *Shopping in Space* appropriate Hell's phrase "blank generation" for the work of the New York literary scene in the 1980s. For Young and Caveney, the term links this literature to its origins in Punk and conveys the affectless or "stunned" quality of the writing (iii). James Annesley in *Blank Fictions* extends the term to US literature of the 1990s in which "there is an emphasis on the extreme, the marginal and the violent. . . . a sense of indifference and indolence . . . The limits of the human body seem indistinct, blurred by cosmetics, narcotics, disease and brutality" (1). Annesley approaches this fiction with an eye to its relationship with commodity culture and contemporary capitalism's relentless dialectic of articulation and co-option.

For Annesley, as for Young and Caveney, Robert Siegle's *Suburban Ambush* is an important resource for establishing blank fiction's origins in the 1970s and 1980s New York downtown scene. But Siegle's book, subtitled "the fiction of insurgency," contributes something else: it articulates the complex relationship between Punk's ethos of resistance to an unacceptable status quo, and the pervasive quality of late twentieth-century US material culture in which resistance can never be more than a fiction. As Siegle puts it, "[i]nsurgency is a 'fiction' in comparison with our metaphysically inspired liberationist politics, the utopian dream of liberation with full sensation" (3). By forcing together the urgency of resistance and the inevitability of its failure, and locating the very real effects of social, economic, and political reality in fiction, the literature of the Blank Generation—whose authors include David Wojnarowicz, Lynne Tillman, and Dennis Cooper, as well as Ellis—underscores the stakes of the violence, subversion, and extremism that characterize many texts in this genre, and of which *American Psycho* is the most vehement example.

Less Than Zero and *The Rules of Attraction*: Ellis's Early Work

Though Ellis insists that his novels are not autobiographical, Clay, the narrator of *Less Than Zero*, shares with the author some important similarities. Both were raised in the affluent suburbs of Los Angeles, both have two younger sisters, both are children of divorced parents, and both attend a small liberal arts college in New England. The novel is an account of Clay's return to Los Angeles for Christmas vacation, where he becomes reacquainted with his sometime girlfriend Blair, attends an interchangeable series of parties, consumes a wide range of narcotics, engages in passionless sex with members of both sexes, and discovers that his childhood friend Julian has become a prostitute to pay the debt incurred by his drug habit.

Less Than Zero is structured as a series of vignettes, all in first person, all in present tense, that circle around similar and repeated themes—parties, sex, drugs, television, clubs, driving—punctured by moments of extreme violence: a snuff film, a dead body in an alley, a young girl tied to a bedpost and gang-raped. Phrases like "people are afraid to merge," "wonder if he's for sale," and "Disappear Here" function as leitmotifs, accruing significance and menace with each recurrence. Two worlds—the world of limitless privilege and the chasm of utter despair—are kept in equilibrium through the point of view of the narrator Clay. Though his name connotes malleability and impressionability, and invites us to expect traditional teleological character development, Clay is primarily a spectator: a numbed and passive witness to the dysfunction, self-destruction, and alienation that pervade the lives of his family and friends and which reach a crux in his relationship with Julian. Toward the end of the novel, Clay participates in a sexual act involving Julian and a client; Clay's role is to watch: he is to see and hear "everything," a role he assumes willingly because, as he puts it, "I want to see the worst" (172).

Clay's attitude toward "the worst" is a combination of fascination and disgust which puts him in an ambiguous moral position. He is drawn to the gory parts of movies and pauses to watch a coyote die after being hit by a car. But he walks out of the snuff film and, when invited to participate in a rape, Clay refuses, stuttering "It's [. . .] It's . . . I don't think it's right"—the only recognizable moral code in the entire novel, and a notably inarticulate one. Clay's friend Rip responds to this tentative gesture toward morality with an assertion of power: "What's right? If you want something, you have the right to take it. If you want to do something, you have the right to do it" (189). As the negative moral code (Clay can only articulate morality by defining it as what it isn't) is countered with a discourse of self-determination and enfranchisement—"you have the right"—the conflation of power and morality in the dual definition of what's "right" effectively undercuts *any* moral position. As the Blank Generation knows so well, when power creates its own morality, there can be no moral agent to applaud goodness or condemn evil. Hence, while Clay functions as the focalizer for the action, his tendency to walk out of the room, to turn away, to "disappear here" undercuts any role he might play in critiquing the worldview of the other characters or the society of excess in which he lives. When Blair says to Clay in the final pages of the novel, "it was like you weren't there. . . . You were never there" (204), the ethos of disaffection so characteristic of Generation X articulates both existential despair *and* narrative technique.

Though Ellis's second book, *The Rules of Attraction*, was something of a critical and commercial flop, the novel's experimental form, which presages his more radical work in *American Psycho* and *Glamorama*, merits attention. Set in Camden College in New Hampshire, *The Rules of Attraction* is structured as a series of monologues by a wide range of characters, including Sean Bateman (whose brother Patrick is the main character in *American Psycho*), Victor (the narrator of *Glamorama*), Lauren Hynde (who also appears in *Glamorama*), and Clay, who is referred to by others as "that dude from LA" and granted a brief monologue. The narrative's decentered quality—within the polyphony of voices and points of view, there is no one with whom we can more or less identify and to whom we can look for hints as to the novelist's attitude toward the people and actions described— enhances the moral incoherence of the characters' world. If Clay's disgust and dismay in *Less Than Zero* enabled that novel to gesture toward some kind of social critique (even though that critique, as demonstrated above, is counterarticulate and futile), the multiple accounts that comprise *The Rules of Attraction* undercut even the possibility of such a gesture. The effect is not only moral incoherence but epistemic instability: Sean's relationship with Paul Denton, for example, is described in loving detail by Paul and explicitly denied by Sean. This instability will prove crucial for *American Psycho*, as the extent to which the horrifying violence in that book is merely fantasized by its narrator is ultimately unclear.

The Rules of Attraction provides, with *Less Than Zero*, important insight into what will make Ellis's later work so fertile a ground for critical dispute. The two books together establish a fictional world that is tantalizingly coherent and recognizable. Camden College in New Hampshire is a thinly disguised version of Bennington College in Vermont; characters from one novel appear in subsequent novels; characterization takes second place to style, as different people sound the same and are concerned with the same issues: sex, drugs, music, and their own ennui. Writing of the cast of characters that Ellis establishes in his early work, Julian Murphet notes that

[t]his ongoing elaboration of Ellis's fictional *milieu* is one of the keys to his ambitions as a writer . . . this insistence on the same

names, faces and above all the same language style, drives home
the point for his long-term readers that, fundamentally, nothing
changes from scale to scale. (14–15)

Like the recurring phrases in *Less Than Zero* ("people are afraid to
merge"; "Disappear Here"), "Clay," "Sean," "Lauren," and "Victor" refer
less to well-rounded characters than to the effect of repetition.
Individuality gives way to indifference, with crucial implications for
language and for identity—as Murphet points out, "the 'names' in
Ellis's work may or may not refer to the 'same' characters" (15). This
aspect of Ellis's writing will become crucial in *American Psycho*,
in which people are constantly mistaken for each other and are
treated as fundamentally interchangeable, and in *Glamorama*, in
which individuality is constructed and deconstructed by media.
With *Lunar Park*, Ellis joins his own cast of characters: a final, and
most radical extension of this fictional world into our own.

American Psycho: The Controversy

On July 15, 1987, Ellis wrote a note to his literary agent describing his
newest project:

> The new novel is tenatively [sic] titled "American Psycho" and
> it follows in the course of a year, its narrator, Patrick Bateman,
> a twenty-six year old investment banker who leads the quintes-
> sential yuppie Manhattan existence, haunting the nightclubs,
> healthclubs, restaurants, bars. On the face of it Patrick Bateman
> (good-looking, successful, well-off) seems fairly normal, even
> boring. But he starts killing people. ("Note")

So bland an account gives no hint of the book's graphic violence or of its
ambitious social critique. The excessive quality of the former, and the
elusive nature of the latter, played a central role in the controversy that
was ignited when sections of the book were leaked to the press and
published in *Spy* and *Time* magazine. The book—for which Ellis's publisher Simon & Schuster had laid out a reported six-figure advance—
was in the final stages of production: in addition to the advance, the
press had invested a significant amount of money and labor in the form
of editorial work, proofreading, text design, advertising, typesetting,
and printing. In light of the growing controversy and fearing negative
publicity, Simon & Schuster cancelled publication in a breach of contract,
forgoing the advance already paid to Ellis and forfeiting the editorial,
marketing, and production labor already invested in the book. Within

48 hours another publisher, Knopf (a subsidiary of Random House), rightly wagering that the controversy would boost sales, purchased the manuscript and speedily published it in March of 1991.

The publication of *American Psycho* by Knopf elicited outcry from activists who argued that the book's violence against women reinforces long-standing problems of assault and abuse, and who noted that in the press' cynical move to capitalize on the growing controversy, misogyny is proved, once again, not only legitimate but profitable. Tammy Bruce, then president of the Los Angeles chapter of National Organization of Women (NOW), called for a boycott of Knopf because of their decision to purchase and publish the book. Bruce allegedly described the novel as a "how-to book on the torture and dismemberment of women" and argued that "the publication of *American Psycho* is socially irresponsible and legitimates inhuman and savage violence masquerading as sexuality" (qtd. in Freccero 50). Artists and intellectuals responded to both the publication and to the boycott with concern about corporate censorship and its effects on artistic integrity and free speech, pointing out that the decision to publish or not publish the book was made by corporations and dictated by profit margins, not literary merit. In each case, the book's *value* was very much at stake: literally—its value in the marketplace and its value to its author, who benefited from a significant advance from Knopf in addition to the one forfeited by Simon & Schuster—and figuratively, as the sexism, racism, selfishness, and narcissism in the book were attributed to its author and treated as uncritical expressions of Ellis's own values (or lack thereof). Murphet accurately characterizes the discourse as "sub-intellectual . . . revolv[ing] around the speculation that Ellis was evidently a warped and deranged individual, bleating his masturbatory fantasies unto the page for his own self-aggrandizement" (71). More sophisticated assessments of the novel's artistry were offered by Norman Mailer and Christopher Lehmann-Haupt: both concluded that the novel does not rise to the moral challenge posed by the extensive violence it depicts.

Of course, the assumption that depictions of violence pose a moral challenge of any sort assumes the existence of stable moral categories and misses a fundamental quality of Generation X: an aversion to preestablished systems of thought, ideals, or "isms." And the attitude that the publication of *American Psycho* must be met with resistance—to corporate censorship or to Knopf—ignores the predicament of Blank Generation fiction: there is no outside, no definable enemy to conquer or resist. Tellingly, both the anticensorship and the pro-boycott groups appropriated the antidrug slogan "just say no" (developed by Nancy Reagan and in wide use during the 1980s and 90s) to articulate their take on the *American Psycho* controversy. Robert Brannon concludes his defense of the boycott by stating: "We must try to do something about the growing popularity and legitimacy of violence against women—to work together to stop it. . . . Let's just say 'NO' to Knopf" (244). John Irving, pointing out that the boycott is itself a form of censorship, reminds readers of Reagan's slogan and applies it to the controversy: "writers and other members of the literary community *should* just say no to censorship in any and every form" (25). But in a society characterized by complicity and co-option, "just say no" is an empty gesture. In *American Psycho*, Patrick's secretary Jean asks him how she should respond to invitations from Ted Madison and James Baker to meet at "Fluties," and Patrick's instructions parody the slogan:

> "Jean." I stand up to lead her out of the office. "What . . . do . . . you . . . say?"
>
> It takes her a little while but finally, frightened, she guesses, "Just . . . say . . . no?"
>
> "Just . . . say . . . no." I nod, pushing her out and slamming the door. (106)

Patrick's reference to the antidrug slogan is especially ironic because he is "hung over from a coke binge" (105). His and Jean's repetition of "just say no" underscores the extent to which resistance as such has been co-opted; emptied of its political and moral content, it circulates in the most banal of contexts. The appropriation of the slogan by both sides of the controversy only underscores the irrelevance of resistance and reflects the evacuation, recirculation, and commodification that characterize not only the world in which the book is set but the language in which it is written. This relentless dialectic of co-option, and the challenge it poses to ethics, extends from the book to its author: as Ellis puts it, "The things that are accepted in popular culture constantly shock me. But then I'm stuck in this position: What do you do when you're part of it?" (Love 51).

After *Psycho*: Ellis's Mature Work

Elisabeth Young has characterized the trajectory of Ellis's early novels as "a search-and-destroy mission" (93). She notes how, as Ellis moves from one setting to another, each novel comments on its predecessor, undercutting and devaluing what the previous novel had posited, however tentatively, as salvation. "In *Less Than Zero* the otherness of the text, the *hope* of the text, lay on the East Coast, in college education, all of which was systematically destroyed and revealed as depthless and banal in *The Rules of Attraction*"; in the first chapter of *American*

Psycho, she continues, Ellis is saying "goodbye to college life, to bohemian life" and the novel "moves us deliberately into his previously signalled other, the adult, world" (93–4). Young, who wrote before the publication of *Glamorama*, could not foresee the turn this trajectory would take: *Glamorama* attacks the very celebrity, fame, and notoriety that accrued to Ellis in the course of the *American Psycho* controversy; *Lunar Park*, which turns further inward, toward "Bret Easton Ellis" himself, reframes Young's "search-and-destroy mission" as a suicide attack.

In 1994, Ellis published a fourth book, *The Informers*. Ellis has described *The Informers* as material he had been working on since 1983 which he sent to Knopf to make good on a deadline while he continued to work on *Glamorama* (Amerika and Laurence). While the book does seem to hark back to Ellis's early period (it reads like a series of five-finger exercises in alienation and disillusion), *The Informers* contributes to the "search and destroy" trajectory Young describes by undercutting the formal qualities of Ellis's previous novels which, however fragmentary and experimental, ultimately adhered to classical unities. *The Informers* possesses no unity of action: alternately described as a collection of short stories and as a novel, it consists of a series of monologues with discernable connections between some but not all of the characters. In its treatment of time, *The Informers* also differs from Ellis's earlier works, each of which was delimited by a specific, definite period (Christmas break in *Less Than Zero*, the academic year in *The Rules of Attraction*; roughly a calendar year in *American Psycho*). Finally, each of Ellis's previous novels was set in a single, distinctive locale (Los Angeles; New England; New York City), while *The Informers*, which ranges from Los Angeles to Tokyo, anticipates the international scope of *Glamorama*.

Glamorama, the first major novel Ellis published after *American Psycho*, shares with that work a number of important features: an obsessive listing of brand names, a cast of rich and famous people, and a flirtation with epistemic instability. If, in *American Psycho*, the reader is ultimately unsure whether Patrick fantasized some, or all, or none of the violent murders he describes himself committing, *Glamorama* extends this unreliability from specific events in the novel to the narrative point of view that ranges from limited first person to omniscient. Victor, the protagonist and occasional narrator, is by turn clued-in and clueless; he is alternately the star of a film, an extra, a witness, a secret agent, a double agent, or the target of relentless media scrutiny and a nebulous terror plot. Like photographs in the text, which are constantly being digitally altered, references to scripts, extras, and props blur boundaries between what is real and what is fake: a terror attack on the Paris métro leaves "body parts—legs and arms and hands, *most of them real*—skidding across the platform" (364, emphasis mine). At the same time, the fantastic and the surreal elements that haunted *American Psycho* (in which a Cheerio is interviewed on a talk show and a park bench follows Patrick for a couple of blocks) also appear in *Glamorama*, where mermaids are sighted, flies buzz in freezing rooms, and confetti is inexplicably omnipresent.

Glamorama also shares with *American Psycho* the explicit and horrifying images of violence that have—perhaps unfairly—become associated with Ellis and his work. But violence, and its relation to style, form, and theme, functions differently in each novel. If *American Psycho*'s aesthetic credo is best captured in Patrick's lament, "Surface, surface, surface, was all that anyone found meaning in" (375), *Glamorama* is motivated by Victor's declaration: "in is out. Out is in" (17). Thus, in *American Psycho* Patrick penetrates the bodies of his victims—not only with his penis, but by cutting, slicing, drilling, biting, and (in a notorious scene) with a hungry rat; in *Glamorama*, violence erupts outward: buildings, aircraft, and people explode. *American Psycho* notes the shallow quality of image-obsessed culture; surface and the superficial are dissected and cuttingly critiqued. In *Glamorama*, flesh, blood, and viscera carpet city streets and computer screens; surfaces are permeable (poison is a popular weapon), malleable (images are digitally altered), and, ultimately, indistinguishable from depth: the "specks" that obsess Victor in the opening pages of the book, specks that look artificial but that grow, glow, and multiply, morph into the "real" stars in the mural behind a hotel bar in the final chapter.

After the terror attacks of 9/11, which have been widely described in terms of the merging of real violence and media spectacle, *Glamorama*'s approach to terror as orchestrated spectacle, and to spectacle (film, fashion, the party scene) as orchestrated terror, is uncannily prescient: "The shock, the sirens, a hundred wounded—it's all so familiar" (*Glamorama* 349). This uneasy straddling of the past and the present, the familiar and the strange, characterizes Ellis's 2005 novel *Lunar Park*. The novel is a ghost story in the style of Stephen King's early work, and its narrator is and is not Bret Easton Ellis. Its setting is in affluent suburbs like those of Ellis's childhood to which the narrator, Bret, and his wife Jayne relocate in the wake of the attacks on the World Trade Center and the Pentagon (Ellis continues to split his time between Los Angeles and New York City). Bret's marriage to Jayne represents an attempt to escape from a surreal world in which "suicide bombers were blowing themselves up in crowded Burger Kings and Starbuckses and Wal-Marts and in subways at rush hour" (27), and to live a wholesome family life with bedtime stories read on CD-ROM and children dosed with a range of "stimulants, mood stabilizers, the antidepressant Lexapro [. . .]

Adderall for attention-deficit/hyperactivity disorder and various other anticonvulsants and antipsychotics" (28).

Lunar Park's epistemic instability (a trait it shares with *American Psycho* and *Glamorama*) extends from the novel's relationship with its status as fiction to the plot, many elements of which are disbelieved or disavowed by other characters. Its violence (also a facet of Ellis's previous work) is characterized by replication (murders are reenactments of *American Psycho*'s gory scenes) and mutation: not only does Bret find himself "changing" as a result of this "vaguely unreal" life (29), the house in which he lives with his family morphs into the house where Bret, and Ellis, grew up. An ugly doll (originally a prop from a horror movie) is also occasionally a fanged, clawing, flapping nightmare that attacks Bret and the children. Victor, a character from *The Rules of Attraction* and the narrator of *Glamorama*, appears here as the family dog, and further mutates into a lupine-faced winged thing. In its emphasis on replication and mutation, *Lunar Park*'s violence reflects its themes: Ellis's relationship with his father, Bret's uneasy role as both father and son, and the novelist's relationship with his own unruly body of work (both published and unpublished)—a convergence of legacies gone awry. Ellis's forthcoming novel *Imperial Bedrooms* (due to be released in Summer 2010) further builds on this idea of a legacy that is haunted and haunting: Ellis has described it as a sequel to *Less Than Zero*—both novels take their titles from Elvis Costello's work—commenting ruefully, "The past haunts" (Toal).

The Value of Bret Easton Ellis

For a novelist who, as critics and reviewers like to remind us, has established his reputation on "less than zero," the question of value is real and pressing. Did this author, whose literary debut promised a meteoric career, fizzle into opportunism, sensationalism, self-indulgence? Some critics and reviewers have insisted that each of Ellis's novels is progressively worse than the first; others claim that Ellis's achievement in *American Psycho* marked the apex (still others the nadir) of his career. But as the controversy around that book made clear, and as the billing of *Imperial Bedrooms* as a sequel to *Less Than Zero* promises, negativity generates interest in every sense of the word and can, it seems, appreciate in value.

Ellis's work teaches us that literary values, like monetary and moral ones, merit interrogation and demand, at times, revision. Whether or not the author, or his novels, are traditionally "good" or "bad" may not be the most interesting, important, or relevant question to ask. Generation X uncovered and undercut the investments (emotional, political, and economic) of its predecessors; the Blank Generation challenged the assumption that the object of critique can be distinguished from its critic and in doing so subverted the very concept of critique. Confronted with such formidable dissolutions, literary criticism finds itself in uncharted territory and on unstable ground. The scholars in this volume trace Ellis's patterns of flight away from the comfortable, the familiar, the recognizable, the real. It is difficult work, but remember: "No one said being a Bret Easton Ellis fan was easy" (*Lunar Park* 21).

PART I

American Psycho

Introduction

"What's left to say about *American Psycho* that hasn't already been said?" writes Ellis in *Lunar Park* (12). And yet, the hysteria and vehemence that characterized the reception of that novel—a phenomenon in itself—did give way to more sober assessments and analyses. Though some of this work (Tighe's, Tanner's) retained the tenor of censure that characterized the controversy, for other scholars the novel and the debate it engendered was an opportunity to examine the nature of censure (Abel, *Violent Affect*) and its manifestation as censorship (Hutchings, Eberly, Kauffman). Part of this work involved situating *American Psycho* within broader cultural and literary trends of the 1980s. For Freccero and Gomel (*Bloodscripts*), these included the fascination with serial killers that was reflected in the sensationalist coverage of mass murderers Jeffrey Dahmer and Ted Bundy and in the popularity of films like *The Silence of the Lambs*. For Annesley (*Blank Fictions*), Messier, and Baelo-Allué ("Serial Murder"), the novel's alignment of mass murder with serial consumption served as an indictment of the excesses of capitalism in Reagan's America. Other critics (Helyer, Story, Schoene) read *American Psycho* as a fundamentally postmodern novel in which existing literary traditions and subject formations are parodied. In the course of this work, Ellis's novel has been compared with the work of the Marquis de Sade and Leopold von Sacher-Masoch (Mandel), Emile Zola (Schneider), and Scottish poet and novelist James Hogg (Cojocaru).

Each of the three chapters in this part is in dialogue with this critical tradition. Michael Clark's "Violence, Ethics, and the Rhetoric of

Decorum in *American Psycho*" revisits the tendency to condemn Ellis's novel by examining how censure is elicited and eluded in the text. With "The Soul of this Man is his Clothes," Elana Gomel counters *American Psycho*'s reliance on the serial killer narrative and the detective story by identifying Patrick Bateman as a version of the *fin de siècle* figure of the dandy. For Alex Blazer in "*American Psycho, Hamlet*, and Existential Psychosis" the myth of Oedipus, Shakespeare's *Hamlet*, and Ellis's own oeuvre join the literary context within which the novel figures. To make their arguments, the chapters draw on very different interpretive frameworks. Clark situates the novel within a tradition of decorum, tracing the concept from antiquity through Renaissance and Neoclassical theories of poetry and poetics to contemporary work on art's relation to its readers and to the world. Blazer works with Freud's and Lacan's theories of psychic formation, the Oedipus complex, and the function of language and of law. For Gomel, who ranges from narrative and genre theory to contemporary work on fashion, *American Psycho*'s unlikely interlocutors are Henry James's *The Turn of the Screw* and Oscar Wilde's *The Picture of Dorian Gray*.

As the chapters in this part enter into the tradition of literary criticism around the novel, they also confront the unique problems that *American Psycho* poses to literature and to criticism. This is a book, after all, that challenges the very foundation of critique, and that (as its detractors insist) has but a tenuous claim to be a work of art. The extreme violence of the text cannot be dismissed, but the possibility that the violence in the novel may be hallucinated by its protagonist blurs the line between fact and fantasy, leaving the reader unsure whether, by registering the violence, she is affirming reality or departing from it. The text urges us to judge, discriminate, and make distinctions, but because the novel does not offer its reader any ground from which to distance herself from the point of view of its protagonist, and no position from which to condemn his violent actions, the critic must work without the comfort of established conceptual, moral, or epistemological grounds.

The three chapters in this part offer a variety of approaches to this dilemma. For Clark, decorum regulates how a reader or viewer evaluates or judges a representation of the world, work that relies on an existing set of standards and values, including, crucially, the stability of language and its function as a medium of signification and communication. Given the absence of such values in the postmodern era, rhetorical relations between speakers and listeners establish and maintain a social bond that approximates this work, generating sociality, coherence, and ethical responsibility. Patrick's attempts to provoke a response from those around him—he repeatedly identifies himself as a psychopath and confesses his crimes to a number of people in the novel—appeal to this bond, and the failure of other characters to judge, condemn, or even recognize him testify to its absence. The novel stresses the importance of response in a world devoid of response-ability, and the ethical charge falls to the reader, who is enjoined not to condemn or judge Patrick but simply to respond to his address.

For Blazer, the father—his law, his power, his ability to dictate, control, and socialize—offers a crucial standard not only for human behavior but for language, and the absence of a father manifests, in the novel, as the deterioration of reference and realism that traps Patrick in a delusional world in which neither sign nor symbol offer the order or meaning he craves. Blazer's psychoanalytical approach departs from the general tendency to treat Ellis's characters as effects of narration rather than as fictional personalities with emotional complexity, personal history, and depth. In doing so, his reading grants *American Psycho*'s narrator a degree of humanity that puts Patrick in the company of that paradigm of humanism, Hamlet. Both wrestle with dead or absent fathers, and for both the dictate to murder the father (Oedipus) and to obey his commands (Hamlet) battle for primacy in the son's psyche. Thus, concludes Blazer, Patrick confronts an existential abyss similar to Hamlet's, but without the stability of language and law, his existentialism takes the form of psychosis.

Gomel, like Clark and Blazer, focuses on the necessity of stable criteria for judgment. For Gomel, Patrick's profound unreliability leaves the novel's reader, like the reader of *The Turn of the Screw*, unable to determine which of the events is real; at the same time, the novel's intertextual relationship with *The Picture of Dorian Gray* underscores the temptation to view violence as a way to break through the artificiality of the image. Patrick, Gomel argues, is a failed dandy whose violence represents an attempt to counter his artificial, superficial, fashion-obsessed world with the unmistakable reality of the body. But since we can never determine whether the murders are real or fantasized, the truth of the text perpetually evades the reader, and fashion—in the form of the coded vocabulary of brand names—is the only stable referent within the novel's narrative, generic, and representational unruliness. Ironically, its rigid dictates offer the sole source of human recognition and social responsibility in the novel.

Each of these chapters, then, is concerned with epistemic stability (or its absence) in the ultraviolent world the novel presents, and with the possibility—however elusive—of ethics, recognition, and responsibility within this world or toward it. Ellis's next novel *Glamorama* will push these issues further, offering a world permeated by its representation in which neither torn body parts nor the shock they elicit can permeate the "surface surface surface" of the contemporary scene.

CHAPTER 1

Violence, Ethics, and the Rhetoric of Decorum in *American Psycho*

Michael P. Clark

Described by one critic as "one of the most shockingly violent novels ever published" (Baldwin 36), *American Psycho* challenges the limits of acceptable discourse and flaunts its disregard for ordinary standards of decency and taste. "Taste" in the form of designer clothes and Zagat-rated restaurants is the primary value and consuming obsession of Patrick Bateman, the narrator of the novel and perpetrator of the most heinous acts described in the book. As the principal source of his identity and self-respect, taste is defended by Patrick zealously. He ruthlessly criticizes the dress and manners of his friends, and he takes any criticism of his own taste as a personal attack that demands retribution. When Bethany, a friend from Harvard, visits Patrick's apartment and giggles that he has hung a painting upside down, he tells us that he picks up a nail gun and attacks her viciously. His account of the attack concludes with a passage that exemplifies the extreme language that some critics have denounced as an act of violence in itself for its brutal effect on the reader:

> I take advantage of her helpless state and, removing my gloves, force her mouth open and with the scissors cut out her tongue, which I pull easily from her mouth and hold in the palm of my hand, warm and still bleeding, seeming so much smaller than in her mouth, and I throw it against the wall, where it sticks for a moment, leaving a stain, before falling to the floor with a tiny wet slap. Blood gushes out of her mouth and I have to hold her head up so she won't choke. Then I fuck her in the mouth, and after I've ejaculated and pulled out, I Mace her some more. (246)

Faced with that passage and others like it, some readers have declared *American Psycho* to be obscene and as immoral as the acts it describes. They have gone so far as to argue that the novel must be condemned, banned, and even avenged, either by boycotting its publisher, "snuffing" the book (Rosenblatt), or doing away with the man who wrote it (Baxter and Craft). In striking contrast to those arguments, other critics have praised *American Psycho* as a satire of 1980s America. They interpret the violent scenes as fantasies of the protagonist's psychosis, which James Annesley describes in *Blank Fictions* as "the natural product of a society in which rampant consumerism intersects with the hyperreality of a media society" (19). Annesley goes on to defend Ellis for "trying to arouse moral indignation and inspire a critical response to contemporary capitalism and media institutions," though he concludes that the graphic violence of Ellis's novel undermines that objective because it "mimics the very processes he is criticising" (20–21).

As this radical divergence of critical opinion suggests, the status of *American Psycho* as a work of art depends on a distinction between the vile actions described in the narrative and the description of those actions as an act of narration or *récit*. Even for readers with the most anti-establishment sympathies and transgressive sensibilities, however, passages such as the one quoted above are so repellant, so extreme in their diction, so graphic in their portrayal of violence, and so deliberately provocative that they tend to render that aesthetic distinction beside the point, even twee. It is therefore useful to consider this debate in light of a concept that has a long and distinguished history in literary theory: the standard of decorum. Today, decorum is most often understood as a minimal standard of social behavior similar to good manners or propriety. Ellis explicitly invokes that standard in the epigraph from Miss Manners that opens *American Psycho*, where she says "One of the major mistakes people make is that they think manners are only the expression of happy ideas. There's a whole range of behavior that can be expressed in a mannerly way. That's what civilization is all about" (Ellis n.p.). It is unlikely, of course, that the range of behavior Miss Manners had in mind extended to Patrick's rages, and in the hands of Ellis's most vehement critics, decorum has been reduced to issues of "taste" and "decency" as those terms are used to regulate discourse and the circulation of images considered obscene. Nevertheless, the association of manners, expression, and civilization in this epigraph suggests a more nuanced concept of decorum than can be found in the denunciations of Ellis's work, and a brief consideration of the theoretical roots of that concept can help us understand the significance of *American Psycho* as a work of art and can explain why the novel has generated such strong and divergent responses from its readers.

Decorum and the Ethics of Representation

The concept of decorum is most often traced to the Roman poet Horace, who claimed that the job of the poet was to teach and delight through an exact imitation of nature that was coherent, plausible, and pleasing to readers' aesthetic sensibilities as well as compatible with their moral, social, and even political standards. When the doctrine of decorum was revived by the European Neoclassicists in the seventeenth century, this mimetic standard had hardened into the concept of verisimilitude. Pierre Corneille, for example, argued that the time and space occupied by a play on the stage must correspond exactly to the time and space required for the actions it represented because the audience's response to actions on the stage was the same as it would be to actions in the world. In that sense, moral and aesthetic judgments were the same. Represented actions led to real responses.

It is just such a naive realism that drives some critics of *American Psycho* to equate the effect of representations of violence on readers with the effect of actual violence on victims in the world. The problem with such claims, however, was noted by Sir Philip Sidney almost one hundred years before Corneille. Even a child, Sidney says, knows that he is not in Thebes when he goes into a theater and sees "Thebes" written on the stage (103). That conundrum led British Neoclassicist John Dryden to describe decorum as the product of a rhetorical relation to the audience that depends on the *difference* between words and the actions they represent, rather than on an exact correspondence between the work and the world. Dryden makes this point in his "Essay of Dramatick Poesie," which is presented as a dialogue among four friends who have rowed out in the Thames to listen to a battle between the English and Dutch navies. The character Lisideius laments the spate of wretched war poetry and tragic drama that will surely follow an English victory because such work

> renders our Stage too like the Theaters where they fight for Prizes. For what is more ridiculous than [. . .] to see a Duel fought, and one slain with two or three thrusts of the foyles, which we know are so blunted, that we might give a man an hour to kill another in good earnest with them?
> I have observ'd that in all our Tragedies, the Audience cannot forbear laughing when the Actors are to die; 'tis the most Comick

part of the whole Play. [. . .] there are many *actions* which can
never be imitated to a just height: dying especially is a thing which
none but a *Roman Gladiator* could naturally perform on the Stage,
when he did not imitate or represent, but do it; and therefore it is
better to omit the representation of it.

[. . .] When we see death represented, we are convinc'd it is but
Fiction; but when we hear it related, [. . .] we are all willing to
favour the sleight when the Poet does not too grossly impose on
us. (39–40)

Lisideius then invokes Horace's warning—"Medea shouldn't kill her
sons before the audience / or evil Atreus cook human guts in public
view / [. . .] Anything like that you show me I'll disbelieve and hate"—
and explains: "those actions which by reason of their cruelty will cause
aversion in us, or by reason of their impossibility unbelief, ought
either wholly to be avoided by a Poet, or only deliver'd by narration"
(Horace ll. 185–88; Dryden 41).

For Dryden, the audience's response to the play is thus determined
by the way the work positions the audience rhetorically in relation
to the action being imitated. Confronted with the immediate visual
display of an action, the audience will normally judge the work morally
as if it were the world, and that judgment has the effect of disengaging
the audience from the play. On the other hand, reading or hearing
the verbal description of an action in narration foregrounds the
differentiation between the world and the words that represent it. That
difference preserves decorum and demands the audience's attention
by mediating the action through the rhetorical structure of a speaker
(either character or playwright) addressing a listener or reader. The
bond established in this narration of the action transcends the representational limits of illusions on the stage and situates the play and the
audience in history and the world beyond the theater. In Dryden's essay,
that situation is manifest in the clash of the naval battle that echoes
behind Lisideius's claim that representation reaches its limit in scenes of
extreme violence and death.

This more complex understanding of decorum can shed light on
the significance of *American Psycho* as a work of art. Rather than
simply reflecting the empty mores of a consumerist society, Ellis
uses descriptions of extreme violence to mark the limit of representation and so establish a relation with readers that can serve as the basis
for ethical responses that would otherwise be impossible in a world
lacking any transcendent standard or shared set of values. The absence
of such standards is painfully evident in the world of Ellis's novel, and
it is characteristic more generally of what Jean-François Lyotard

has described as the "postmodern condition" of contemporary society (*Postmodern Condition*). In that condition, Lyotard argues, society depends on a purely rhetorical relation between speakers and listeners (or writers and readers) to provide the basis for ethical response and just action (*Just Gaming*). That relation closely resembles what Kenneth Burke called the "rhetoric of address," that is, the rhetorical connection that is constituted when someone addresses another person in speech, writing, or performance. "Such considerations," Burke says, "make us alert to the ingredient of rhetoric in all *socialization*, considered as a *moralizing* process" (39). For Lyotard, the socialization inherent in the rhetoric of address takes the form of an ethical obligation to reply to the address that constitutes a social bond, which in turn makes possible and indeed demands a response in the absence of moral absolutes, individual "character," or meaning itself. The importance of *American Psycho* lies in Ellis's daring dramatization of that obligation at the limit of representation.

The limits of representation in *American Psycho* are evident in Patrick's accounts of violence when he confuses words and images (signifiers) with what they represent or signify (signifieds). That confusion makes true signification or communication impossible. It creates in place of signification an illusion of immediacy and presence— Corneille's verisimilitude—that precludes social interaction with others, isolating Patrick and making ethical responses impossible. Like a clumsy playwright staging an unconvincing death scene, Patrick flaunts signs of his crimes in hopes of provoking a response that will relieve his isolation, but those violations of decorum only succeed in confusing Patrick's audience when they pay attention to him at all. What limited character development or plot there is in the novel focuses on Patrick's increasing frustration over the failure of such efforts, especially as they involve direct confession and the flagrant display of evidence from the violent acts he describes.

Understood rhetorically in light of Dryden's theory of decorum, Patrick's frustration may be read as the effect of a utopian impulse toward engagement with others that is realized in the rhetorical connection Patrick's act of narration establishes with the reader. Within the story that Patrick tells, characters are isolated from one another by the words and images that separate Patrick from the world and even from himself. The impulse to engage with others in any form is manifest only as momentary disruptions in Patrick's illusion of autonomy, power, and authority. As Ellis presses the representational limits of Patrick's displays of violence, however, depictions of violent acts that would merely repulse us if we encountered them in the world lead to a recognition of the reader's place in relation to the act of description and, more generally, the *récit* itself. That recognition evokes the obligation to reply that under-lies the social bond and therefore makes possible a genuinely ethical response to *American Psycho* by positioning readers as subjects respon-sive to, and so responsible for, others through the rhetoric of address.

"surface, surface, surface"

The lack of depth or meaning is the most readily identifiable motif in *American Psycho*. That lack is most obvious in the characters' com-pulsive recitations of brand names and designer labels, shibboleths of superficiality and the empty values of excessive consumerism, and in the reduction of their identities to their corporate roles and even, at one point, to the card-stock on which their business cards are printed (44). The dislocation of words from any stable base of meaning or significance is evident in the opening lines of the book. As many critics have noted, *American Psycho* begins with an allusion to Dante's words over the gates of Hell in the *Inferno*, "ABANDON ALL HOPE YE WHO ENTER HERE" (3); but instead of directing us to their context in Dante's work as a literary citation, here the words are plastered as graffiti on the side of Chemical Bank. Timothy Price notices them as he is passing by in a cab, but before he has time to reflect on their meaning a bus bearing a large poster for *Les Misérables* blocks his view—and ours. Similarly, in the next par-agraph the word "FEAR" appears "sprayed in red graffiti on the side of a McDonald's" (3), but just as Timothy's cab passes the word his view is blocked again by another bus with a similar poster, though this one has been defaced by the word "DYKE" scrawled across the face of Eponine, one of the characters in the play (3–4). Timothy is talking to his friend Patrick Bateman and idly counting the homeless people he sees from his cab when a third advertisement for the play distracts him again. He turns away from the bums and idly asks Patrick, " 'Did you read about the host from that game show on TV? He killed two teenage boys? Depraved faggot. Droll, really droll' " (6).

In this opening scene, words and images denoting fear, violence, suffering, and judgment are literally mobile, disconnected from any context, referent, or speaking subject that would lend them substance and immediacy. Whatever ironic significance the allusion to the *Inferno* may bear when associated with Chemical Bank is lost on Timothy and readers when his view of the words is interrupted by the poster for *Les Misérables*. That poster is a doubly mediated image of suffering, thepicture of a play (based on a novel) about homeless poverty in nineteenth-century Paris that in 1980s New York has become a vehicle of consumer pleasure and a generator of wealth. The poster and playbills associated with this doubly mediated relation to poverty and suffering appear throughout the novel, often in pieces literally floating through air or blown by the wind. They usually appear at moments when the characters' failure to connect with others leads to accounts of horrible violence. In the cab riding to Patrick's apartment just before the attack described above, for example, Bethany fans herself with a playbill from *Les Misérables* that someone left in the back seat. It should not be surprising, then, that after glancing at the poster Timothy fails to respond to the immediacy of the bums on the street, or that his assessment of the teenage boys' murder by a game show host would be more aesthetic than moral. Similarly, later in the novel Patrick sees a torn playbill tumbling down the street just before he describes his horrible mutilation of a homeless man and his dog. After teasing the bum cruelly with offers of money and expressions of compassion, Patrick says he stabs him repeatedly, cutting his eyes and crushing them in the sockets before slicing the bum's face and stomping on the dog's legs. "I can't help but start laughing," Patrick adds. "I linger at the scene, amused by this tableau" (132).

Like the spectators described by Lisideius who laugh when they see actors dueling on stage with blunt swords, Patrick laughs here because the bum's body appears unreal to him, as if it were merely an image in a tableau. Conversely, just as he treats the bum's body as a mere image, at other times he treats images as the things they represent. Sick and disoriented at one point, Patrick leans against a defaced poster of *Les Misérables* at a bus stop and says "I kiss the drawing of Eponine's lovely face, her lips, leaving brown streaks of bile smeared across her soft, unassuming face and the word DYKE scrawled beneath it" (151). As the novel progresses, Patrick appears to lose any sense at all of the distinction between signs and things until, one evening at Harry's bar with his friends, he finds himself silently obsessing with the idea of "faxing Sarah's blood I drained from her vagina over to her office in the mergers division at Chase Manhattan" (395).

We cannot know whether Patrick is so deluded that he thinks real objects are transmissible as faxes, or if his violent acts are just fantasies and the only blood Sarah has shed is an image in Patrick's mind. The point is that such distinctions do not matter to Patrick. Throughout the novel, he has trouble distinguishing between words or images and the objects and people they denote because the line between fantasy and reality is vague to him. "I'm really dreaming all this," Patrick says at one point (231), and he warns his secretary, Jean, that "the lines separating appearance—what you see—and reality—what you don't—become, well, blurred" (378). Without a stable point of reference in the world, words cannot lead us anywhere beyond the illusion of their immediacy. The novel illustrates that point vividly in Patrick's account of a murder scene in Paul Owen's apartment, where he says he has dipped his hand in blood and written on the wall "I AM BACK and below it a scary drawing which looks like this" (306). There is, of course, nothing there on the page after the word "this." The words have been stripped of their referential and expressive functions; they offer no clue to a way out of the maze. The violence associated with these words cannot be located in the world. Instead, the site of violence should be located on the line that Patrick draws between appearance and reality—what Jacques Lacan would call the bar between signifier and signified ("L'instance")—and "reality" should be understood here precisely as what cannot be seen from or admitted to the world of appearances and empty signs that the characters inhabit.

Cut off from any anchoring point in the world, words and images drift loose in *American Psycho*, realigning in highly unstable and contradictory associations that make nonsense of ordinary values and categories of meaning. (On the anchoring point or "point de capiton," see Lacan's "Subversion" and *Seminar III*. Lacan describes such linguistic instability as a form of psychosis.) Characters are constantly calling each other by the wrong names; even Patrick's fiancée has trouble telling him apart from his friend Timothy. Those pervasive misnomers are matched by equally frequent errors of attribution, as when Patrick is showing off his cultural knowledge about popular tourist sites that show "various spots where Columbus landed"—in 1590 (140). He says he considers the saddest song in the world to be "You Can't Always Get What You Want" by the Beatles, rather than the Rolling Stones (371); and he refers to the pop duo Milli Vanilli as "Milla Vanilla," a solecism that is doubly ironic because the duo was discredited for lip-synching to songs sung by other people and because it reduces their exotic and marketable ethnicity to vanilla-whiteness (257). Similarly, Sri Lanka is mistaken for a "cool club in the village" (14); Bedlam a "new club in midtown" (17); and AIDS a "new band from England" (34).

The din of noise and confusion that swirls around Patrick and his friends in clubs and restaurants confounds the conversation at the phonetic level as well. When Patrick comments on the T-shirt slogan "Science Equals Death" (which is probably his misreading of the ACT-UP slogan "Silence = Death"), his friend thinks he is offering advice about hair products—"Silkience Equals Death" (331); a character who likes to party becomes a "pâté animal" (398); and decaffeinated coffee is ordered as "decapitated coffee" (372). Even at a quiet lunch Patrick cannot quite control such slippage: admonished by his friend Bethany to "Calm down" he responds "I'm clam. I mean calm" (232). When he tries to pin language down on a date with Jean by explaining the etymology of the word "panic," his (accurate) connection of the word to the god Pan quickly dissolves into nonsense, "Blah blah blah" (264).

Just as words are cut off from referential connections to things in the world, from categories of value or meaning, and even from their own histories, so too are words disconnected from any speaking subject whose feelings or desires they might express. The semantic drift produces only distorted illusions of expression and revelation, as when some of Timothy's friends are teasing him:

> "Price," Van Patten says. "You're priceless."
> "Watch me act thrilled," Price says [. . .]
> "Whoa," McDermott says. "And he's dressed to im*press*."
> "Hey," Price says. "I'm depressed, I mean impressed." (41)

Ordinarily, Price's association of "depressed" and "impressed" would suggest a Freudian slip indicating an interior psychological state, but in *American Psycho* words resist such constraint to an individual psyche just as surely as they evade connections to the world. Whatever expressive functions words might have has been reduced to pure display, the theatrical gesture of Price's sarcastic "act" of expression that emphasizes its distance from the emotions it represents. As Patrick explains, "there is no real me, only an entity, something illusory [. . .] *I simply am not there*" (376–77).

The failure of language both as denotation and as expression profoundly disorients the characters and leaves them incapable of meaningful relationships with others. Characters are promiscuous in the novel because "everyone is interchangeable," as Patrick tells us (379). If Patrick's discourse fails to provide stable points of authority and expression from which he might speak to others, it also fails to direct him toward others as stable and meaningful objects of desire. Their bodies are as fungible as their images, as Patrick explains: "I masturbate, thinking about first Evelyn, then Courtney, then Vanden and then Evelyn again, but right before I come—a weak orgasm—about a near-naked model in a halter top I saw today in a Calvin Klein advertisement" (24). Thus Patrick directs his lust toward a defaced poster; a boy falls in love with a box of soap (297); and when Bethany asks Patrick whom he is seeing, he replies, "A very large bottle of Desyrel" (238). Throughout the novel, desire floats as freely as the words, attaching to objects almost at random, directed to, literally, nothing: "'I want it,'" Patrick shouts to Paul Owen at one point when they see two girls smoking grass near them at dinner. "'You want *what*?' he shouts back. 'Marijuana?' 'No. Nothing,' I scream" (148).

Lacking both an origin in the subject's desire and a destination in the world beyond the words, conversations in this novel circle back upon themselves, trapping both speakers and listeners in a maze from which there is no exit: later at another dinner with Evelyn, when Patrick gets up to leave and she asks him where he is going, he tells us:

> I make no comment, lost in my own private maze, thinking about other things: warrants, stock offerings, ESOPs, LBOs, IPOs [. . .] a book of matches from La Côte Basque splattered with blood, surface surface surface [. . .] To Evelyn our relationship is yellow and blue, but to me it's a gray place, most of it blacked out, bombed, footage from the film in my head is endless shots of stone and any language heard is utterly foreign, the sound flickering away over new images. (342–43)

Slipping across a screen of images to which it has no clear connection, incomprehensible and foreign, the language Patrick describes here has no clear place for him as speaker, no subject-position from which he can address others and engage them effectively. Consequently, his authority as the narrating "I" grows increasingly unstable as his narrative unfolds. That instability registers at the grammatical level in a shift from first-person to third-person narration when Patrick is running from the police who have heard the explosion of his gun (or so he imagines) (349–52). A similar slip occurs later when Jean's persistent desire to please him leads him to snap, "'You shouldn't fawn over him. . . .' I pause before correcting myself. 'I mean . . . me. Okay?'" (372–73).

These grammatical shifts suggest a much deeper instability of language in *American Psycho*. Words have drifted loose both from a world they would designate and from the mind of a speaker whose ideas or feelings they might express. Whatever expressive origins they may have had in their original contexts are withered into vestigial associations that mock the very possibilities of expression or intention. Not only is it impossible to tell who is speaking, it is not even certain that the speaker will be human:

> The conversation follows its own rolling accord—no real structure or topic or internal logic or feeling; except, of course, for its own hidden, conspiratorial one. Just words, and like in a movie, but one that has been transcribed improperly, most of it overlaps. I'm having a sort of hard time paying attention because my automated teller has started *speaking* to me, sometimes actually leaving weird messages on the screen, in green lettering, like [. . .]

"Feed Me a Stray Cat," and I was freaked out by the park bench that followed me for six blocks last Monday evening and it too spoke to me. (395)

No wonder Patrick cannot get reservations at the restaurant "Subjects" (137). The ceaseless slippage of signifiers over any point of reference in the world or expressive origin leaves no room for a stable speaking subject and the coherent identity that speech would define, nor for other subjects to whom that speech might be addressed.

"not . . . a . . . game"

For much of the novel, Patrick cynically embraces the isolation of signs and images as freedom from constraint, and he manipulates the free-floating signifiers to establish his power over others. "Disintegration— I'm taking it in stride" he brags, and he tells us that he just wants to "keep the game going" (394–96). However, that freedom eventually leads to a sense of isolation that finally grinds Patrick's cynical fluency down into silence as discourse approaches its limits in his increasingly blatant displays of violence and death.

Ellis portrays those displays explicitly as Patrick's efforts to provoke a response from his listeners, seeking beneath the moral condemnation that Dryden predicted what Marco Abel calls an "affect," an emotional response that would establish contact across the meaningless words and empty images that isolate characters from one another and thereby "constitute the social" (*Violent Affect* 59). The displays often take the form of direct confession, which is repeatedly undermined by language's incapacity to lead to anything beyond itself. At a dinner one night in No Man's Land, Patrick admits "'Listen, guys, my life is a living hell,' [but] they utterly ignore me" (347). At other times, his companions just hear what they want to hear, translating his admissions into ordinary table talk. At dinner with a model, Daisy, Patrick says "'So it was really hot out today, wasn't it?' 'It was,' Daisy agrees, and then adds "'So what do you do?' [. . .] 'I'm into, oh, murders and executions mostly,'" Patrick responds with a shrug. Daisy, unfazed, answers "'Do you like it? [. . .] most guys I know who work in mergers and acquisitions don't really like it.'" Patrick corrects her but then gives up: "'That's *not* what I said [. . .] Oh, forget it'" (205–06).

Frustrated with this lack of response, Patrick takes to flaunting evidence of his atrocities, as when he uses pieces of his victims' bodies on his costume for the office Halloween party. "I went as a mass murderer, complete with a sign painted on my back that read MASS MURDERER [. . .] and beneath those two words I had written in blood

Yep, that's me and the suit was also covered with blood, some of it fake, most of it real" (330). Despite additional accoutrements (a hank of hair taken from one of his victims and a finger bone pinned next to his boutonniere), Patrick's costume does not lead to his anticipated social triumph, and the award for the best costume goes to someone dressed as convicted financier Ivan Boesky.

Patrick becomes increasingly agitated at the failure of others to respond to, or even to notice, his crimes. Several months after Patrick says he murdered his friend Paul Owen and starting using Paul's apartment as a killing ground, he returns to the scene of the crime and has an unsettling encounter with a real estate agent, Mrs Wolfe, who is showing the apartment to prospective buyers. The walls are spotless, the furniture carefully arranged,

> but it doesn't make me forget what I did to Christie's breasts, to one of the girls' heads, the nose missing, both ears bitten off [. . .] the torrents of gore and the blood that washed over the apartment, the stench of the dead [. . .]. "Can I help you?"

the real estate agent asks, interrupting his reverie, and he is plunged into confusion:

> All frontiers, if there had ever been any, seem suddenly detachable and have been removed, a feeling that others are creating my fate will not leave for the rest of the day. This . . . is . . . not . . . a . . . game, I want to shout, but I can't catch my breath though I don't think she can tell. I turn my face away. I need rest. I don't know what to say. Confused, I reach out for a moment to touch Mrs. Wolfe's arm, to steady myself, but I stop it in midair, move it to my chest instead, but I can't feel it, not even when I loosen my tie; it rests there, trembling, and I can't make it stop. I'm blushing, speechless. (368, 370)

Patrick's embarrassment, his alienation from his own body, and his speechlessness all register the effect of social pressure that is otherwise invisible on the smooth surface of images, brand names, and empty signifiers where he lives his life. As he has told us earlier, reality is what we don't see, but he nevertheless confronts the effect of the Real as a limit to the representational power of words and images that sustains his illusions and supports his authority and power over others. That limit is evident in a similar scene at the end of the novel when Patrick confronts Harold Carnes, to whom he has confessed his crimes in a voice message left on Carnes's answering machine. When Patrick asks

Carnes if he got the message, Carnes (who mistakes Patrick Bateman for a man named Davis), says "'Jesus, Davis. Yes, that was hi*lar*ious. That *was* you, was it? [. . .] Bateman killing Owen and the escort girl?'" He keeps chuckling. "'Oh that's bloody marvelous. Really key, as they say at the Groucho Club'" (387). Aggravated that his declaration of brutality has not moved Carnes to anything more than qualified praise for what Carnes thought was a weak joke, Patrick tries to force Carnes to acknowledge the truth of what he revealed in his message on the answering machine:

> "*I* killed him. *I* did it, Carnes. *I* chopped Owen's fucking head off. *I* tortured dozens of girls. That whole message I left on your machine was *true*." [. . .]
> "But that's simply not possible," he says, brushing me off. [. . .] "Because . . . I had . . . dinner . . . with Paul Owen . . . twice . . . in London . . . *just ten days ago*." (388)

Flummoxed by Carnes's appeal to the Real, Patrick just stares at him in silence, and when Patrick finally finds the nerve to speak, he can no longer recognize himself as the speaking-subject of his own words:

> I finally have the nerve to say something back to him but my voice lacks any authority and I'm not sure if I believe myself when I tell him, simply, "No, you . . . didn't." But it comes out a question, not a statement. (388)

Carnes's direct appeal to the world outside of words dislocates Patrick from his position of authority and power and alienates him from his speech just as the social pressure of Mrs Wolfe's question "Can I help you?" left Patrick standing in embarrassed silence, unable to control or even feel the body he has cultivated at such lengths in the gym.

Few of the other characters in *American Psycho* address Patrick in this way from beyond the limit of representations that sustain his narcissistic illusions of power and autonomy. In addition to Mrs Wolfe and Carnes, only his secretary Jean seems capable of eliciting a response from Patrick that goes any further than the incantatory recitation of nonsense that characterizes his usual conversation, and he is repelled by his sporadic responsiveness to her: when Jean hugs him at one point, Patrick begins to respond but immediately defends himself against any meaningful reaction by imagining they are merely actors in a hackneyed movie scene (265). Later in the novel, Patrick responds similarly as he and Jean gaze into a baby carriage during one of their walks: "The baby stares at Jean and me. We stare back. It's really weird and I'm experiencing a spontaneous kind of internal sensation, I feel I'm moving toward as well as away from something" (380). As his narrative continues, Patrick becomes increasingly susceptible to the ambivalence he feels in this scene as the object of the baby's gaze. Eventually, that ambivalence invades even his relationship with his friend Timothy Price when at the end of the novel they are watching a speech on television by former President Reagan and Timothy suddenly appeals to the distinction between appearance and reality as a ground for ethical judgment:

> "How can he lie like that? How can he pull that *shit*? [. . .] I don't believe it. He looks so . . . *normal*. He seems so . . . out of it. So . . . *un*dangerous. [. . .] He presents himself as a harmless old codger. But inside . . ." He stops. My interest picks up, flickers briefly. "But inside . . ." Price can't finish the sentence, can't add the last two words he needs: *doesn't matter*. I'm both disappointed and relieved for him. (396–97)

Patrick is disappointed because Timothy cannot cynically reject the notion that there should be a connection between appearances and reality that would warrant the ethical judgment Timothy tries to exercise here. Their conversations and the illusion of community that discourse supports depend on the ability to say such a connection "doesn't matter." Unable to say that, Timothy cannot say anything. At the same time, Patrick is relieved by Timothy's refusal to accept the subordination of reality to appearance that underlies the popular impression of Reagan's innocence. Patrick recognizes in that refusal a kindred impulse to his own repeated attempts to confess his crimes, provoke judgment, and so find his way out of the maze of empty images and meaningless discourse that isolates him and makes ethical judgment impossible. For a moment, Timothy's effort seems to have made a difference: " 'Inside? Yes, inside?' Craig asks, bored. 'Believe it or not, we're actually listening to you.' " But when Timothy asks Patrick what he thinks of this issue, "I look up, smile, don't say anything. [. . .] I sigh, shrug, whatever. 'That's, uh, a pretty good answer,' Price says" (397–98).

The conversation quickly returns to the usual concerns with reservations, Rolexes, and random factoids until it dissolves into meaningless blather, an empty echo of the ironic self-denigrating references to yuppie excess we have heard earlier: " 'yup yup yup yup yup yup . . .' I think it's me who says," Patrick adds, " 'I have to return some videotapes' " (398). The next word spoken has drifted loose entirely from its sources and its referents—"someone asks, simply, not in relation to anything, '*Why*?' "—and Patrick answers, "for no reason, just opening my mouth, words coming out [. . .] this is what being *Patrick* means to me, I guess, so, well, yup, uh . . . ." The novel then concludes as it began with another allusion to a literary hell, this time to Jean-Paul Sartre's play *No Exit*, looming above the dark room in red letters : "THIS IS NOT AN EXIT" (399).

The Rhetoric of Address and the Ethics of Alterity

Some critics have interpreted Patrick's inability to provoke outrage and judgment as evidence that his violent acts are all in his imagination and never extend to the bodies of his purported victims. Yet, *American Psycho* offers no reliable basis for that claim, no immediate point of reference that is out of play in the game Patrick would perpetuate. Patrick has no "inside," no interior depth in which such fantasies could play out in isolation from the words that describe them, nor do those same words reliably designate objects and actions in the world outside the text. Even readers are caught up in this indeterminable situation at times when Patrick addresses the implied reader as "you" and so dislocates us from the privileged position of outsider that normally authorizes judgments about characters in a novel. On his way to the dry cleaners, for example, Patrick says he steps on the foot of a blind, crippled bum and then asks, "Did I do this on purpose? What do you think? Or did I do this accidentally?" (82). Similarly, when Patrick is being questioned by the private detective Donald Kimball, who has been hired to investigate the disappearance of Paul Owen, Patrick muses,

> Kimball is utterly unaware of how truly vacant I am. There is no evidence of animate life in this office, yet still he takes notes. By the time you finish reading this sentence, a Boeing jetliner will take off or land somewhere in the world. I would like a Pilsner Urquell. (274–75)

Like the opening scene of the novel, which conflates the space of reading and the words of the text by identifying the reader's point of view with that of Timothy, so this paragraph identifies the time of reading with the time of Patrick's narration through the rhetoric of address.

Designated grammatically in the second-person pronoun, the reader's perspective is constructed in these passages as what Naomi Mandel calls "a vision of alterity that literally renders Patrick answerable to the question, '*why?*'" at the end of the novel (18). This alterity is not in the text *per se*. It derives from a rhetorical bond between the text and the reader that is entailed in the process of reading rather than designated in what is read. It is the same alterity with which Dryden seeks to maintain decorum by abandoning the illusions of the stage and addressing the audience directly to describe actions beyond the limits of representation and illusion. That address engages the audience ethically by distinguishing clearly between the actions described in the text and description as a rhetorical act, with its direct appeal to the audience and inherent obligation to reply that the appeal imposes on those to whom it is addressed.

A similar distinction can be made between readers' relation to Patrick's narration and the relation of characters to Patrick in the text as he speaks to them or about them as objects of violence. Those characters are positioned in Patrick's discourse through his imaginary conflation of words and images with the acts and ideas those words represent. The illusions stemming from that conflation free him from responsibility to those imaginary others and the empty signs that surround them, but the illusions also isolate him by foreclosing the possibility of establishing a relation to others through expression or confession. The limits of illusion are evident in Patrick's inability to shock others with accounts of his violent acts, or to evoke the fear and condemnation that his actions would elicit if encountered in the world. This failure of what Corneille called verisimilitude in Patrick's discourse undermines his delusions of power and authority; when confronted with pressure from the world beyond his words, Patrick is struck silent, motionless, desiring nothing. Mrs Wolfe, Carnes, and a few other characters who are not caught up in the illusions literally distance themselves from Patrick and reject his efforts to communicate, much like playgoers described by Dryden who scoff at unrealistic death scenes and otherwise dismiss the action on stage when decorum is breached.

As illustrated by Ellis and Dryden, the consequence of that breach is not so much an ethical response as a smug moralistic occlusion of any responsibility for the violence relegated to the other side of the bar that separates representations from the real. That complacent moralism is evident in readings of *American Psycho* that insist on conflating the act of narration with the violent acts the narrator describes, or that dismiss Patrick's accounts of violence as psychotic fantasies or a sick joke. Both responses are really strategies for not reading, for refusing the obligation to reply that distinguishes ethical reading from moral condemnation. Ellis precludes such easy moralism by using Patrick's most extreme accounts of violence and death—such as the one quoted at the beginning of this chapter—to establish the representational limits of discourse and then portraying the transgression of that limit as a rhetorical gesture addressed to others from whom Patrick seeks recognition rather than judgment. Instead of then calling for assent or condemnation, that appeal positions readers as subjects in, and to, an ethical obligation in the world that transcends the illusions of the text and the imaginary relation to signs that sustain them.

Dryden's defense of decorum enables us to locate Ellis's rhetorical strategy within the literary and aesthetic traditions that inform our understanding of extreme fictions in any age, just as Lyotard's effort to establish a rhetorical basis for the social bond helps us to articulate the possibility of ethical action in a postmodern world without moral absolutes. The social importance of these issues is suggested by yet another theoretical source invoked by Ellis himself near the end of the novel after Patrick is robbed at gunpoint by a cab driver and stripped of his beloved Rolex and Wayfarer sunglasses. As he is walking back to the highway, Patrick is accosted by an old woman who steps from behind a poster for *The Threepenny Opera* and tells him to get a haircut. Unlike the earlier allusions to the kitschy suffering of *Les Misérables*, which enables Patrick's cruelty, this reference to Brecht's play recalls the alienation effect (*Verfremdungseffekt*) Brecht sought by deliberately breaking the illusion of the stage. By forcing the actions on stage to their representational limits, Brecht intended to stimulate the critical faculties of the audience and direct its attention away from theatrical illusions and toward the social injustice and political conflicts that surround the theater in the world. So, too, Dryden reminds his readers of their role in the historical struggles of empires as the clamor of battle rages behind the aesthetic debates in his "Essay on Dramatick Poesie." Ellis seeks the same end in *American Psycho*. By exposing the limits of representation in scenes of violence, he turns our attention from the illusions of the narrative text itself to the act of narration as it creates a social bond with the reader in the rhetoric of address and so makes ethical reading both possible and obligatory.

CHAPTER 2

American Psycho, Hamlet, and Existential Psychosis

Alex E. Blazer

[. . .] looking back at my hand, the specks of blood under the nail on my thumb, the photograph of my father, when he was a much younger man, on my mother's bedside table, next to a photograph of Sean and me when we were both teenagers, wearing tuxedos, neither one of us smiling. In the photograph of my father he's wearing a six-button double-breasted black sport coat, a white spread-collar cotton shirt, a tie, pocket square, shoes, all by Brooks Brothers. He's standing next to one of the topiary animals a long time ago at his father's estate in Connecticut and there's something the matter with his eyes.

American Psycho 366

Some consider Bret Easton Ellis's *American Psycho* tedious and unreadable. Tedious because its narrator, Patrick Bateman, spends hundreds of pages comprehensively detailing the designer wardrobes of everyone he meets, providing us with entire chapters on his grooming rituals, and recounting in detail the inanity of his conversations on the phone and in restaurants with his friends and lovers. Unreadable due to the half dozen meticulously described and emotionally arid sex scenes and half dozen nauseatingly exacting torture scenes involving acid, batteries, Habitrails, and cannibalism. However, the paragraph above distinguishes itself from Patrick's ceaseless, monotonous, and affectless 400-page monologue by providing a glimpse of the psychotic serial killer's family life. The scene is an asylum called Sandstone where his mother resides, suffering from some unnamed disorder. The father appears only in a photograph. The Bateman brothers, in a separate photograph, gaze unsmilingly at the camera, unable to pose with a grin despite the festive implication of the tuxedos they are wearing.

The Bateman men—the father and, in a separate frame, the sons—are accessible only through the photograph. As Roland Barthes has noted, the photograph offers a semblance of presence that ineluctably denotes the absence of the thing it represents (*Camera Lucida*). It testifies to a loss of presence; it is an image separated, if not divorced, from reality. What does this tell us about the Bateman clan? Is Patrick's father dead, available only through the memorializing image? Or does he rule his family through intermediary lawyers and managers from atop some Wall Street skyscraper? Patrick's obsession with appearance and status may well be inherited from this simulacrum of a father, who valorizes Brooks Brothers and girds his sons in tuxedos. The father comes from a long line of moneymakers, as evidenced by the reference to his father's (Patrick's grandfather's) estate. But despite the information we can glean from this brief description of an image, Patrick's attitude toward this man remains a cipher. Does Patrick respect the authority of his father? Does he love him, miss him—if indeed either man is capable of love?

The passage provides a palpable hint to this thicket of questions. Oedipus was perhaps the first character in Western literature to have "something the matter with his eyes." After unwittingly fulfilling his prophetic fate to marry his mother and kill his father, he blinds himself as retribution for transgressing the fundamental laws prohibiting incest. The passage's fleeting hint of the Oedipus story offers a way into the psychic terrain of this "American Psycho": the inaccessibility of the father, the absence of his law, assume the form of psychosis as Patrick inflicts his inner paternal confusions upon the world in torturous and murderous form.

They Ate Their Own Children

Critics have noted that the father figure is a problematic presence in each of Ellis's novels. Julian Murphet asserts that "Avatars of this figure appear in most of the novels, fathers who are as culpably implicated in the shallow consumerism of the culture as their cynical sons and daughters" (11). Ellis's first novel, *Less Than Zero*, set in the alienating and arid city of his birth, is populated by broken families, parents who, as Peter Freese describes, are

divorced or separated, occupied by their passing affairs, intent on their success in the Hollywood industry, and obsessed by their futile attempts at preserving eternal youth, [they] have no time for and no interest in their children, have never provided them with a functioning value system, and try to absolve themselves of their responsibility by generously writing cheques.

In her discussion of "The Existential Dilemma in *Less Than Zero*," Nicki Sahlin similarly emphasizes the impact of parental absence and inaccessibility on the inner life of the characters: "That these characters are virtually abandoned by their parents, while hardly registering the fact consciously, accounts for some of their more generalized feelings of anxiety and malaise" (27). Significantly, Sahlin focuses on the role of the father: "The character who should be Clay's strongest source of identity is instead a depersonalizing force. . . . The values presented by his father are patently transient, and Clay clearly must look elsewhere for any meaning in his life" (29). Ultimately, concludes Sahlin, "Ellis shows that Clay's parental encounters are at best empty of useable values and at worst more like confrontations with the existential void" (29).

What Clay finds back East with Sean Bateman, Lauren Hynde, and Paul Denton in *The Rules of Attraction* is an endless bacchanal replete with sex and drugs yet devoid of pleasure. Here, too, parents are notably absent, and the majority of the characters are reeling from the impact of their decimated home lives. One of the characters, Paul Denton, takes pride in his singular status as an exception to this rule:

> I liked the fact that my parents were still married. Whether the marriage was any good was anyone's guess, but just the fact that most, or all, of my friends' parents were either divorced or separated, and my parents weren't, made me feel safe rather than feeling like a casualty. (31)

Predictably, though, Paul is informed by his mother in the course of the novel that his parents plan to divorce (158) and he, like his schoolmates, is condemned to replace a home life with the dubious "havens of shelter" described by Sean's unnamed crush:

> *I stayed with my brother one night and visited a recently widowed aunt on Shelter Island and I stayed in tons of motels, motels that were pink and gray and green and that glowed in the Hamptons light. I stayed in these havens of shelter since I could not bear anymore to look at my father's new girlfriends.* (127)

As Sean puts it in the final pages of the novel, "Home was gone" (282).

Hailing from financially stable but emotionally insecure, if not loveless, homes, this class of students, like the characters in *Less Than Zero*, seek oblivion through perverting pleasure: alcohol becomes mind-numbing binging, lovemaking turns into "dreaded fucking" (114), and climax yields crying and disillusionment (115). Lauren barely registers that Parents' Weekend is cancelled (131), and her self-destructive relationship, a bizarre love triangle, with Paul and Sean terminates in an abortion (the father of the fetus is uncertain). Though Lauren concludes that "it doesn't matter" (265), the annihilating impact of the experience is represented as a blank page in the text (268). The abandoned children of absent, self-absorbed, and unavailable parents in *Less Than Zero* have transformed, in *The Rules of Attraction*, into the progenitors of their existential angst: they have become their parents. The graffiti that Lauren sees in the abortion clinic ("Feminine Chaos. End of the term— things only other girls from the college had written" [265]) situate her and her schoolmates as the addressees of the graffito Clay notices on a bathroom wall in *Less Than Zero*: "Fuck you Mom and Dad. [. . .] You both can die because that's what you did to me. You left me to die" (193). Both pieces of graffiti echo the theme of the absent, but murder- ous parents that haunt Clay in the final pages of *Less Than Zero*:

> The images I had were of people being driven mad by living in the city. Images of parents who were so hungry and unfulfilled that they ate their own children. Images of people, teenagers my own age, looking up from the asphalt and being blinded by the sun. (208)

American "Psycho"

Because Ellis populates his intertextual, fictional world with one funda- mental character type (the existentialist alienated by the vapidity and sameness of commercial culture) but also the very same characters at different stages of their lives (home, college, work, middle age), one can follow the hollow family relationships in general and fatal paternal function in particular throughout Ellis's work. While neither *Less Than Zero*'s Clay nor *The Rules of Attraction*'s Sean could be accurately described as a "fucking evil psychopath" like *American Psycho*'s Patrick Bateman (*American Psycho* 20), the emotional distance between the three first-person narrators is quite small.

The first-person narratives of Ellis's work would seem to eschew any potential for character development, stylistic innovation, or psychic depth. Rather, as Murphet puts it, Ellis's narratives articulate "a kind of *non-self*, a self defined not by freedom and the open horizon of the undetermined, but by repetition and tunnel vision" (25). Ellis's novels, Murphet continues, offer "an interminable monologue of the non-self, which is, at some hypothetical sociopsychological limit, the lived 'self' of everyday life in contemporary America" (25). The "non-self" articu- lated by so monotonous, repetitive, and affectless a voice hardly lends itself to a psychoanalytical approach. And yet, the Oedipal theme suggested in Ellis's early works—as well as the *Hamlet* theme that emerges explicitly in *Lunar Park* (in the paternal haunting, the identification of Patrick Bateman with Ellis's father, along with the symbolic location names Elsinore Lane, Ophelia Boulevard, Claudius Street)—indicate that such an approach has the potential to yield new insight into *American Psycho* in particular, and Ellis's oeuvre in general.

Previous attempts to account for the "psycho" in *American Psycho* have linked Patrick to the excesses of capitalism and consumer culture or to a culture of simulation detached from any grounding in the Real. John W. Aldridge, for example, connects Patrick's excessive detailing of brands, sex, and violence to an effort to ground his unhinged psyche:

> Bateman, in short, is clearly psychotic about procedural decorum in all its expensive, trendy, state-of-the-art manifestations. It is an obsession that provides him with constant reminders of who he is because it tells him that he is what he possesses, and it serves to shift his consciousness away from the vacuum that yawns beneath his peaked lapels. (142–43)

My own previous work on *American Psycho* argued that Patrick was consumed by a Baudrillardian postmodern hyperreality composed of consumer goods, signs with no relationship to concrete reality: "He has no feeling for humanity, just for products. . . . Consequently, he kills indiscriminately in order . . . to shock some feeling, any feeling, into the hollow image that constitutes his very psychic identity" ("Chasms"). Carla Freccero and Bertholde Schoene have both noted the Oedipal reverberations in the novel. Freccero, who suggests that Patrick enacts his inner feelings of Oedipal confusion and fury upon the outer world (53), ultimately reads Patrick as a sadist in the sense articulated by Gilles Deleuze in his "Coldness and Cruelty." For Schoene, the image of Patrick's parents "only hints at profound familial estrangement while foreclosing any more detailed psychological or psychoanalytic profiling" (381). Schoene argues that postmodern culture, with its emphasis on body image and status, radically challenges traditional masculinity, turning normal Oedipal feelings into murderous acts of sexual aggression.

This chapter differs from previous work on the topic (including my own) by focusing on the notable absence of parental figures in Ellis's third novel. Despite the prominence of this theme in his previous work, and his statement, in *Lunar Park*, that *American Psycho* "had been about my father (his rage, his obsession with status, his loneliness)" (121) the emotionally absent parents of *Less Than Zero* and *The Rules of Attraction* have been reframed, literally, as a photograph in an asylum in *American Psycho*. And yet, the absent presence of Patrick's parents is fundamental to his psyche and define his psychosis. I treat the absent father as existential catalyst and psychotic trigger through two interrelated lenses: the tragic relationship between ghostly fathers and melancholic sons in William Shakespeare's *Hamlet* and the theoretical relationship between symbolic fathers and psychotic sons in Jacques Lacan's psychoanalytic conceptualization of psychosis. Just as *Hamlet* is a play about a son who, bound by his dead father to avenge his murder, finds himself paradoxically adrift, able to do almost anything but fulfill the ghost's injunction, *American Psycho* can be read as a novel about an emotionally abandoned son adrift and searching for meaning in a confusing, contradictory world.

Unlike Oedipus, who transgressed a fundamental law and suffered the consequences, Patrick has inherited the world of Ellis's previous novels, a world in which parents destroy their children, children wish death on their parents, and no law—written or unwritten—surfaces to exonerate or condemn. Because of the absence of this law, the novel operates according to Jacques Lacan's definition of psychosis, which is characterized by a lack of paternal prohibition and symbolic castration. Hence, while Hamlet is bound by the father's dictate to revenge and remember, Patrick has no moral imperative that binds him to the world, its values, or other people. Hamlet responds to the father's injunction "remember me," by vowing to empty his mind of all save his father's commandment: "thy commandment all alone shall live / Within the book and volume of my brain" (1.5.98–103). Patrick has no injunction to structure his psyche: his interiority circles an innate emptiness:

> Desire—meaningless. Intellect is not a cure. Justice is dead. Fear, recrimination, innocence, sympathy, guilt, waste, failure, grief, were things, emotions, that no one really felt anymore. Reflection is useless, the world is senseless. Evil is its only permanence. God is not alive. (375)

Father and Sons: Freud

The spirit of the dead, always already absent father haunts Patrick's unconscious, and such paternal neglect structures his psyche. Noting that children's first desires are for their opposite sex parents, and that "Accordingly, the father becomes a disturbing rival to the boy and the mother to the girl" (*Interpretation of Dreams* 291), Freud theorizes what happens to these initial, admittedly "childish" sexual desires by turning to literature where dreams are writ large. The prophecy of Oedipus killing his father and marrying his mother in Sophocles's play

Oedipus Rex, according to Freud, shows how desire is dreamed and symbolically represented:

> King Oedipus, who slew his father Laius and wedded his mother Jocasta, merely shows us the fulfillment of our own childhood wishes. But, more fortunate than he, we have meanwhile succeeded, in so far as we have not become psychoneurotics, in detaching our sexual impulses from our mothers and in forgetting our jealousy of our fathers. Here is one in whom these primeval wishes of our childhood have been fulfilled, and we shrink back from him with the whole force of the repression by which those wishes have since that time been held down within us. While the poet, as he unravels the past, brings to light the guilt of Oedipus, he is at the same time compelling us to recognize our own inner minds, in which those same impulses, though suppressed, are still to be found. (296)

Why are these taboo wishes relegated to the unconscious? Because, in the case of boys (the male psyche is Freud's dominant model), the father serves as a more powerful rival to the son for the mother's affections. The Oedipal father functions as the voice of prohibition; he is the lawgiver who compels the son's adherence to the rules of civilization. In order to live at peace with the respect of the authority of the father, we relegate our primordial, childish wishes to the recesses of our unconscious. In short, the rivalry with the more powerful father instills guilt.

But Patrick's father is never described as a powerful rival to his sons. In *The Rules of Attraction*, Sean recounts an evening in which the son proves more sexually potent than his father:

> two women in their mid-twenties tried unsuccessfully to pick up on my father and I [. . .] What was strange about that situation was not the pick-up itself, for my father had always been quite adept at casually picking up women. It was that my father, who would normally have flirted with these two, didn't. (232)

Later Sean has sex with a girl in his father's suite at the Carlyle while his father sleeps (233). In *American Psycho*, Patrick feels neither remorse nor desire for the abject things he does, because he has no care for justice and no belief in the law (of God or the father). Patrick's psychosis is connected with his unresolved Oedipal feelings—unresolved because the father does not temper the son's aggression and civilize his mind. Patrick is devoid of feeling and conscience because he was never introduced to the laws of society by society's familial representative, the father.

Unlike *Hamlet*, in which the father presents his injunction in the form of a ghost, *American Psycho* offers conflicting information as to whether Sean and Patrick's father is, indeed, alive. Hints of the father's status, and the sons' relationship with him, are offered in *The Rules of Attraction*: Sean, Patrick's brother, recalls a weekend in New York as "the last time I saw my father" (231) whom he describes as "noticeably dying" (232). In a later scene in *The Rules of Attraction*, Patrick enjoins Sean to be "the son your father wanted," and Sean responds by laughing: "You think that thing in there even cares?" (239).

In *American Psycho*, Patrick and Sean meet again for Sean's birthday dinner. The Batemans' father's accountant and estate trustee tell Patrick to question Sean about his life. Besides suggesting that the father is dead, the money men's roles in the sons' lives imply that they, rather than the patriarch proper, are and were responsible for household authority. Moreover, the fact that Sean is staying in his father's suite at the Carlyle Hotel while in New York City (225) signifies that the spirit of the deceased paterfamilias lingers.

References to Patrick's father also serve as a site of a vexed conversation between Patrick and Bethany, an old girlfriend from his Harvard days whose murder will later be described in excruciating detail:

> "You're at . . . P & P?" she asks.
> "Yes." I say.
> She nods, pauses, wants to say something, debates whether she
>   should, then asks, all in a matter of seconds: "But doesn't your
>   family own—"
> "I don't want to talk about this," I say, cutting her off. "But yes,
>   Bethany. Yes." [. . .]
> "But—" she's confused. "Didn't your father—"
> "Yes, of course, I say interrupting. [. . .]
> "Patrick," she says slowly. "If you're so uptight about work, why
>   don't you just quit? You don't have to work."
> "Because," I say, staring directly at her, "I . . . want . . . to . . . fit . . .
>   in." (236–37)

Here, too, whether or not the father is alive or dead remains somewhat uncertain. Either Patrick's father currently owns/controls his company, thereby entailing the son's feeling of dispossession, or his deceased father left him more than well-off in no need of a job. In any case, the impact of the father's absence on Patrick's psyche is reflected not only in the fractured sentences and the obvious reticence of both Patrick and Bethany (who presumably knows something about his past) to speak of him, but also by the urgency of Patrick's need for socialization: "I . . . want . . . to . . . fit . . . in."

Where is the Bateman matriarch? In Sandstone, a sanitarium. Though the exact nature of her psychological disorder remains unknown to the reader, the brothers' two-sentence conversation regarding their mother suggests that she has some sort of mental illness, perhaps a degenerative madness. When Patrick states, "Things are worse at Sandstone," Sean replies, "Like what? Mom ate her pillow?" (224). When Patrick actually visits Sandstone, his hands are shaking and he's "not surprised at how much effort it takes to raise [his] head and look at her" (365). For stability, he regresses to describing his designer, status-conscious clothes but here, too, Patrick is haunted by a whiff of uncertainty: "I'm wearing a two-button wool gabardine suit with notched lapels by Gian Marco Venturi, cap-toed leather laceups by Armani, tie by Polo, *socks I'm not sure where from*" (365 emphasis mine). Even more significant, the conversation regarding Christmas (it's April) fades away as he hides in plain sight—in a mirror: "I don't say anything. I've spent the last hour studying my hair in the mirror I've insisted the hospital keep in my mother's room" (365). However, the mirror reveals not his solipsism, but his primordial, imaginary identification with his mother, for his gaze oscillates between his hair and hers. "'You look unhappy,' she says, more quietly this time. She touches her hair, stark blinding white, again. 'Well, you do too,' I say slowly, hoping that she won't say anything else" (365).

Hair and unhappiness *bind* mother to son. However, the identification does not stop at the imaginary level. Significantly, the mother's hair *blinds* the son. Oedipus ultimately blinds himself for marrying his mother and killing his father. In effect, Patrick's mother has more Oedipal power over her son than his absentee father. Patrick represents what happens when the father abdicates his duty and leaves his son unbound to the law: the blinding of the son by the mother. The son's civilized identity is forged in sand, or rather Sandstone. Given this, it is possible to understand Patrick's violence against women in particular as a raging against feminine usurpation of Oedipal power.

The problem, however, is that Patrick's mother's psyche is itself fragmented; therefore, the ontology he seeks to reconstitute must fail for the imaginary space he seeks to reconstruct was already fractured. The degeneration of the mother's psyche places even greater import on the father, who himself persists as loss. In Patrick's 400-page monologue consisting of dinner conversations in which he flails for alpha male status, product descriptions in which he vies for social status, monotonous pornography in which he eludes satisfaction, and sadistic violence in which he commands power, this telling scene in Sandstone reveals the basic lack of the father. The patriarch holds no law-giving authority over the son and therefore cannot socialize him into the normal symbolic order, civilized society. The crazed matriarch's inconceivable homecoming deceives and disappoints, and the ghostly patriarch's financial stability affords no recompense. The mad mother and the impotent father spawn the madness of death: the pathological, if not murderous, psychosis in the son. If the Bateman patriarch taught his son Patrick anything (and we are not sure if he did) it was a lesson in consumption to fill the lack: Patrick devours the elite, symbolically meaningful brands in order first to stave off his original alienation and primal aggression, and then to refind his imaginary sense of being with his mother. But the "Mom [who] ate her pillow" (225) perverts even the notion of consumption.

In Freudian psychoanalysis, the mother constitutes the child's first love; and in the boy's Oedipal struggle, the father functions as a stronger love rival who lays down the law and turns the boy's loving gaze outside the home. But "home" is a vexed concept in Ellis's novels: there is nowhere from which to turn the loving gaze. In *The Rules of Attraction*, Sean abandons the college campus reflecting, "Home was gone" (282). In *American Psycho*, Sean stays at his father's suite at the Carlyle, though whether the father is alive or dead is ultimately uncertain: like the castle at Elsinore, it is haunted. For Patrick, who lives alone in an anonymous skyscraper where even his doorman does not recognize him, "home" threatens to turn him into a ghost like his father: "I am a ghost to this man," thinks Patrick, "I am something unreal, something not quite tangible" (71). Perhaps it is no surprise, then, that Patrick turns his murderous impulses toward the homeless. While Patrick wants to fit in with his oblivious family and friends (237), he protests too much in distinguishing himself from the abject, excremental, and miserable homeless like Al: "You *reek*," I tell him. "You *reek* of . . . *shit*. [. . .] I'm sorry. It's just that . . . I don't know. I don't have anything in common with you" (130–31). Patrick's inner rage, a shattering admixture of self-hatred and self-flagellation, reappears in the Real as a self-projection which must be murdered by himself because there is no other, no law, no Oedipal father to rival him, to castrate him, to blind him:"I pull out a long, thin knife with a serrated edge and, being very careful not to kill him, push maybe half an inch of the blade into his right eye, flicking the handle up, instantly popping the retina" (131). A ghost in his own home, he pursues and punishes reality, a tangible quality, in the bodies of his victims.

Language and Psyche: Lacan

For Lacan, who interprets Freud linguistically, the dyadic relationship with the mother constitutes the pre-symbolic imaginary stage of being, the realm in which image structures self and deploys affect. By contrast, the father cuts into the primal, unspoken, ideal bond between mother and child with language and thereby introduces the child into the symbolic world in which signifiers substitute for signified things. The paternal function is not only Oedipal but also symbolic: the father drives the child from the lure of the imaginary, the seduction of self-illusion, to the laws of language in which significance is differential and constructed. In the Lacanian mode, the father functions linguistically, as symbol of the law of language and social order: "It is in the *name of the father* that we must recognize the support of the symbolic function which, from the dawn of history, has identified his person with the figure of the law," writes Lacan (*Écrits* 67). Moreover, language—the Law of the Father—itself inaugurates one's feeling of lack not only due to the separation from the imaginary unity with the mother but also because words represent but do not equal the things they signify.

In *The Interpretation of Dreams*, Freud explicitly connects the story of Oedipus with Shakespeare's *Hamlet*, linking each to the modern subject's vexed relationship with the paternal and his law-giving function. If *Oedipus* notes the role of the father in the social structure, *Hamlet* attests to the implications of repressed Oedipal identification:

> Hamlet is able to do anything—except take vengeance on the man who did away with his father and took that father's place with his mother, the man who shows him the repressed wishes of his own childhood realized. Thus the loathing which should drive him on to revenge is replaced in him by self-reproaches, by scruples of conscience, which remind him that he himself is literally no better than the sinner who he is to punish. (Freud 299)

Hamlet, who is "bound to hear" by his father (*Hamlet* 1.5.10) and adept at speaking daggers at his mother, is in a very different relationship to language and its law than Patrick. Both protagonists' existential thoughts are marked by the ghostly presence, or absence, of their fathers' symbolic law. As we have seen, Patrick's father leaves his son adrift, with no guidance and no direction in the sea of shifting codes, thereby compelling Patrick to forge his own hollow law and superficial order, one devoid of emotion and desire, replete with apocalypse and nihilism. Hamlet, bound to his father's law, uses language to inquire into and clarify his relationship with the world ("To be or not to be" [3.1.55]) and to confess his inner failings ("what a rogue and peasant slave am I" [2.2.550]). Patrick's monologues, on the other hand, are ultimately a series of confessions that mean "*nothing*" (377) and are described by

Murphet as so much linguistic play: "Bateman has [. . .] done nothing but write, speak, construct himself in a variety of language games, none of which is any more 'real' than the others" (49).

Lacan's distinction between neurosis and psychosis helps us to understand the difference between Patrick's and Hamlet's relationship to the world:

> In the neuroses it's meaning that temporarily disappears, is eclipsed, and goes and lodges itself somewhere else, whereas reality itself remains. Such defenses are inadequate in the case of psychosis, where what is to protect the subject appears in reality. The subject places outside what may stir up inside him the instinctual drive that he has to confront. (*Seminar III* 203)

Without a powerful father figure to enculturate his basic self-destructive instincts, Patrick evacuates his annihilating impulses in the form of self-preservational delusion. Rather than dream, fantasy, or, as Murphet suggests, linguistic game, the violence that haunts Patrick reappears in the Real—as delusional thinking. Although the reader could presumably distinguish Patrick's thoughts from reality by paying attention to time shifts within chapters, and by simply asking herself what kind of slaughter a maid would have to clean in his apartment, Patrick himself cannot; this by definition makes his thinking not fantasy, not dream, not escape, but a delusion in which he remains trapped. Lacan clarifies:

> What is the psychotic phenomenon? It is the emergence in reality of an enormous meaning that has the appearance of being nothing at all—in so far as it cannot be tied to anything, since it has never entered into the system of symbolization—but under certain conditions it can threaten the entire edifice. (*Seminar III* 85)

Patrick's father, the one with the problematic eyes, failed to sever his son from the imaginary link with the psychotic mother and introduce him to the symbolic world. In an effort to stabilize his identity and diverge from his self-destructive rage, Patrick grasps on to the prominent signifiers in his world—the trendy, faddy, and ultimately empty brand names that replace his dead father and in effect become his all-meaningful god. When that chain of signifiers fails, for instance, when Patrick merely glimpses the "existential chasm" underlying its hyperreality that puts him into a panic (179), he protects himself with delusions of power and control that separate him from this terrifying and chaotic world: "All I have in common with the uncontrollable and the insane, the vicious and the evil, all the mayhem I have caused and my utter indifference to it, I have now surpassed" (377). It is the others, the men and women whom he tortures and dismembers, who are inchoate and powerless.

Let us apply this final structural distinction of Lacan's to Hamlet and Patrick: "In neurosis, one always remains inside the symbolic order. [. . .] Delusions occur in a completely different register. They are legible, but there is no way out" (*Seminar III* 104–05). Throughout the play, Hamlet is ensnared by the machinations of his father, his mother, his uncle, his girlfriend's father, and so forth. Even upon death, he instructs Horatio to tell his story to the world. Patrick Bateman is caught not in the symbolic order but in the delusional world of his own making. Even at the end of the novel, not only has his "confession [. . .] meant *nothing*" (377), but his narrative also runs on an infinite loop inside his morning rituals, his brand name locutions, his effusive torture. While any previous "conscience [. . .] pity [. . .] hopes disappeared long ago [. . .] if they ever did exist" (377), eventually the force of language of a narrative of his own making forecloses upon the reality of his existence: he is trapped in a world without an exit (399). Consequently, though both Hamlet and Patrick see the life before them as an existential abyss (a grave in Hamlet's case, a chasm in front of the Clinique counter in Patrick's), they do so for very different psycho-existential reasons.

Bret, Hamlet, and Patrick: *Lunar Park*

Lunar Park fully realizes, at least in fictional form, the theme of fathers and sons in *American Psycho* that this examination has attempted to exhume. The novel plays with metafictional horror by commencing as Ellis's own memoir before devolving into a fanciful yet intertextual ghost story in which Patrick Bateman haunts the author, the details of whose real life and fictional world are confused. The only certainty in this psychological horror tale is the fictional effect of the author's real father, Robert Ellis, on his son. Ellis's first-person narrator asserts, "My father created me, criticized me, destroyed me" (*Lunar Park* 7). In reality, Ellis based Patrick Bateman on his father; in fiction, the conventional demands of the horror genre link Patrick first to the father and then to a primordial, terrifying thing: "someone—*something*—else took over and caused this new character to be my only reference point during the three years it took to complete the novel" (*Lunar Park* 13). The ghost story becomes "an elegy, a description of the anguish inflicted by an uncaring father, a testament to the pain of lost love and an account of the frustration of unexpressed admiration and remorse. And finally, it is an exorcism, a reexamination of Mr. Ellis's life and work, in which he does, eventually, answer some of the questions he has deflected for years" (Wyatt). In *American Psycho*, Patrick kills because he rages for order, because he was not parented and cannot fit into the symbolic world; in *Lunar Park*, Patrick Bateman, in the form of Robert Ellis, is a very-much-present father, repeatedly emailing the narrator at the exact time of his death. *Lunar Park* documents the return of the repressed— first, of the father, second, of the narrator's denied anger at his father over his father's fatal abandonment, and, ultimately, of the primal aggression Lacan teaches. The repressed also returns in inverted form from *American Psycho*'s dispersed father and psychotic son, as the child- less real author imagines himself as a father with a stepson whom he cannot save from disappearance:

> I didn't know what to say. I was now my father. Robby was now me.
> I saw my own features mirrored in his—my world was mirrored
> there: the brownish auburn hair, the high and frowning forehead,
> the thick lips pursed together always in thought and anticipation,
> the hazel eyes swirling with barely contained bewilderment. Why
> hadn't I noticed him until he was lost to me? (*Lunar Park* 160)

Bret Easton Ellis, the narrator, may not have wanted to return to the raging Patrick Bateman and the status conscious Robert Ellis, but Patrick (the fictional, delusional son) and Robert (the real, dead father) reappear in frightening fantasy. The willless, delusional world of *American Psycho* transforms into the supernatural, dream world of *Lunar Park*. The dead father of *American Psycho*, the one who instigates the physical dismemberment and psychological fracture, returns to terrorize *Lunar Park* as a ghost.

Earlier I referred to Hamlet's response to his own ghostly father's injunction to "remember me" with this promise: "From the table of my memory / I'll wipe away all trivial fond records / All saws of books, all forms, all pressures past / That youth and observation copied there" (*Hamlet* 1.5.98–103). This passage serves as an epigraph for *Lunar Park*. If Patrick's psychosis in *American Psycho* was defined by the absence of the father, of his law, of the Oedipal complex's structuring role in the psyche, the father and law return to haunt the narrator in *Lunar Park*. Addressing the ashes of his father and his past, the narrator offers this promise: "you will be remembered, you were the one I needed, I loved you in my dreams" (*Lunar Park* 308).

CHAPTER 3

"The Soul of this Man is his Clothes": Violence and Fashion in *American Psycho*

Elana Gomel

[. . .] believe this of me: there can be no kernel in this light nut; the soul of this man is his clothes. Trust him not in matter of heavy consequence.

Shakespeare, All's Well that Ends Well *2.5.42–45*

The Body of Fashion

Whether condemned as a sexploitation joyride or praised as a social satire, Bret Easton Ellis's *American Psycho* is regarded as a serial-killer novel, part of what Mark Seltzer calls America's "wound culture": an apparently limitless fascination with motiveless violence indicative of the deep pathology of postmodernity. In this chapter, I will argue that *American Psycho* is an *anti-serial-killer novel*, one that playfully undermines the narrative conventions of the serial-killer genre. Despite its graphic descriptions of murder and mutilation, *American Psycho* is not "about" violence at all. The novel's real concern is not with the body but with fashion; not with the psychology of guilt but with the sociology of appearance; not with ethics but with aesthetics. It is a postmodern novel of manners, tracing the disintegration of the cultural paradigm of depth and secrecy and the emergence of a new paradigm of surface and spectacle.

As befits a postmodern text, *American Psycho* is highly intertextual. It is a franchise rather than a finished product: its progeny include a cinematic adaptation by the director Mary Harron, a series of fictional emails the protagonist Patrick Bateman exchanges with his therapist, and a number of fan websites. But it is also intertextual in a more traditional way, referencing a number of elite and popular texts, from Dante and Sartre to pop groups and men's magazines. Of all these many strands of allusion in the novel I will focus on its implicit dialogue with the *fin-de-siècle* Gothic, epitomized by Oscar Wilde's *The Picture of Dorian Gray*, published in 1890, and Henry James's *The Turn of the Screw* (1898). Both texts offer interesting narratological and thematic parallels with *American Psycho*. In particular, I will argue that Ellis's appropriation of the *fin-de-siècle* figure of the dandy illuminates both similarities and differences between the modernist depiction of the West End in *The Picture of Dorian Gray* and the postmodernist depiction of Wall Street in *American Psycho*. The locus of these similarities and differences is the conjunction between violence and fashion.

The *fin-de-siècle* Gothic developed a poetics of violence that have been appropriated by the twentieth- and twenty-first-century serial-killer novel. (On the nature of serial killing, see David Schmid's *Natural-Born Celebrities* and my own *Bloodscripts*.) Central to this poetics is the distinction between surface and depth; between social appearance and psychological reality; between the superficiality of manners and the metaphysics of murder. The Gothic novel strives to uncover what Joel Black calls "murder's undetermined, metaphysical dimension" (6). The significance of violence is rooted in the physical body, in "the incontestable reality" of corporeal suffering (Scarry 27). The modernist poetics of violence probes what Slavoj Žižek calls the "void[s] in a symbolic structure" through which the reality of the body penetrates representation (*The Sublime Object* 169). In contemporary serial-killer entertainment, the aesthetic of what, in *Bloodscripts*, I call "the violent sublime" still shapes the graphic descriptions of butchered bodies in popular thrillers by Patricia Cornwall, Thomas Harris, and John Connelly and informs the special effects of R-rated movies. Without their shock value, such movies and novels would not reach their multi-million sales figures, but this shock value is dependent on the notion that murder is not only socially unacceptable but also incontestably real. Murder, in this context, provides a glimpse into some hidden dimensions of social, psychological, and metaphysical evil.

American Psycho, on the other hand, represents violence as contestable, ephemeral, and inconsequential. Patrick Bateman's attempts to access the truth of the body through violence only further trap him in the Wall Street world of vacuous chatter, day trading, and brand-name fashion. The social symbolization of his world effortlessly repairs the slashes of his knife, preserving intact its glittering surface. As the roster of Patrick's victims grows, the reader becomes less and less convinced that he has killed anybody at all or that even if he has, it matters.

Ellis's aesthetics are based on surface, rather than depth; on the comic, rather than the sublime; on manners rather than murders. Patrick's violence is nostalgia for the Real, a modernist and therefore old-fashioned affect in the postmodern world of fashionable simulacra. It is this nostalgia, rather than the violence itself, that dooms him to a Sartrean version of hell, from which killing "IS NOT AN EXIT" (Ellis 399). Patrick is not a successful serial killer, escaping punishment for his barely believable crimes. He is a failed dandy.

By calling Patrick a "dandy" I refer to the cultural genealogy that links the *fin-de-siècle* figure of the man of fashion with the postmodern concept of celebrity. Both the dandy and the celebrity are what Rhonda K. Garelick calls "a personality that encompasses its own mechanically reproduced versions, and eventually seems indistinguishable from them," and each is predicated on "the performance of a highly stylized, painstakingly constructed self, a solipsistic social icon" (*Rising Star* 3). But while the most famous dandy-turned-killer in literature, Oscar Wilde's Dorian Gray, successfully resorts to violence in order to break out of the artificiality of his constructed image, Patrick remains trapped in his role as social icon. If *The Picture of Dorian Gray* ends with a mutilated body whose reality exposes the artificiality of Dorian's dandy persona, *American Psycho* ends with a dandy futilely trying to establish the reality of the many mutilated bodies he has supposedly produced. The hell that Patrick is in is generated not by his violence but by the fact that violence, both socially and epistemologically, is less consequential than the choice of a wrong tie.

American Psycho reverses the traditional configuration of fashion and the body. Fashion in the novel becomes the only stable discourse underpinning the postmodern flux of identities and desires. It is not that sexual mutilation, torture, and cannibalism reveal the shady reality underneath the brand-names-world of Wall Street. Rather, the brand names constitute the *only* reality in the world of simulacra. Ellis's *fin de siècle* is a threshold into the world in which, in Baudrillard's words, "events follow on illogically from one another, with a total equanimity towards the greatest inconsistencies, with a profound indifference to their consequences" ("Precession" 372). This is a world without depth, truth, or knowledge; a world in which clothes and appearances become the only currency of social and epistemological exchange.

I will analyze the relation of body and fashion in the novel along three narratological axes: narrative reliability, intertextuality, and the cultural code. The latter, as Roland Barthes defines it in *S/Z*, encompasses communal and shared codes of knowledge. I will use this term to designate the novel's discourse of brand names, which is central to its aesthetics. The three axes are interdependent and together they produce—to paraphrase Richard Corliss—a slasher novel Miss Manners could love.

The Serial Killer and the Governess

American Psycho belongs to the category of narratives in which the meaning of the text vacillates between two different modalities depending on the reader's evaluation of the first-person narrator's reliability. "Reliability" is a narratological rather than moral or psychological concept; it asks simply whether we can rely on the narrator to report accurately the events that constitute the plot. The most famous example of an irreducibly ambiguous text, in which the reliability of the narrator cannot be established with any degree of certainty, is Henry James's *The Turn of the Screw*.

American Psycho shares many structural similarities with *The Turn of the Screw*. Like James's governess, Patrick describes a series of violent and outrageous events; like hers, his reliability is compromised but never completely undermined. The governess may be fighting the evil ghosts in Bly or she may be hallucinating about them. Patrick may be killing a large number of people or he may be suffering a series of delusions brought about by overdoses of legal and illegal drugs. Our evaluation of the overall meaning of the text crucially hinges on our answer to the question of Patrick's narrative reliability. While *American Psycho* has been excoriated as violent pornography and praised as a keen satire of Wall Street, the relationship between these two approaches to the novel depends on who Patrick is. If he is an unfortunate victim of violent hallucinations, the target of the satire is the psychological damage done to the "yuppies" by the materialistic emptiness of their lifestyle. If he is a serial killer preying upon the homeless, women, and children, the target of the satire is the actual damage perpetrated by Wall Street on the rest of society. In the first case, we eventually pity Patrick as a poor rich boy. In the second case, we abhor him as an apocalyptic monster.

A narrator's unreliability, as Shlomith Rimmon-Kenan writes in her lucid exposition of classic narratology, can be of several different kinds: cognitive ("the narrator's limited knowledge"), emotional ("his personal involvement"), and moral ("his problematic value-scheme") (100). The first kind, cognitive unreliability, should be expanded to include hallucinating or frankly insane narrators such as the murderer in Edgar Allan Poe's "The Tell-Tale Heart." Both James's governess and Patrick may belong to this category: both may be seen as "unreliable, neurotic narrator[s], unwittingly reporting [their] own hallucinations" (Rimmon-Kenan 103). What further emphasizes the similarity between the two is that the temporal progression of their narratives tilts the balance of ambiguity toward the insanity pole. We tend to believe both at the beginning; disbelieve both at the end. When at the end of *The Turn of the Screw* little Miles dies in the governess's arms, we begin to suspect that she, rather than the putative ghosts, is the real danger to the children in Bly. When toward the end of the novel Patrick reports watching a Cheerio interviewed on a talk show (386) or being tailed by a park bench (395) it is hard to accept him as a reliable witness. However, immediately after describing the incident with the bench, he says: "Disintegration—I'm taking it in my stride" (396). Serial killers commonly enter what is known as the "disorganized stage" as their minds buckle under the strain of their actions. If Patrick is aware of his insanity, does it not make him sane and therefore reliable?

The answer is "not necessarily," since unreliability is a narratological, not psychological, concept. Patrick may suffer from acute schizophrenia and yet accurately report the actual murders he commits—or he may be legally sane and simply drugged out of any sense of objective reality. Nevertheless, there are strong indications in the text that he is, in fact, unreliable and the murders have never actually taken place. Just as our confidence in the governess is shaken when Mrs Grose proves unable to see the ghosts in *The Turn of the Screw*, our confidence in Patrick's lurid confessions is undermined when Paul Owen's apartment (where Patrick has supposedly committed grisly murders) turns out to be on the market in pristine condition and Owen himself, whom Patrick describes killing, is reported by Carnes to be alive and well in London (388). Perhaps, then, only *some* murders are real. But if so, which ones?

If the (un)reliability of the narrator cannot be established, then it is this ambiguity itself that becomes a focus of narratological study, as Tzvetan Todorov argued in *The Fantastic*. The problematic of *The Turn of Screw* is epistemological: how can we know the history behind the story, the reality behind the simulacrum? The problematic of *American Psycho* is social: what kind of society does not know the difference between reality and simulacrum and does not care?

In *The Turn of the Screw* the governess's first-person narrative is embedded in Douglas's story about her, addressed to the audience that includes yet another unnamed first-person narrator. This elaborate structure is meant to place the implied reader in the position of a sleuth, trying to piece together the real events of the story from biased, limited, or incomplete testimonies. Precisely because both Douglas and the narrator of the embedding frame are unsure about the governess's veracity, so should we be. But in *American Psycho*, the characters who receive Patrick's confessions are totally uninterested in whether they are true or not. When Patrick tells his girlfriend Evelyn (preparatory to breaking up with her) that his "*need* to engage in . . . homicidal behavior on a massive scale cannot be, um, corrected," she responds by positively refusing to have breast implants (338). When he bellows to Carnes's face, "I-killed-Paul-Owen-and-I-liked-it," his interlocutor responds: "But that's simply not possible [. . .] And I'm not finding this amusing anymore" (388). And even when Detective Kimball shows up to interrogate Patrick, he not only disregards his patently guilty behavior but actually provides him with an alibi for the night Owen was (supposedly) killed. Like the governess, Patrick is trying to prove his narrative reliability, but unlike her, he has his attempts thrown back into his face as irrelevant, embarrassing, and "not amusing."

The interaction with Kimball is particularly significant, because in the classic detective story and in its offshoot, the serial-killer mystery, the detective represents the narrative's epistemological desire for the truth. His main function is to restore order from chaos, to tear away the web of appearances, and to reach the bedrock of reality. Kimball's friendly treatment of Patrick seems to be the opposite of what is expected of literary detectives, who "search for the overarching plot pattern that governs and organizes the relations among the parts," moving within the "hermeneutical circle" of the text (Pyrhonen 68–9). But his inexplicable laxity becomes logical if we assume that the novel's truth-discourse is the opposite of the truth-discourse of the conventional mystery. It is not the body of the victim that functions as the ultimate guarantor of the Real but rather the clothes of the perpetrator.

As Kimball is walking into Patrick's office, the latter pretends to be talking on the phone, delivering a fashion lecture to a nonexistent interlocutor: "There are definitely *dos* and *don'ts*, good buddy, of wearing a bold-striped shirt" (267). Kimball (who is wearing an Armani suit not unlike Patrick's) is instantly reassured of his witness's unimpeachable truthfulness. The discourse of the body—dead or alive, lost or found—is slippery, unstable, and provisional. It is the discourse of fashion, with its clear-cut rules, epistemological procedures, and hierarchies of expertise that provides the foundation of the social reality-picture. Patrick's attempts to speak publicly the language of corporeal violence are both irrelevant and embarrassing, as he insists on appealing to the ontological and epistemological frameworks that are no longer even comprehensible to those around him.

Jean, his secretary/date, tells Patrick that he is "sweet" (378) because he is "shy" (378) and "concerned with others" (377). Rather than regarding Jean's evaluation as a grotesque misreading of Patrick's character, perhaps we should take it at face value. Patrick is indeed "concerned with others" in a way that is unique in his society because he is concerned with them as bodies rather than as conglomerates of clothes. Because of his proficiency in the language of fashion, he can easily blend in, appearing as a supreme authority on the "*dos* and *don'ts*" of Armani suits, Hugo Boss ties, and Christian Lacroix bustiers. And yet when Patrick is trying to parley this authority into proof of his narrative reliability, he fails miserably.

The irresolvable ambiguity of Patrick's narrative function is a means to portray him as an exception in his society—not because he is a serial killer but because he thinks that it matters whether he is or is not. He is the only one to worry about the actuality of the murders because he still inhabits the same modern world as James's governess, the world in which, as he puts it, "the lines separating appearance—what you see—and reality—what you don't—become, well, blurred" (378). But Jean and most other characters live in the postmodern world of simulacra, in which the line is not blurred but nonexistent. What you see is all there is. Jean tells Patrick that she used to think like him but no longer does. And Patrick suddenly perceives his secretary as stronger than himself, "wanting to take me into a new and unfamiliar land—the dreaded uncertainty of a totally different world" (378). But he cannot cross into this "totally different world" because he is irrevocably divided between his postmodern fashion sensibility and his modern old-fashioned preoccupation with the body. And though he is aware that "[s]urface, surface, surface was all that anyone found meaning in," he still remains half-committed to the paradigm of depth (375).

Words of Prophets on Subway Walls

American Psycho is bracketed by famous quotations: "Abandon all hope ye who enter here" and "This is not an exit." The first one is a graffito; the second a sign placed by the authorities. Just as lawlessness and the law are collapsed in the welter of urban experience, low and high culture are collapsed in the irreverent heterogeneity of the novel, whose three epigraphs place Fyodor Dostoyevsky side by side with the alt-rock group Talking Heads (whose greatest hit is called "Psycho-killer") and with Miss Manners. This obtrusive and yet self-deprecating invocation of high culture emphasizes another postmodern aspect of Ellis's novel: its self-conscious intertextuality.

Mikhael Bakhtin has defined intertextuality (or the dialogical imagination) as a property of a certain kind of narrative poetics, specifically of the "polyphonic" poetics of Dostoyevsky. Graham Allen expands Bakhtin's concept of polyphony from "relations and dialogues between characters" to "a world in which all characters, and even the narrator . . . are possessed of their own discursive consciousness" and posits the concept of "the polyphonic novel" that "presents a world in which no individual discourse can stand objectively above any other discourse" (23). Also drawing on Bakhtin, Julia Kristeva expands intertextuality further, positing it as an inherent property of literature, an invocation of interpretative codes, genres, and discourses. Intertextuality situates the individual text "within (the intertext) of society and history" (37). Clearly, *all* literature is intertextual, but intertextuality assumes different forms. Ultimately, and given Barthes's distinction between "readerly" and "writerly" texts (*S/Z*), it has become common to see polyphony and self-conscious intertextuality as features of postmodern narrativity.

American Psycho is intertextual in a number of senses. The novel does indeed present a world in which, as Allen puts it in his gloss on Bakhtin, "no discourse can stand . . . above any other." Dante, Sartre, and Dostoyevsky rub shoulders with pop and rock groups, video-rental porn flicks, and lifestyle magazines. This collapse of different cultural levels may, of course, be read as a satirical deprecation of the shallowness of the "yuppie" society. But it may also be seen, in Kristeva's terms, as a clash of different hermeneutical codes, creating the same *aporia* of meaning on the level of the novel's overall message as Patrick's (un)reliability creates on the level of its plot. Aporia, in the sense I am using here, signifies an irresolvable paradox or a quandary with no solution.

Cued by the high-culture quotations, the implied reader may be tempted to read the novel as a serious meditation on the "hell" of existential loneliness. In fact, Patrick himself occasionally makes grandiloquent claims to the effect that "Some kind of existential chasm opens before me while I'm browsing in Bloomingdale's" (179). But this "chasm" is quickly plugged by more shopping and Patrick's self-congratulatory awareness that he is "wearing a cashmere topcoat, a double-breasted plaid wool and alpaca sport coat" (180). This bathetic resolution does not undermine the validity of the high-culture discourse but juxtaposes it with another discourse, that of lifestyle magazines, which offers an alternative reading of Patrick's momentary angst as stemming from his worries over the tracking device on his VCR rather than from his remorse at his treatment of Evelyn. Since the polyphonic, intertextual character of the novel, together with Patrick's fragmented consciousness, make it impossible to privilege one discourse over the other, they constitute parallel tracks of interpretation, offering a shifting perspective on the same events. Like the famous rabbit–duck illusion, in which the brain switches between seeing a rabbit and a duck in the same picture, the novel forces the reader to switch between a high-culture and a pop-culture hermeneutic without being able to choose either.

At one point Patrick falls victim to a rabbit–duck misreading of a social situation. Seeing a "very pretty homeless girl sitting on the steps of a brownstone on Amsterdam, a Styrofoam coffee cup resting on the step below her feet," he is overcome by charity and puts a dollar bill into the cup, only to realize it is full of coffee, the girl is reading Sartre, and she is a Columbia student rather than a beggar (85–6). What might have constituted a moment of redemption, rather like the meeting of Raskolnikov and Sonya in Dostoyevsky's *Crime and Punishment*, turns into an embarrassing faux pas resulting from the misinterpretation of social performance clues. For Patrick this moment marks a breakdown of the distinction between reality and delusion: "Lunch at Hubert's becomes a permanent hallucination in which I find myself dreaming while still awake" (86). The Sartre-reading girl who should have been part of the high-culture intertext becomes instead incorporated into the discourse of brand names (it was her unnoticed Columbia book bag that should have alerted Patrick).

The dizzying collage of allusions, quotations, references, and voices in *American Psycho* creates a carnivalesque textual body, to use another term from Bakhtin. In *Rabelais and His World*, Bakhtin set out the important distinction between the classic and the grotesque or carnivalesque body. The latter is open, leaking, untidy, promiscuous, and challengingly disharmonious, as opposed to the "closed," proportionate, and disciplined classic body. The text of Ellis's novel, with its sudden shifts between incongruous discursive registers, is decidedly carnivalesque. Patrick's logorrhea and his over-the-top verbalization of his supposed atrocities, instantly followed by petty worries about his dry cleaners and face moisturizers, generate textual hybridity: "a clash of 'languages' occurring within the same utterance" (Allen 30). Patrick's entire narrative is a discursive chimera, stitched together from the urban heteroglossia which embraces Sartre, graffiti, porn, talk shows, and Miss Manners in no hierarchical order. The carnivalesque body of the text is the carnivalesque body of the city, speaking through Patrick.

Patrick's generation of grotesque physical bodies by killing and mutilating his alleged victims is analogous to his generation of the grotesque textual body of his narrative. Intertextuality run amok is to the text what (serial) killing is to the body: it rips apart a coherent, balanced, unified whole. Perhaps a fitting image of this mélange of clichéd allusions and body parts is Patrick's description of a vagina lying in his locker with "a blue ribbon from Hermès tied around" it (370). The shock of this graphic description is that it is not really shocking, since by this point the implied reader has become habituated to the most incongruous juxtapositions of violence and triviality. Startling at first, violent images become just another kind of quotation, referencing the discourse of X-rated pornography, sensationalist news media, and serial-killer biography, all very much part of Patrick's cultural milieu. While waiting for Patricia to show up for their date, Patrick is leafing through a new book by Garrison Keillor, listening to a hit by the Lovin' Spoonful, and considering whether to gouge Patricia's eyes out (he eventually decides not to) (76). Placed on the same level, the three discourses become interchangeable. The pervasive violence of the urban media infiltrates Patrick's narrative in the same way as do pop-music or high-brow culture. To kill or not to kill is not an earth-shattering moral decision but an arbitrary ascendance of a particular strand of social polyphony within the hybrid, heterogeneous, and grotesque body of the text. As Patrick points out, "This is simply how the world, *my* world, moves" (77).

The Philistine Dandy

The only discourse that stabilizes Patrick's erratic narration is the discourse of fashion. Even as his sanity and social standing become increasingly suspect in the eyes of his acquaintances, they still defer to his fashion judgment as unimpeachable. In the last chapter Patrick is out with his buddies, thinking about the necklace he made from "the bones of some girl's vertebrae," while they pepper him with questions, such as "Are the rules for wearing a pocket square the same as for a white dinner jacket?" (395). Even though his mind is on other things, he is capable of triumphantly guiding his friends through the thicket of fashion rules.

Patrick is a dandy, a man of fashion, whose self-consciously crafted social persona depends on the manipulation of the cultural code of clothes. The dandy has become a cultural hero of postmodernity by offering an image for "the shifting, laminate conception of personhood we now refer to as postmodern" (Fillin-Yeh 6). And though dandyism as a social praxis goes back to the Regency's Beau Brummell, while the dandy's articulation as a cultural icon rests on Charles Baudelaire and Walter Benjamin (*Charles Baudelaire*), the centrality of the self-conscious (wo)man of fashion in cultural studies today testifies to the fascination with the concept of identity as construction. The dandy, originally an elite, aristocratic role, merges with the contemporary cult of the media celebrity, which is also predicated on what Garelick calls the "layered" performance of the self through codified behavior, narrative, and external appearance ("The Layered Look" 37). Patrick's self-performance is equally layered; like a celebrity, he is aware of the different registers he deploys in presenting himself to the world. He is constantly monitoring his own appearance: "I am wearing a two-button single-breasted chalk-striped wool-flannel suit, a multicolored candy-striped cotton shirt and a silk pocket square, all by Patrick Aubert" (87).

He positions himself as a guardian of social propriety by going to all the right restaurants and clubs, buying all the right gadgets, knowing all the right people. But his greatest authority is in the realm of clothes. He appears genuinely affected when his friends commit fashion faux pas, wearing a wrong tie or flaunting the rules of taste in color coordination. While interacting with a girl in a video store, Patrick is shocked by the fact that she is "actually wearing a baggy, nondescript sweater— definitely *not* designer" and generic sneakers (112). This is no mere snobbishness because for Patrick the lack of social class is inextricably tied to the lack of classiness in clothes. The girl is disturbing not because she is poor but because she is not interested in fashion; she fails to "recognize" Patrick for what he is: a fashion guru, a trendsetter, an arbiter of taste (113).

However, Patrick conspicuously fails to embody the most interesting and provocative feature of the dandy: his ironic, playful, disruptive sensibility. The dandy's "resistance to norms" expresses itself in the subtle or not-so-subtle subversion of gender and social codes (Fillin-Yeh 3). Cross-dressing, camp, parody, edgy glamour, appropriation of marginalized racial and social personae characterize famous dandies, from Benjamin Disraeli and Baudelaire to Andy Warhol and Madonna. The dandy is a person who "design[s] himself as a visual object to assert an intractable independence" (Ratcliff 115). Like Lord Henry Wotton, a fashion-conscious aristocratic wit in *The Picture of Dorian Gray*, a true dandy is "Prince Paradox." Against this literary genealogy of anarchic wit and artistic creativity, Patrick stands out as staid, conservative, and philistine. If the true dandy, as Garelick writes, "longs to recreate himself as an emblem of complete originality" (*Rising Star* 19), Patrick wants to be like everybody else, only better. If the dandy constantly subverts and manipulates the fashion codes of his society, Patrick declares himself their guardian. If the dandy is charming and seductive, Patrick is abhorrent and pathetic.

The reason for this departure is precisely Patrick's panicky clinging to the accepted fashion codes as the only stabilizing influence in the chaotic world of simulacra. If the novel seems curiously old-fashioned, it is partly the result of Patrick's insistence on treating the yesteryear *Vogue* as holy writ. Fashion provides him *not* with a stage for multiple self-performances but with a set of rules to hold together his disintegrating psyche. His pronouncements on fashion are curiously pedantic and scholarly, bolstered with reliance on such real-life gurus as "Bruce Boyer [. . .] the author of *Elegance: A Guide to Quality in Menswear*," which he apparently has studied with true dedication and genuine understanding (154). Upset at his friends' mockery of this Bible of good taste, Patrick is further discomfited when Luis, whom he tries to strangle in a men's bathroom, misinterprets his actions as a sexual come-on. While sexual ambiguity and cultivated androgyny are part of the true dandy's persona, Patrick is conservatively homophobic. Shaking and close to tears, he escapes the embarrassing scene and only manages to compose himself when one of his acquaintances felicitously asks: "Hey Patrick, what's the right way to wear a tie bar or clasp?" To this Patrick can give a perfectly polished answer, no doubt quoting Boyer or a similar manual of good taste: "While a tie holder is by no means required businesswear, it adds to a clean, neat overall appearance" (160). Surely "a clean, neat overall appearance" is the last thing a dandy would strive for.

Patrick's predilection for expensive brand names is more than a yuppie's unthinking materialism. The emergence of haute couture in the *fin-de-siècle* was a twofold phenomenon. On the one hand, expensive brand names reinstated the social distinctions of dress undermined by textile industry and mass retail. On the other hand, paradoxically, by opening the possibility of cheap knockoffs and imitations, haute couture contributed to the democratization of fashion and its mass deployment as a means of self-fashioning. As Garelick puts it, "haute couture, an elite art form, wound up creating something of a democracy of style, weakening clear-cut visual distinctions of social class that had long been held in place by sumptuary laws" ("The Layered Look" 38). One no longer needed to be as rich as Disraeli to be a dandy. But for Patrick, haute couture functions precisely as "an elite art form," meant to shore up the "clear-cut distinctions" that are so sadly lacking in his world. His profound indignation when confronted with knockoffs and his insistence on "the real thing" are part of his anti-dandyist dandyism. He values brands not because they function as a proof of his wealth; he values wealth because it allows him to buy genuine brands and thus prove that something is still real within what Jean Baudrillard has called the precession of simulacra. Fashion in *American Psycho* functions not as a means of multiplying identities as modes of being, in the way it functions in *The Picture of Dorian Gray*, but rather as a means of stabilizing the already shaky, multiple, and disintegrating self of the postmodern subject. Fashion is the discursive corset worn over the grotesque body of the text.

The Body and the Suit

In "The Precession of Simulacra" Baudrillard composes a lament for the Real, drowned in the postmodern production of simulacra, copies without original, which shatter "every ideal distinction between true and false" and undermine the principle of referentiality (360). It is not merely that simulacra make it impossible to tell the difference between "being and appearances . . . the Real and its concepts"; they make this distinction meaningless (343). According to Baudrillard, the horror of postmodernity comes from its willing acceptance of the postulate that "the truth, reference, and objective causes have ceased to exist" (344). In such an episteme, to use Michel Foucault's term for a cultural formation, emotions are flattened into an insatiable voyeuristic desire for visual stimulation. The only genuine feeling remaining is nostalgia: "When the real is no longer what it used to be, nostalgia assumes its full meaning," writes Baudrillard ("Precession" 347). But even here postmodern society is unable to come to terms with its nature: "none of our societies knows how to manage its mourning for the real, for power, for the *social itself*" (361).

American Psycho may be read as a similar lament for the reality of the Real, a nostalgic search for nostalgia, a violent exploration of the irrelevancy of violence. And yet it may also be read as a counter-argument to Baudrillard's lament for the Real by suggesting that the acceptance of the simulacrum as the new order of epistemological and social organization might, in fact, become a foundation for a new cultural and moral code. Since, as Baudrillard recognizes very well, the return to the truth principle is impossible, the postmodern subject has to come to terms with its own provisional and artificial status. Patrick's violence is not, as Baudrillard suggests, "the violence of a civilization without secrets" ("Precession" 350); it is a violence that attempts to restore the truth principle and the aesthetics of depth by manufacturing secrets. But it leads nowhere. The dead end of the search for the Real is fittingly epitomized in the scene in which Patrick becomes "obsessed with the idea of faxing Sara's blood I drained from her vagina over to her office in the mergers division at Chase Manhattan" (395). If blood can be faxed, it is no more significant than a printer's ink.

Patrick's quest for the truth in/of the body ends in the hell of narrative unreliability for him and in the confusion of clashing hermeneutical codes for the reader. But just as the discourse of fashion offers the only respite from his increasing epistemological "disorganization," it also, surprisingly, offers the only possibility, albeit narrow, of a genuine human connection. In the book's penultimate chapter, Patrick is robbed by a cab driver who seems to recognize him as a killer (a scene that supports ambiguity rather than outright unreliability as Patrick's narrative modality). Walking back to the highway and sobbing, he is accosted by a sick beggar woman. Instead of (imagining) killing her as he usually does with the unfortunate and the poor, Patrick meekly asks her to go away. And in an unexpected response, she tells him to get a haircut, proving that somebody truly *looks* at him without the hidden agendas of mockery and/or social games of his Wall Street buddies (394).

Significantly, the beggar woman emerges from "behind a *Threepenny Opera* poster" rather than that of the ubiquitous *Les Misérables*: a faint intimation of some genuine social involvement and awareness, not (yet) reduced to a bland commercial hit.

In this fleeting moment of stranger interaction, Patrick's obsession with his appearance, so easily reviled as the yuppie's narcissism, becomes a meeting point across the divide of class and gender. If religion or metaphysics of suffering can no longer provide the foundation for social solidarity, all that remains is appearance and spectacle. The depth paradigm of *fin-de-siècle* modernism has been discredited. In digging into his own violence-obsessed psyche, Patrick gains "no deeper knowledge about myself, no new understanding extracted from my telling" (377). The search for the truth in confession ends in meaningless anomie. But surfaces do matter. As the Miss Manners epigraph to the novel suggests, social codes of behavior, no matter how conventional or superficial, are the only way to restrain violence: "If we followed every impulse, we'd be killing each other" (Ellis n.p.).

Instead of seeing the soul as the reverse of the surface, we should perhaps be willing to accept the surface at face value. After all, Patrick, no matter how narcissistic, is capable of changing his clothes to suit another person's taste:

> The Julian might be a little too warm for May but if Patricia's wearing this outfit by Karl Lagerfeld that I *think* she's going to, then maybe I *will* go with the Julian, because it would go well with *her* suit. (76; emphasis in the original)

Perhaps Jean's assessment of Patrick as a person who is "concerned with others," no matter how tentative and incoherent, is ultimately justified (377). His search for connection through violence ends in the emptiness of simulacra, phantoms of intertextuality run amok. But his search for connection through fashion and appearance may yet succeed. *Vogue* may not be much of a foundation for social solidarity. But it is better than nothing.

PART II

Glamorama

Introduction

In many ways *Glamorama* was ahead of its time. The novel was published in 1998, and its treatment of image manipulation, virtual identity, and celebrity anticipated the ubiquity of Photoshop, Facebook, and reality TV. Its graphic depictions of spectacular terror bombings foreshadowed, of course, the events of September 11, 2001. But like *American Psycho*, the book was also very much *of* its time. Its exhaustive catalogues of famous people and brand names cement the novel to its era; the technology to fabricate images was widely available at the time of writing; terror attacks both within and outside the US were not foreign to the 1990s. In any case, what prescient qualities *Glamorama* may possess were not readily apparent to its early reviewers who, schooled by Ellis's reputation as literary "it-boy" and the *American Psycho* controversy, stressed its setting among the privileged and noted its mounting body count. Like its protagonist Victor Ward for whom, Steven Shaviro writes, "to be is to be perceived" (*Connected* 74), the novel's historical acuity is largely, if not entirely, the product of its critical perception.

Glamorama's uneasy relation to its historical moment (five of its six parts progress through descending chapter numbers) is reflected in scholarly work on the book, much of which was published after 9/11 and which retrospectively situates the novel in relation to the events of that day. Punter, Colebrook, and Ayers, who wrote before 9/11, draw on the work of Frederic Jameson, Gilles Deleuze, and Jean Baudrillard, whose publications in the 1990s offered scholars a language with which to describe the erosion of authenticity and the subsumption of the real by the image. For Michaels, Stephenson, Houen, and Peterson, 9/11 provided a framework through which to read *Glamorama*'s treatment of terrorism, spectacle, and politics; conversely for Woods and, later, Blazer ("*Glamorama*"), terrorism in the novel offers insight into postmodern, decentered, fragmented subjectivity. Nielsen ("Telling Doubles") identifies the locus of this fragmentation in the novel's vexed relation with its own first-person narrative voice. For all, *Glamorama* is the quintessence of the postmodern, charting the evaporation of subjectivity as a coherent, stable locus of meaning, sensation, or emotion.

The chapters in this part offer new dimensions to this tradition of critical work. David Schmid's "The Unusual Suspects: Celebrity, Conspiracy, and Objective Violence in *Glamorama*" notes Ellis's use of the conspiracy narrative that promises, but withholds, revelation. Schmid situates *Glamorama* within the cultural context of the period (when *Twin Peaks* and *The X-Files* were popular) but argues that the primacy of Jameson and Baudrillard in readings of *Glamorama* needs to be supplemented by Slavoj Žižek's work on 9/11 and Alain Badiou's retrospective reflections on the twentieth century. With " 'It's Really Me': Intermediality and Constructed Identities in *Glamorama*," Sonia Baelo-Allué examines the references to other media (music, cinema, photography) within the first-person narrative framework. Focusing on the novel's structural and stylistic aspects, Baelo-Allué uncovers, in its fragmented narration and disjointed form, both a reaffirmation of art and a demarcation of its limits. Arthur Redding's " 'Merely Political': Glam Terrorism and Celebrity Politics in Bret Easton Ellis's *Glamorama*" examines the novel's retrospective alignment with spectacular terrorism and geopolitics which he contrasts with the narrative's disjointed, fragmented quality that belies temporal progression or narrative coherence. Redding treats the novel as both sign and symptom of the challenges to political engagement and efficacy in a world in which engagement, efficacy, and even the political can be effectively simulated.

Glamorama's own explorations of politics, violence, spectacle, and, via Victor, the subject's implication, or imbrication, in them is addressed in each of the chapters in this part. All are concerned with the nature of contemporary subjectivity, the qualities of the medium through which this subject is (re)presented, and the implications—political or personal—for such a subject inside and outside of a literary text. For Schmid, *Glamorama*'s multiple film crews and Victor's perennial confusion about what is happening are not evidence of Ellis's continued obsession with surface and simulacra but, rather, suggest his willingness to consider the real possibility that something lies beneath: not the spectacular violence perpetrated by the group of terrorist supermodels but the structural, determinative power wielded by Victor's father, a US Senator who is considering a run on the White House. The significance of the paternal and its power has already been hinted at by Blazer and will be examined further by Nielsen in this volume. For Schmid, the fact that this power, and the violence it represents, reveals itself only in glimpses underscores his point: although *Glamorama* is concerned with a world of surfaces, this novel comes closer than Ellis has ever done to suggesting that there is a level of deeper meaning beneath the glitz.

Baelo-Allué traces the infiltration of the novel's first-person narrative voice by other media (music, cinema, photography) and, drawing on the work of Guy Debord and Baudrillard, explores the implications of this engagement for the increasingly virtual world in which the book is read. She traces the permutations of Victor's point of view throughout this long book and shows that as the plot progresses, Victor's narrative voice is increasingly permeated by other media, to the point at which a computer-generated double has apparently replaced Victor as narrator. But despite this ascendency of the image, argues Baelo-Allué, *Glamorama*'s literary medium retains the distinction between narrated and simulated events and stresses the value of the real. This aspect of her argument echoes Clark's approach to *American Psycho* in the previous part; Karnicky's chapter on *Lunar Park* will further explore the uneasy relation between reality and art in Ellis's work. And yet, as Baelo-Allué concludes, Victor's persistence in twenty-first-century cyberculture testifies to the extension—or assumption—of this fictional world into the virtual.

If, for Schmid and Baelo-Allué, *Glamorama* values depth and honors the fundamental, though elusive, distinction between work and world, Redding—like Gomel in the previous part and Annesley's chapter on *Lunar Park*—affirms the novel's embrace of the superficial. Taking as his starting point the retrospective investment of *Glamorama* with political relevance, Redding extends this unraveling of cause-and-effect to the novel itself, in which representations of events precede their occurrence. Victor's failure to make sense of what is happening to him mirrors, Redding argues, a more generalized situation of post-9/11 geopolitics in which the act is detached from its outcome and ideological causes are unlinked from their realization. *Glamorama*'s challenge to the reader is not to attempt to make sense of this world but to register her reluctance, or aversion, even to try. For Redding, the novel's treatment of terror and politics enables this timely text to float free of the historical and sets the stage for an exploration of postmodern empathy.

For each of the scholars in this part, *Glamorama*'s labyrinthine plot, its uneasy situation within its cultural and historical context, and its flirtation with cyberculture open the text and extend its work beyond the covers of the book. Unlike *American Psycho*, which was bracketed with literary references to hell, *Glamorama* begins and ends with evaluations of magnitude: "specks" is the first word of the novel, "mountain" the last; the reader must situate herself within a dizzying terrain. With *Lunar Park*, Ellis's conceptual expansion, and the challenges it poses, will take one further step.

CHAPTER 4

The Unusual Suspects: Celebrity, Conspiracy, and Objective Violence in *Glamorama*

David Schmid

In contrast to the public outcry provoked by *American Psycho*, Bret Easton Ellis's fourth novel, *Glamorama*, received relatively little attention. Although there are certainly many connections between *Glamorama* and Ellis's previous novels (including the reappearance of certain characters and the use of certain themes and techniques), this chapter will focus on what is distinctive about *Glamorama*. I will argue that this novel represents a definite advance over Ellis's earlier work, and that the nature of this advance helps to explain why *Glamorama* has been both misunderstood and underappreciated.

The key to understanding why *Glamorama* has been undervalued so persistently can be found in the following quotation from *American Psycho*, which far too many readers have assumed can also be applied to the world of *Glamorama*:

> He continues talking as he opens his new Tumi calfskin attaché case he bought at D.F. Sanders. He places the Walkman in a case alongside a Panasonic wallet-size cordless portable folding Easa-phone (he used to own the NEC 9000 Porta portable) and pulls out today's newspaper. "In one issue—in *one* issue—let's see here . . . strangled models, babies thrown from tenement rooftops, kids killed in the subway, a Communist rally, Mafia boss wiped out, Nazis." (4)

At first glance, this passage seems to be a perfect description of the world inhabited by *Glamorama*'s protagonist, Victor Ward. Although the novel contains an occasional token acknowledgment of an outside world in which violence and tragedy happen, Victor's environment in the first part of *Glamorama*, like Victor himself, is saturated with ephemera: products, fashion modeling, nightclub openings, and celebrity parties. Both seem to be dominated entirely by surface and to possess no hidden depths of any kind whatsoever. Even when Victor moves to London and then Paris and becomes involved with a group of supermodel terrorists who plan and carry out a series of spectacular bombings, there still seems to be little basis for detecting a deeper meaning to these events. In this respect, the continuities between the sterile and hyperviolent reality of *American Psycho*'s Patrick Bateman and *Glamorama*'s Victor Ward seem both obvious and substantive, and it is precisely these continuities that led so many critics to dismiss *Glamorama* as another paean to banality. "*American Psycho*," writes Daniel Mendelsohn in a typical such dismissal,

> was a bloated, stultifyingly repetitive, overhyped novel about a fabulously good-looking and expensively dressed Wall Street sociopath who tortures and dismembers beautiful young women [. . .] *Glamorama*, as anyone can see, is a bloated, stultifyingly repetitive, overhyped book about an entire gang of fabulously good-looking and expensively dressed sociopaths who torture and dismember both women and men. (8)

I want to argue, however, that these similarities are misleading. They disguise the extent to which *Glamorama* is a much more traditional novel than *American Psycho*. Containing both a stronger narrative component and greater emphasis on character development than anything Ellis had written up to this point, *Glamorama* is committed, despite its seeming preoccupation with surface, to the belief that what happens to Victor over the course of the novel both matters and can, at least to some extent, be untangled and explained. In contrast to *American Psycho*, which leaves its readers in a state of suspension concerning whether any of the narrated events actually took place (and if it matters whether they did or not), *Glamorama*, while still containing a significant degree of undecidability, cares much more about the distinction between truth and falsehood, about the ability to say what happened and why.

I am aware that these are unlikely claims to make about Ellis, who has for years been held up as the poster boy of American literary postmodernism (in both an approving and a pejorative sense). My intent is not to rehabilitate Ellis as a proto-modernist, but rather to explain how, through its use of the themes of celebrity, conspiracy, and violence, *Glamorama* explores the stakes of defining and describing reality in a manner unprecedented in Ellis's work. The novelty of the attempt also means that those theorists whose work has traditionally been used to interpret Ellis's novels (Fredric Jameson, Jean Baudrillard, and Guy Debord) may still be useful, but they need to be supplemented by other theoretical resources. Drawing on Slavoj Žižek's distinction between subjective and objective violence, and exploring Alain Badiou's concept of the "passion for the real," I will show how *Glamorama* presents Victor Ward as an unlikely seeker after truth; although that truth may never be unequivocally or authoritatively revealed, Ellis's reader is meant to appreciate the stakes of the search more than she has ever done before. My use of Žižek and Badiou is also indicative of the double meaning of my title: the "unusual suspects" refers both to Ellis's conceit of supermodel terrorists and to my displacement of the triumvirate of postmodern critics (Jameson, Baudrillard, Debord) with the supplementary and revisionary presence of Žižek and Badiou.

Celebrity, Terror, and the Unbearable Lightness of Victor

Before discussing the more innovative aspects of *Glamorama*, I would like to elaborate on those elements of the novel that are reminiscent of Ellis's previous work, partly because they help to explain why *Glamorama* was so disliked by most critics. As I mentioned earlier, the first part of the novel, which details Victor's life in New York City as an up-and-coming supermodel and wannabe nightclub owner, bears the closest resemblance to *American Psycho* and for some critics, this was the strongest part of the novel. Adam Begley, for example, argues that "A radically shortened *Glamorama*, amputated before the 200-page mark, would have been delightful: a fine satire, funny, bleak, biting." Even the critics who appreciated the satire of celebrity-saturated 1990s Manhattan, however, seemed to hate Ellis's protagonist. Although Victor Ward was unlikely to provoke the same kind of outrage as Patrick Bateman (he is, by virtue of his more or less forced participation in the terrorist group, more victim than predator), he is presented as such a vacuous, uninteresting, and banal character that he makes Patrick look complex, three-dimensional, and engaging by comparison.

There is no doubt that Victor is, to put it mildly, dim and shallow. Ironically, one of the first comments he makes about himself is "I . . . know . . . nothing" (7) and Victor's lack of knowledge is confirmed again and again as well as commented on by other characters throughout the novel. "We like you, Victor," says Bobby, the leader of the supermodel–terrorist gang, "because you don't have any answers" (327) and "because you think the Gaza Strip is a particularly lascivious move an erotic dancer makes" (359). Victor's vacuousness may be one of the main reasons that *Glamorama* did not enjoy greater success, but, at the risk of stating the obvious, the vacuousness is entirely deliberate on Ellis's part and, as the novel progresses, even works to make Victor something of a tragic figure. When we first encounter the phrase that Victor uses repeatedly, "The better you look, the more you see" (31, 63), our initial reaction is to sneer at Victor's shallowness. As Victor becomes more deeply embroiled in conspiracy, however, this shallowness comes to seem more and more like a tragic flaw as we realize just how totally unequipped he is to cope with what is happening to him—a point reiterated by another haunting phrase, "It's what you don't know that matters most" (390, 459). Despite his many annoying attributes, Victor is meant to be a sympathetic figure, and in particular the reader is meant to identify with his increasingly frustrated desire to figure out what is happening to him, despite the fact that he is completely incapable of doing so.

The stakes of whether or not the reader is sympathetic to Victor are suggested by the consequences of those critical analyses that tend to pathologize both Victor's unreliability as a narrator and his inability to understand. Angela Woods, for example, has diagnosed Victor as "an exemplary postmodern schizophrenic." For Woods, Victor's "schizophrenic narrative voice" has the effect of making meaning "undecidable": "that events might in fact be figments of a psychotic imagination utterly destabilizes the delineation of reality from representation, truth from delusion." Similarly, William Stephenson writes that "Victor's perception of the world as alternately simulation and reality is so rapid as to allow him to make no firm distinction between them, or even to characterize such a distinction as problematic" (285). Such blanket dismissals of Victor's doomed attempts to understand what is happening to him miss the text's problematic relation to "reality" and its potential to offer a critique of that reality. Victor does not wander schizophrenically among the simulacra (as Jameson or Baudrillard-inflected readings would have it). *Glamorama* is an anti-Baudrillardian, anti-simulacra book (it is terrorist mastermind Bobby Hughes who possesses a copy of Debord [302]), and Victor consistently, if ineffectively, attempts to determine the difference between what is real and what is not. The Victor who, in the opening section of the novel, moans "I don't care what's real anymore" (79) will, by the end, dismiss his girlfriend as "reality-challenged" (512). Though he never learns the truth, his quest does uncover the multiple forces that inform our mediated world and—even more important—*that the distinctions between these forces matter*. Put differently, to identify with Victor is to remain open to the novel's political and critical dimensions. This is a point to which I will return later.

Rather than anatomizing Victor's shortcomings, a more productive direction for discussion is to consider Victor's obsession with celebrity status (he's "semi-famous" [13], "*not* a top male model" [90, emphasis mine], who needs to identify himself to his agent as "the guy everyone thought David Geffen was dating" [34]) and how celebrity functions more generally in *Glamorama*. On an obvious level, of course, celebrity acts as the perfect symbol for the triviality and shallowness that is the subject of Ellis's satire, though the assumption that Ellis's use of celebrity merely mimics that shallowness rather than critiquing it is another reason many critics dismissed *Glamorama*. While the conceit of terrorist supermodels is patently absurd ("My fingers fail me: The stupidity of the premise induces instant arthritis" writes Begley), the novel does offer justifications for why models make such good terrorists: "as a model all you do all day is stand around and do what other people tell you to do [. . .] it was an analogy that made sense" (352). Ellis has commented on what he sees as the connections between the worlds of fashion and terrorism:

> I think the connection I'm making has to do with the tyranny of beauty in our culture and the tyranny of terrorism. Of course that's a metaphor and the idea of models actually blowing up hotels and airlines is farfetched. But the idealization of beauty and fame in our culture drives people crazy in a lot of ways: we resent it, we want it, we love it, we hate it . . . Fashion—and what makes us attracted to it—is all about insecurity . . . The point of terrorism is to make us insecure about our safety. What I did in *Glamorama*—or what I propose—is that these two things can be linked; there is a connection. ("Interview")

Whether or not one agrees with the connections Ellis asserts is less important than recognizing that Ellis has reasons for using celebrity as a backdrop in *Glamorama* other than its association with the shallow and the trivial. Indeed, celebrity is the means by which we can access another equally important dimension of *Glamorama*: Ellis's use of conspiracy. It should come as no surprise that Ellis sees the world of celebrity fashion models as a convenient, almost logical, way of transitioning into the subject of a terrorist conspiracy:

> Fear—that was the leap I was making between terrorism and fashion. Also, it interested me to ask what would be a perfect smoke screen for a terrorist conspiracy. Would it be a world where image and surface were the only truths? Could that be the smoke screen? (Blume)

As this quotation implies, *Glamorama* is dominated by a very strong sense that the apparent ubiquity of surface, a surface epitomized by the world of celebrity and fashion, in fact works as a screen narrative, obscuring a deeper level: the terrorist conspiracy. In turn, as we shall see, the terrorist conspiracy also acts as a kind of screen narrative, masking what will be revealed as the novel's ultimate stakes.

Glamorama as Conspiracy Narrative

If celebrity gives Ellis a way of signifying and exploring both shallowness and depth, conspiracy is the factor that makes *Glamorama*, formally speaking, the most traditional novel Ellis had written up to this point of his career. Ellis has described *Glamorama* as sharing his earlier works' concern with "certain elements of my generation . . . by ridiculing the things we seem to find important or the way we're obsessed with surfaces and glamor and status" ("Interview"), but he has also explained how the presence of conspiracy introduces another dimension to his work:

> Well, to put it bluntly, it has a plot, or at least an identifiable narrative that my other novels really don't have . . . as I've gotten older, the idea of narrative appeals more to me . . . I think that as you get older you start to see that lives have a certain narrative shape to them that when you're younger and haven't had that much experience you don't see. And I think that affects your work. Also, if you're writing about a conspiracy—which is really what *Glamorama* is about—you can't help but have a narrative. The conspiracy dictates it. ("Interview")

If Ellis presents his return to narrative as part of his evolution as a novelist, he also presents himself as the passive instrument of the conspiratorial emphasis in his narrative. Much like his protagonist's, the author's encounter with conspiracy compels him to abide by its dictates: he works with conspiracy, *therefore* he is compelled to produce a more traditional narrative. Of course, Ellis's turn to conspiracy also reinforces his reputation as a cultural barometer: during the 1990s, when Ellis was writing *Glamorama*, conspiracy narratives were becoming mainstream (*The X-Files* was an immensely popular program at the time).

In *Aliens in America* (published in the same year as *Glamorama*), Jodi Dean points to the political potential of conspiracy culture:

> We have moved from consensus reality to virtual reality. Politics itself must now be theorized from within the widespread

dispersion of paranoia that has supplanted focus targets such as "Jim Crow" laws, Richard Nixon, and the Vietnam War. Insofar as its practitioners can link together varieties of disparate phenomena to find patterns of denial, occlusion, and manipulation, conspiracy theory, far from a label dismissively attached to the lunatic fringe, may well be an appropriate vehicle for political contestation. (8)

Such political potential, though, in no way amounts to cogent critique. In fact, as Peter Knight explains, conspiracy narratives in the 1990s, unlike those of the 1960s and 1970s, enact a kind of "default skepticism" rather than provide a counter-narrative: "Conspiracy culture is thus no longer a symptom of a naïve and fervent demonology, but a very knowing acceptance of suspicion as a default mode—including even a cynical and self-reflexive skepticism about that suspicion itself" (*Conspiracy Culture* 55). This ambivalence about the political potential of conspiracy narratives is most evident in *The X-Files*. According to Douglas Kellner, *The X-Files* combines the two types of paranoia that define conspiracy thinking: "populist paranoia that demonizes irrationally institutions [sic] and often projects evil onto occult and supernatural figures, and a critical paranoia that is rationally suspicious of hegemonic institutions like the state, the military, or corporations" (205). The combination of both types of paranoia, argues Kellner, has mixed consequences for politics: "*The X-Files* combines rational social critique and mistrust with occultist projection onto the supernatural that deflects attention from the real sources of social oppression" (205). *The X-Files* thus advances potentially radical social critique but also undermines that critique through its supernaturalism, leading to a situation in which the series promises, but never delivers, the revelation of the ultimate source of power/conspiracy and the final truth.

For Ellis, this deferral of ultimate meaning in conspiracy narratives, or what Peter Knight describes as "a principle of *différance*" (*Conspiracy Culture* 223), reflects *Glamorama*'s pursuit of an ever-elusive meaning or truth. "By its very nature conspiracy doesn't really make sense. One element leads to another that leads to another that leads to another, and there seems to be no final answer. To me, a conspiracy is an essentially meaningless thing" (Blume). *Glamorama* may share with conspiracy narratives like *The X-Files* an emphasis on the deferral of meaning, and no ultimate meaning is attained by the end of the novel, but meaning as such is not discarded—it remains, if only under erasure. The novel wavers between utter undecidability and cogent critique; its power and value come precisely from this combination.

Subjective vs. Objective Violence

What connects the themes of celebrity and conspiracy in *Glamorama* is the novel's use of violence. On one level, Ellis uses violence in *Glamorama* in the same way he has used violence throughout his literary career, as a way to "break out of a flat, affectless world and try to find some approximation of meaning" (Blume). In the "meaningless" context of conspiracy, violence punctures the surface of things and hints at hidden depths. But there are different levels of violence in *Glamorama*, and the role of violence in the novel is best understood through Žižek's distinction between subjective and objective violence in his 2008 book *Violence: Six Sideways Reflections*. Subjective violence is "obvious" and "clearly visible": "acts of crime and terror, civil unrest, international conflict" (1). Objective violence, on the other hand, resides in "the contours of the background which generates such outbursts" and consists of "the often catastrophic consequences of the smooth functioning of our economic and political systems" (1, 2).

In *Glamorama*, subjective violence is easily identifiable as the spectacular, highly visible devastation wrought by Bobby Hughes and his gang of supermodel terrorists. The ubiquitous camera crews that record it underline its visibility. But this very visibility, Žižek continues, enables subjective violence to obscure the presence of objective violence, which is much more difficult to detect:

> Is there not something suspicious, indeed symptomatic, about this focus on subjective violence—that violence which is enacted by social agents, evil individuals, disciplined repressive apparatuses, fanatical crowds? Doesn't it desperately try to distract our attention from the true locus of trouble, by obliterating from view other forms of violence and thus actively participating in them? (*Violence* 9)

Ellis's goal, in *Glamorama*, is to connect this spectacular violence with the invisible, objective violence that characterizes the ordinary functioning of the system. It is this attempt that establishes *Glamorama* as a significant departure from Ellis's previous work. Most striking is the fact that the relays between subjective and objective violence in *Glamorama* are not established in any easy, unambiguous, or instrumental fashion, as we can see if we look more closely at the role played by Victor's father, a US Senator with Presidential ambitions. On the surface of the novel, Victor's father plays a minor role, but of course, given the conspiracy scenario, this is exactly what draws our attention to him. Over the course of the novel a plot emerges and Victor's father is revealed to be close to the center of the conspiracy. The first time Victor's father is mentioned in the novel, Victor himself dismisses him as a "contrivance" and a "plot device" (41). Although some critics have taken Victor at his word here, and have seen Victor's father as nothing more than a plot element that Ellis has taken and satirized from the thriller genre, I want to suggest that the role played by this character is much more complex than Victor's throwaway comments suggest. Victor's father points to the operation of objective violence in *Glamorama*.

The first hint the reader gets of these complexities comes early in the novel as Victor has lunch with his father in Manhattan. In this scene, we learn that Victor's father works in Washington, DC, and that Victor's activities and statements to the press are both a potential and real source of embarrassment to his father: "What you say and do actually affects my life, and because of what my life is like, it can be acutely embarrassing for me" (92). At this point of the novel, the reader does not learn exactly what Victor's father does for a living, but his identification with the center of US political power is enough to associate Victor's father with the system in the broadest sense of the word, and the details of this association will become much more specific later in the novel.

During the same lunch meeting with Victor, his father makes some cryptic or apparently banal comments, the significance of which will also become clear much later in the novel: "You just need to find yourself [. . .] Find—I don't know—a new you?" (90). Victor's father has already initiated this process by suggesting that Victor change his last name from Johnson to Ward (presumably so Victor won't be associated with his father). When the second part of the novel begins with Victor being sent to Europe by the mysterious figure of F. Fred Palakon on a mission to find an old school friend and bring her back to the US, it seems that Victor will be given the chance to reinvent himself.

Moving Victor and the setting of the remainder of the novel to Europe at this point is an inspired decision on Ellis's part, even though many critics felt that the novel started to go downhill at this point (Begley describes this part of the novel as "300 pages of dreck"). Victor's move evokes a number of previous American journeys to Europe that offer added dimensions and complexity to the plot. What will happen to Victor in the remainder of the novel? Will the person he has been commissioned to recover and return to the US change him, as Lambert Strether is changed in Henry James's *The Ambassadors*? Or will Victor seize the opportunity to reinvent himself and take on a new identity, perhaps even through an act of murder, as the protagonist of Patricia Highsmith's *The Talented Mr. Ripley* does?

The second possibility turns out to resemble much more closely what apparently happens to Victor, although he is the one who is replaced, rather than the one who does the replacing. Toward the end of the novel, when Victor is both trying to leave the group of supermodel terrorists and struggling to comprehend the full complexity of the situation in which he finds himself, we learn that Victor's father is in fact a United States senator who is planning a run at the White House: "Mr. Johnson, your father is leaving the United States Senate [. . .] He is interested in moving on, shall we say?" (458). With Victor's father now identified even more closely with center of systemic political power, his association with the objective violence that defines that system becomes even stronger; more significant than the knowledge of his profession, though, is the revelation that Victor's father has been working with both Palakon and Bobby Hughes, the leader of the terrorist cell, to keep Victor away from the United States and from his father. As Palakon explains to Victor: "your father didn't want you harmed in any way [. . .] He simply wanted you to, well, take a break for a little while. He wanted you . . . preoccupied. He didn't want you in the States. [. . .] Things were discussed. Arrangements were made" (459). It is this link between Palakon and the shadowy figure of the Senator—established with Palakon's simple statement, "I work for your father, Mr. Ward" (457)—that offers, for Victor, insight into Žižek's concept of objective violence. As Victor realizes the full extent of his father's possible complicity in the terrorist conspiracy, he realizes precisely that he is getting a glimpse of what usually remains invisible:

> These men are perpetrators and the table they're sitting behind suddenly seems vaster and they're making plans, they're jotting memoranda, they're casting motives, they're plotting itineraries. Something invisible is forming itself in the cold air in the interrogation room and it's directed at me, wheeling forward. (457–58)

Unfortunately, Victor is not able to do anything with the knowledge he gains because by the end of the novel, it appears that Victor, with the active collusion of his father, has been disappeared and a new Victor has taken over his life. This new Victor fits his father's requirements for a son (he is settling down and attending law school rather than modeling and partying). The positive consequences of this replacement for Victor's father are suggested by the last glimpse we have of the Senator, a glimpse that suggests that the father's political plans are proceeding apace: "Now Dan Rather's interviewing my father in his office. Dad has obviously had a face-lift and his upper-lip-to-nose area has been shortened, droopy lids have been lifted and his teeth are bleached. He's laughing, relaxed" (539). The Senator has also learnt the lessons of transformation; he is willing to change himself, too, albeit not quite so radically as he has apparently changed his son's life.

The Reader's Search for Truth and Reality

Glamorama's conspiracy narrative, in which meaning is constantly deferred, poses crucial challenges to the reader. Every detail of the narrative is subject to question and revision. The reader, like Victor, cannot be absolutely sure what really happened, and this position of skepticism can never be abandoned. There are a number of viable explanations, including the possibility that Victor has had some kind of (possibly drug-induced) psychotic break and is hallucinating many or all of the events. In the remainder of this chapter, my aim is not to argue that there is only one true explanation for the events in the novel, but rather to emphasize the fact that, as long as Ellis holds their real meaning in suspension (and he does so scrupulously), the reader is given the task of choosing from a range of possible interpretations, all of which come with their own set of consequences, and all of which are thoroughly mediatized, that is, contaminated by the possibility that they have been manipulated or wholly created by media technologies and are therefore not true by any conventional standard. The point, however, is that for Ellis, this contamination is not something to be either mourned or fought against; it simply is. As Palakon puts it, "There are different truths" (464).

Ellis's reader and the critic are thus left with a choice that is both sobering and exhilarating: which version of events or reading of the novel are we prepared to endorse, and why? The stakes of this choice become clear if we consider the novel in terms of the terrorism that it so presciently describes. Even though *Glamorama* appeared before 9/11, the events of that day provide a convenient as well as a compelling example of how novelists respond to the imperative to represent, to make sense of, to cast into narrative form, the relationship between violence and reality. In "Welcome to the Desert of the Real!" (2002), an essay that Žižek would later expand into a book that engages in detail with Badiou's concept of the "passion for the real," he urges that we recognize the terrorist attackers as "the distilled version of our own essence" (387). Jamie Fields, recounting how she, and other models, were recruited by Bobby, suggests as much: "it wasn't hard to recruit people . . . everyone wanted to be around us . . . everyone wanted to be movie stars . . . and in the end, basically, everyone was a sociopath" (352). In the book version of "Welcome," Žižek suggests that, in order to achieve this act of recognition, America will need to "finally risk stepping through the fantasmatic screen separating it from the Outside

World, accepting its arrival into the Real world" (*Welcome* 49). "I was told I was destroying lives," Jamie continues, "but it didn't touch me because no one we knew was real . . . people just seemed . . . fake and . . . Bobby liked that I felt that way . . . It 'helped,' he said" (354). Jamie goes on to describe "heads struck with such force they broke open as easily as soft-boiled eggs" and "a form of torture where the victim has to swallow a rope" before the director packs up and leaves (354).

Ellis, in his own way, is responding to this same imperative to confront the Real. Neither he, nor his protagonist, is willing to accept Palakon's matter-of-fact assent to Victor's lament that "everything's a lie" (463). Here lies the political potential of *Glamorama*'s conspiracy narrative. Those who emphasize the undecidability of *Glamorama* are also those who tend to imply political quietism or indifference on Ellis's part. Walter Benn Michaels, for example, in commenting on the use of a quotation from Hitler as one of the epigraphs of *Glamorama* ("You make a mistake if you see what we do as merely political") argues that "In *Glamorama*, however, it is hard to see how 'what we do' or what anyone does is at all political, much less merely political. *Glamorama* is about models and terrorists—about models-slash-terrorists" (105). My objection to such comments is not so much that they misread *Glamorama* (although I think Michaels does not pay enough attention to the conspiracy narrative in the novel) because I agree that it is highly problematic to read *Glamorama* as a political novel in any conventional sense. At the same time, though, the absence of politics by conventional means in *Glamorama* does not leave the novel politically toothless, and critics who, like Michaels, assume that Ellis's preoccupation with image is antipathetic to political content are missing the point.

In an otherwise perceptive article on the novelistic response to 9/11, Alex Houen argues that a revision of realism is necessary for the politically engaged novelist writing after 9/11. Houen believes that such a revision would (re)examine the relation between violence and image; its worst outcome would be the conclusion, by the novelist, that there is "nothing but image," a position that Houen associates with Baudrillard (428). According to Houen, *Glamorama* presents "transferential loops" between the simulacral and the real: "As the novel progresses, it certainly becomes clear that Victor's ability to find a way out of this looping would allow him to regain control of his life. It never happens; he is already too invested in the image world" (428–29). While there is no doubt that Victor's situation at the end of *Glamorama* is bleak, I disagree that the bleakness comes from what Houen seems to see as the mutual exclusivity of image and reality. Rather than acknowledge what appears to Houen to be the ultimate dominance of image, I am inclined to emphasize Ellis's and Victor's insistent engagement with a thoroughly mediatized version of the real. It may be true, as Houen argues, that *Glamorama* confirms the belief that "a culture of simulacra is inescapable" (430), but I see no evidence of fatalism regarding this fact on Ellis's part: after all, Palakon's statement, "there are different truths [. . .] no one cares about 'better.' No one cares about 'worse,'" causes Victor to weep (463–64). *Glamorama* does not celebrate undecidability for its own sake; nor does the novel unproblematically (re)assert the category of the real as if it can be separated magically from representation.

The Passion for the Real in *Glamorama*

In his 2007 book *True Crime*, Mark Seltzer argues that violence has often been used as if it can achieve a kind of unmediated access to the real. "The media," writes Seltzer, "develop possibilities of social communication (social relation) without interaction . . . To the extent that this is experienced as a crime against humanity, violence (and its synthetic witnessing) will . . . be solicited as its antidote" (170). While I agree with Seltzer that many writers have used violence in this manner (and perhaps even Ellis has done so in the past), *Glamorama* posits both violence *and* the real as thoroughly tied up with representation. Real and fake blood, torn limbs and props, victims and extras are indistinguishable. A bombing on the Boulevard Raspail leaves "legs blown off [. . .] skulls crushed [. . .] people bleeding to death in minutes," but "without staring through the lens of the cameras, everything at that distance looks tiny and inconsequential and vaguely unreal" (337). Even the attempt to penetrate beneath the deceiving layers of subjective violence to an objective violence that represents a deeper level must negotiate with the problematic of representation. But throughout the novel, the difference between the deceptive level of subjective violence and the more troubling operation of objective violence *matters*, and the attempt to discern the difference must still be made not only by Victor but also by the reader. In this way, *Glamorama*'s mediatized landscape solicits not violence but, rather, what Alain Badiou has described as the "passion for the real."

According to Badiou, the passion for the real, which is distinguished by the desire to penetrate beneath the deceiving appearance of what ordinarily passes for reality in order to determine the real itself, is "the key to understanding the [twentieth] century" (32). For Badiou, the "passion for the real" is defined by excessive violence and by the effort to represent that violence: "Much of the century's greatness lay in its commitment to thinking the relationship—often obscure at first—between real violence and semblance" (48). Representation is central precisely because the real is unrepresentable. This unrepresentability leads, paradoxically, to an obsession with representation because "the real, conceived in its contingent absoluteness, is never real enough not to be suspected of semblance. The passion for the real is also, of necessity, suspicion. Nothing can attest that the real is the real, nothing but the system of fictions wherein it plays the role of the real" (52).

I do not want to claim that Ellis's novel is a perfectly complete and accurate instantiation of the passion for the real. For example, when Badiou argues that the twentieth century's passion for the real led it to "destroy every density, every claim to substantiality, and every assertion of reality" out of a kind of terroristic nihilism (64), it is clear that Ellis does not share this nihilism, which he relegates to Bobby Hughes and his supermodel/terrorist gang. But *Glamorama* participates in the same conjunction of violence and representation that defines Badiou's passion for the real. Ellis's novel is an effort to understand the stakes of representing reality, especially when that reality appears to be violated or disturbed by an act or acts of violence. At one point in *Violence*, Žižek cautions against what he describes as the "hermeneutic temptation: the search for some deeper meaning or message hidden" within the subjective acts of violence (65). Ellis cannot help but give in to this temptation—*Glamorama*'s concern with celebrity, conspiracy, and spectacular violence is explicit—but unlike Victor, Ellis has no expectation that a deeper meaning can be found. The attempt, however, must be made.

In terms that echo Badiou's argument regarding the unavoidably intimate relation between representation and violence, Žižek explains that the "fundamental paradox" of the passion for the real is that "it culminates in its apparent opposite, in a *theatrical spectacle*" (*Welcome* 9). According to Žižek, however, this does not mean that the passion for the real should be abandoned as a strategy or an ideal; to do so would lead to a situation in which "the only remaining attitude is that of refusing to go to the end, of 'keeping up appearances'" (*Welcome* 24). Like Žižek, Ellis believes that "keeping up appearances" is not an option and that the objective violence that defines the Real must continue to be confronted. But Ellis also believes that this confrontation comes through engaging with representation, not in spite of representation. Consequentially, *Glamorama* accords a crucial role to the reader. The fact that the last we see of Victor's father, the closest we come to a personification of objective violence in *Glamorama*, is a series of televised images (538–40) can only be read as peculiarly appropriate. Of course, these images may be as manipulated and mediatized as everything else Victor witnesses in the novel. There may be another layer to the conspiracy that has not yet been revealed. But it is a mistake to dismiss *Glamorama* as fatally destabilizing any sense of objective reality. The ongoing attempt to connect the spectacular, easily visible image with invisible, objective violence (the violence that characterizes the ordinary functioning of the system) unveils reality as we know it. Even if we, like Victor, are doomed to fail, it is precisely this attempt that defines the true achievement of *Glamorama*.

CHAPTER 5

"It's Really Me": Intermediality and Constructed Identities in *Glamorama*

Sonia Baelo-Allué

Glamorama is a complex novel in both thematic and narrative terms primarily due to Bret Easton Ellis's use of intermediality as an expressive means to construct the personality of Victor, the main character in the novel, and to build up the climate of virtuality that frames the narrative and the terrorist plot. Intermediality—the convergence of literature, cinema, newspapers, television, and other popular culture and media forms—plays different roles in *Glamorama*. Initially, intermediality is firmly framed by the pattern and style of literary narration. References to films, print culture, images, and music contribute to the construction of characters and the depiction of their shallow lifestyles, particularly their obsession with always having an audience. As the novel progresses, intermedial references engulf Victor's narrative voice, reflecting a struggle between different media for narrative control. In the course of the novel, a double of Victor is created that briefly usurps the narrative voice and the novel veers toward the virtuality that Baudrillard describes in *The Perfect Crime*. This double ultimately eludes the novelistic medium and enjoys a virtual life in cyberspace, maintaining a continuous presence on websites and social networks. In a time when media are central and ubiquitous in many people's lives, *Glamorama* displays a love–hate relationship with contemporary media, complicit with but critical of the consequences and possibilities of an increasingly virtual world.

Intermediality and Bret Easton Ellis

Intermediality has always been an aspect of media studies, including the medium of literary texts. According to Jay David Bolter and Richard

Grusin, all media works are connected with other media since no channel of communication works in isolation anymore (*Remediation* 15). As new media have always emerged from older forms, every medium is intermedial (a film, for example, contains 25 photographs per second). Due to the rapid circulation of digital technologies and the conversion from the analogue to the digital, media are increasingly interconnected. Literature is no exception to intermediality: like other mediums, literature may incorporate the effects of other media and may be disseminated in other media. Maddalena Pennachia Punzi states that the way a "literary message" can be reproduced in comic-strip adaptations, audiobooks, movie adaptations, and video games constitutes a form of "literary intermediality" (9). Irina O. Rajewsky distinguishes between three types of intermedial practices: medial transposition (the transformation of a given media product into another medium; e.g., film adaptations or novelizations), media combination (the blend of at least two distinct media or medial forms of articulation that are present in their own materiality and constitute an entire product; e.g., opera, film, or performances), and intermedial references: the use of references to other media by imitating these other media techniques (51–54). This last intermedial practice is most common to literature and it plays a prominent role in *Glamorama*. It is important to keep in mind that the practice of intermedial reference does not involve two different media working together. Only one medium is present—in this case, the literary text—and it contains references to other media. As Rajewsky puts it: "[r]ather than combining different medial forms of articulation, the given media-product thematizes, evokes, or imitates elements or structures of another, conventionally distinct medium through the use of its own media-specific means" (53). This practice has some shortcomings since, due to the specificity of the novel, other media techniques cannot be genuinely reproduced in it; they can only be imitated. However, the effects are visible and worth studying.

Bret Easton Ellis has used intermedial references in all of his novels. For example, *Less Than Zero* was considered an MTV novel because of the techniques from music television that were incorporated in it: short chapters resembling music videos and the montage-like organization of images. In *American Psycho*, Patrick Bateman, the serial killer of the novel, speaks the language of advertisements, tabloids, films, and mass culture references in general, including pornography and horror films. In *Glamorama*, Ellis's interest in the language and expressive possibilities of media produced a novel rich in intermedial references. Written words, visual images, and acoustic references construct Victor's world.

In a thoughtful discussion of intermediality in *Glamorama*, Sheli Ayers argues that *Glamorama* represents the history of imaging technology—especially photography, film, animation, video, the digital media—as a confused totality. *Glamorama* is "a system of textual effects analogous to other scripted spaces: themed architecture, animated digital games, and special-effects films." For Ayers, "to say that *Glamorama* is a novel would be misleading," and Ayers's frame of reference is not the novel but scripted spaces and other allegorical landscapes—she compares Victor to an avatar within an adventure game. My approach to *Glamorama*'s intermediality differs from Ayers's in that I take into consideration the literary context. *Glamorama is* a novel. Though within the medium of a novel, other media are referenced, evoked, and even vie for narrative control, the full implications of Ellis's use of intermediality can only be appreciated if *Glamorama*'s medium is taken into account. It is precisely because *Glamorama*'s medium is the relatively traditional one of a literary text that its use of intermediality, and especially the extension of its intermediality beyond the boundaries of print, is so striking.

Intermediality as Setting, Character, and Theme in the Society of the Spectacle

In the long first part of the novel, intermedial references establish a context in which images substitute for, and even establish, reality. Print, aural, and visual intermedial references establish character, setting, and theme. Magazines, photos, videos, and songs are crucial currency in a world where celebrities construct their selves through their media image. Therefore, references to media are prominent in Part 1, as cameras pop up almost everywhere creating a series of pseudo-events that start to blur the difference between reality and fiction. The term "pseudo-event" (coined by Daniel Boorstin) refers to events which are organized solely for the purpose of being broadcast, such as press conferences or presidential debates. Boorstin describes pseudo-events as "more vivid, attractive, impressive and persuasive than reality itself" (12–17). The opening of the club in the first part of the novel could certainly qualify as a pseudo-event. The club monitors are connected to MTV or have a virtual-reality videotape on (9); the opening of the club is also filmed by MTV, complete with this warning: "This Event Is Being Videotaped. By Entering You Consent to the Cablecast and Other Exhibition of Your Name, Voice and Likeness" (166). The world of the novel is one in which only the events that are reported, those that are recorded or photographed, can be said to have occurred. Thus, for example, after Victor repeatedly asserts that he did not attend a Calvin Klein fashion show, he is confronted with a photograph that documents his presence at the show (68–69). When he protests—"I'm in the here *and* the now, baby"—he is treated with skepticism ("that's not what I hear," he's told [69]).

These intermedial references establish Victor's character. He is a media sponge who absorbs the images and messages that he receives through the media and replicates them in his own speech. Many of Victor's sentences are titles or parts of song lyrics which are used as dialogue. "So what's the story, morning glory" (89, 130), "But that's the way, uh-huh uh-huh, I like it, uh-huh uh-huh" (121) are examples of the way intermedial references to popular music lyrics replace Victor's own language. Advertisements also find their way into Victor's speech: "Baby—come to where the flavor is" (291), he tells Jamie—a line from a Marlboro advert. However paradoxical it may seem, these intermedial references establish Victor's identity: discussing a bouquet of flowers received by Victor's girlfriend Chloe, which Victor denies sending, his assistant JD reports that the card that accompanied the flowers said, "'Ain't no woman like the one I've got' and 'Baby, I'm-a want you, Baby, I'm a-need you.'" JD adds, "That sounds like you" (75).

The intermedial references in the opening part of the novel also establish *Glamorama*'s setting in the society of the spectacle, a term developed in the 1960s by French philosopher Guy Debord to describe the "predominance of appearances" in which "all human life, which is to say all social life, is mere appearance" (14). The novel's depiction of celebrity culture in the 1990s offers a world in which, as Debord puts it, "the spectacle . . . . is the very heart of society's real unreality. In all its specific manifestations—news or propaganda, advertising or the actual consumption of entertainment—the spectacle epitomizes the prevailing mode of social life" (13). The implication of this setting for the novel is evident in Victor's selection of the hip celebrities who will attend the opening of the club. This scene includes long lists that mix real celebrities and fictional characters; the point, for Victor, is not the difference between reality and fiction but the degree of celebrity these people possess. Like Boorstin's concept of the pseudo-event, in the society of the spectacle the difference between reality and fiction falls away.

Despite the destabilization of authenticity, of presence "in the here and the now," and of the distinction between fiction and reality, all performed by intermedial references, one thing remains consistent throughout Part 1 of *Glamorama*: Victor and his point of view are the primary narrative vehicles by which the reader has access to information. Much of the first part of the novel shows Victor attempting to control and manipulate his image as he tries to become famous. Victor is aware of the importance of publicity, public relations, and the power of the mass media to create an image of the self. Confronted with a photo of himself in Miami (though Victor denies having been in Miami) his only concern is "Did I look good?" (91), and the reporter who follows him in the opening pages of the novel is from the appropriately named *Details* magazine, a Condé Nast publication that claims "to define the modern man of our times" ("Mission"). Victor's control over his image extends to the narrative voice in the opening part of the novel: the range of intermedial references are suborned to his point of view. Intermedial references establish setting, character, and theme, but Victor is always the narrator and focalizer.

Intermediality as Virtuality: The Cinema/Prose-Fiction Interface

As Victor leaves New York City on the QE2 in Part 2 of *Glamorama*, the society of the spectacle fades away and is replaced by what Jean Baudrillard terms virtuality. Unlike the spectacle, which, Baudrillard says, "still left room for a critical consciousness and demystification," with virtuality "we are no longer spectators, but actors in a performance, and actors increasingly integrated into the course of the performance" (*The Perfect Crime* 27). As the novel progresses, intermedial references subsume Victor's narrative voice and his centrality as narrator and focalizer begins to fade. By Part 4 of the novel, the reader is unable to distinguish between Victor's point of view and that of a camera. Like the "thin strip of white" on the horizon that Victor sees from the QE2 that can't be identified as land or sky (215), the real gradually disappears as a stable frame of reference.

Baudrillard describes "the very essence of the Virtual" as a coincidence of real time action and recorded information. In a world in which "There is always a hidden camera somewhere" and "You can be filmed without knowing it," there is no clear distinction between reality and its virtual form:

> In any case, the virtual camera is in our heads. No need of a medium to reflect our problems in real time: every existence is telepresent to itself. The TV and the media long since left their media space to invest 'real' life from the inside, precisely as a virus does with a normal cell. No need for the headset and the data suit: it is our will that ends up moving about the world as though inside a computer-generated image. We have all swallowed our receivers, and this produces intense interference on account of the excessive proximity of life and its double, and the collapsing of time and distance. (*The Perfect Crime* 26)

As Victor wanders through London and then Paris, there is always a camera crew nearby, music on the soundtrack, and a script to follow. As a result, the distinction between reality and its filmed double becomes increasingly difficult to discern. Victor's reality becomes indistinguishable from cinematic mise-en-scène. The people he meets are actors cast and recast—like the cruise pianist who also plays the aerobics instructor (261). Objects are also props (334) and even momentary clarity is the product of a fog machine being dismantled (265). His point of view increasingly takes the form of mise-en-shot: handheld cameras (310), circling camera movements (334), intercut shots (362), or close-ups (362) become common narrative references. The editing process is foregrounded: scenes will be cut (313) discarded (265) or made into a montage (367). Sound is also very important, both diegetic (the songs Victor hums or hears [538, 521]) and extradiegetic: "I kept my Walkman on, the Dave Matthews Band's 'Crash into Me' buzzing in my ears through the headphones, spilling over onto the sound track" (265).

This convergence of cinema language and literary language—the cinema/prose fiction interface—both determines the plot and undermines it. The script is central to the narrative and there are constant references to its contents. "Haven't you read the rest of the script?" Felix, the cinematographer, asks Victor, "Don't you know what's going to happen to you?" (221). As the novel progresses, the relation between the narration and the script becomes closer and closer. For example, after Victor brings Sam Ho to Bobby he absently picks up a script where he reads: "descriptions of Bobby calming someone down, feeding me a Xanax, I'm weeping, people are getting dressed for another party, a line of dialogue ('what if you became something you were not') and my eyes are closing" (321). After witnessing Sam Ho being tortured to death, Victor breaks down and the scenes in the script take place: "Bobby keeps feeding me Xanax" (324) and says to Victor, "what if one day you became whatever you're not?" (327). The script—which is constantly referenced, though never summarized—casts over the novel an air of inevitability; Victor seems no longer in control of his actions, emotions, or experience. As Bobby puts it, "You shouldn't be shocked by any of this, Victor [. . .] This is expected. This was in the script. You shouldn't be surprised by any of this" (326).

As the cinema/prose fiction interface increases, the cinematographer and the director, whose presumed authorship of the plot enabled them to offer Victor advice about what his character would or would not do (205), become subsumed by the cinematic references. Felix, the cinematographer, initially warns Victor that the script will put him in danger (221) and that "things are getting out of hand" (222). But after Felix informs Victor that "the movie's over" (399), he joins the many victims of a bomb planted in his hotel room at the Ritz. The bomb "swallows Felix up, vaporizing him instantly. He literally disappears. There's nothing left" (403). The cinematographer vanishes like an image on a film that leaves no residue when it disappears—a moment that (re)defines Felix as a character filmed by a second film crew, this time French, that is also filming terrorist attack scenes, many of which take place without Victor. Summing up, we have a film within a film within a novel, and no stable narrative frame to trust.

The connection *Glamorama* draws between terrorism and film is especially striking in light of the 9/11 terror attacks. In *The Spirit of Terrorism*, Baudrillard defined the attacks as a "Manhattan disaster movie" that combines "the white magic of the cinema and the black magic of terrorism" (29–30). In fact, the way Baudrillard describes the 9/11 events could also be a summary of *Glamorama*'s take on terrorism: "the media are part of the event, they are part of the terror, and they work in both directions" (*Spirit* 31).

Evoking the Perfect Crime: The Disappearance of Reality

The effect of the cinema/prose fiction interface is dual. It simultaneously evokes and undermines virtuality or what Baudrillard calls "the perfect crime":

> The perfect crime is that of an unconditional realization of the world by the actualization of all data, the transformation of all our acts and all events into pure information: in short, the final solution, the resolution of the world ahead of time by the cloning of reality and the extermination of the real by its double. (*The Perfect Crime* 25)

Ellis's use of the cinema/prose fiction interface invites us to read *Glamorama* as a "perfect crime." Increasingly, Victor cannot distinguish between a real camera in a pseudo-event and the camera he imagines is shooting his own life. This is a process that begins early in the novel, just after the disastrous opening of the club and the publication of a photo documenting his affair with Lauren (188). It is at this point that references to film production begin to infiltrate Victor's narrative voice. Statements like "behind me something's being filmed, a camera crew's setting up lights" and references to "someone in the cast I hadn't met yet" (191) all may refer to one of the many films that are being shot in Manhattan (153); at the same time, Victor wonders whether the blows being rained on him by Damien's thugs are in the script (195) and finds himself "waiting for the director to shout 'Cut'" (196).

As the novel progresses, Victor's experience is increasingly indistinguishable from a film. In Part 2, aboard the QE2, Victor discusses the script with Felix the cinematographer and notices "extras" sitting at the bar (263). The devastating bombing in London's Notting Hill that opens Part 3 initially reads as an omniscient narrator describing a terror attack, but as the point of view reverts to Victor's we learn that this is a filmed scene, with "body parts made of foam" and "fake blood" (272). With Part 4, the cinema/prose fiction interface has become primarily cinematic: this part opens with a reference to a camera crew (333), a "circling" camera, props, a soundtrack, and repeated injunctions to "stick to the script" (334). By this point in the novel, the difference between a character and the actor playing that character vanishes in the space of a sentence: "The actor playing Bruce had a promising career as a basketball player at Duke and then followed Danny Ferry to Italy where Bruce immediately got modeling jobs" (334).

This increasing primacy of the cinema/prose fiction interface is reproduced narratively as Victor's point of view begins to fracture: from the first-person narrative in Part 1, to occasional second-person ("You are beyond uneasiness. You force yourself to look at them" [459]), third-person ("A montage of Jamie and Victor walking along Quai de la Tournelle" [367]), and omniscient narration ("Tammy declines a glass of champagne, then reconsiders" [336]), to the climactic explosion of a 747 in the final chapter of Part 4 which is described through a dispassionate, omniscient narrator—certainly not Victor. These changes in narrative voice and the increasing primacy of intermedial film narration underscore the lack of any stable narrative frame that the reader can trust.

The movement toward and away from Victor's point of view that these intermedial references describe have the effect of situating him both within and outside of the film that he stars in (or hallucinates). For David Punter, the effect of this narrative fracturing is that "Victor is not only inside himself experiencing his despair, he is simultaneously part of the audience at the movie of his life, describing his own behavior, his own words, from the outside" (71). Henrik Skov Nielsen suggests that such departures from Victor's point of view are examples of "the impersonal voice" that "breaks with the expected limits of the first-person narrator" to tell us what Victor does not notice ("The Impersonal Voice" 140). In my opinion, the effect is to add perspective and depth while maintaining the shallowness and superficiality of Victor's character. With a sentence like "I walk into the frame, not noticing the black limousine parked across the street, four buildings down, that the cameraman pans to" (193), another dimension is literally added to the narrative and permits the inclusion of information that the self-centered Victor would never have grasped. Ellis has stated that in the course of writing *Glamorama* he attempted to omit the references to film crews, but explains, "I couldn't get around the fact that Victor isn't an aware narrator—and I didn't want to corrupt the purity of his character by making him know more than he would. So I brought the film crews back in" (Clarke 90).

The climax of this cinema/prose fiction interface is the "seamless" integration of reality into media described on pages 406–409 as Bentley, a colleague of the terrorist Bobby, shows Victor the process of image adaptation and falsification. With the help of a "new program" (Kai's Photo Soap) (407), Bentley scans, alters, and revises images. "In five minutes my head—in profile—is grafted seamlessly onto the shoulders of an average-looking guy fucking Sam Ho" (407). Bentley is "adding graininess, he's erasing people, he's inventing a new world, seamlessly" (408). In Baudrillard's terms, the function of both art and technology is "to make reality disappear and, at the same time, to mask that disappearance" (*The Perfect Crime* 5). Punter, discussing this scene, notes that Victor is "watching Bentley construct his own replacement, a replica that is also already a relic, a set of images that perfectly, seamlessly represent a past that never existed; or rather, that existed 'only' in virtuality" (72). The return to New York City and to a stable, first-person narrative in Part 5 of *Glamorama* would seem to suggest that Victor's narrative voice has recovered its primacy over the cinematic intermedial references. But Part 5 is, in fact, narrated by this image of Victor created by Bentley. In other words, the replacement of Victor with Bentley's version of "Victor" as the narrator sets Part 5 of the novel firmly in the virtual.

In the world of *Glamorama* words and images are raw material that can be shaped, replicated, and manipulated. Consequently, individual identity can be generated, shaped, and transformed through media. The narrator of Part 5 is such a construct: he conforms to the social codes of the moment and responds to the political needs of Victor's father, a senator in Washington. Victor has already been presented as a media sponge, whose personality is constructed by fragments, defined by surfaces and commodities and style. The transformation of Victor's double into an ideal son is performed by changing his style and photographing him; his identity is established by generating an image. For a *George* magazine photo shoot, before-and-after shots of the "new" Victor are juxtaposed:

> Before: I'm holding a Bass Ale, wearing Prada, a goatee pasted on my face, a grungy expression, eyes slits. After: I'm carrying a stack of lawbooks and wearing a Brooks Brothers seersucker

suit, a bottle of Diet Coke in my left hand, Oliver Peoples wire-frames. (513)

The juxtaposition of the "before" and "after" shots are not fundamentally different, in their effect, than the doctored photographs that Bentley creates. Since in *Glamorama*'s celebrity world individual essence disappears, the self is continuously constructed and reconstructed by means of very superficial aspects like clothing which are supposed to send the intended, coded message. The image's accoutrements (the books, the glasses) convey this new "improved" Victor, who is less superficial and now cares for his intellectual nourishment.

For many computer interface designers the ultimate goal of virtual reality and digital technology is the creation of a perfect transparent interface. Bentley achieves this transparency with the creation of Victor's double, who can masquerade as the real Victor since the digital interface is hidden and, thus, transparent. This creation has effects not only at the level of the plot but also at the level of the narrative voice. As Nielsen has pointed out, Victor's double not only takes Victor's personality on a thematic level but also takes the "I" of the narration, cutting Victor off from mastery of the first-person narrative ("Telling Doubles" 26–27). In Part 5, the transparency of the transformation is also reflected in the stable first-person narrative voice that is in stark contrast to the shattered narrative framework (alternating between first, second, and third person, and omniscient) of the previous parts. Given that each previous part of the novel showed Victor's narrative voice as increasingly destabilized and, ultimately, erased by the cinema/prose fiction interface, the relatively traditional literary narrative offered by Victor's double in Part 5 would seem to indicate that both narrative and film have been subsumed by the virtual. In the very brief final part of the novel (Part 6), Victor—who is still in Europe—offers an additional, stable, first-person narrative to counter that of his double in Part 5. But he is informed by the director that "Your role is over" (535), and his continued existence after this point is not likely: Davide, his bodyguard, is assassinated, and the novel ends with Victor alone, friendless, and defenseless in Milan.

Undermining the Perfect Crime: Against the Transparency of Virtuality

In *Glamorama*, the digital media represent a challenge to other media and a form of intermediality that David Bolter has named "remediation" since newer and older media forms are involved "in a struggle for cultural recognition" ("Transference" 14). If all media try to offer viewers the most compelling representation of the real, digital media can create "a seamless whole in which the marks of the digital technology are effaced" ("Transference" 16). Bentley commands the digital media and shows Victor how he can alter photos, manipulate videos, and create computer files to incriminate Victor for crimes he has not committed. The goal is, as Bolter puts it, "seamless" representation. Victor, describing Bentley's activities, uses the same terminology: Bentley works "seamlessly" (407, 408). Significantly, "seamlessness" is ascribed not to the digital world Bentley creates (as Bolter would have it) but to the process of creating this world: it is the process of creation, and not the product, that is "seamless." The effect is what Victor Shklovsky calls "defamiliarization": a focus on the process of perception that counters the illusion of transparency and draws our attention to the constructed quality of this virtual space.

Ellis achieves this effect through intermediality: the reproduction of the filmic means of narration in the written medium. Mainstream Hollywood film narration hides all aspects of its cinematography to render the represented world transparent and seemingly unmediated, creating a seamless illusion of reality. As Chiel Kattenbelt claims, "transparency and immersion are the two sides of the same coin: the more transparent the medium, the more we feel surrounded by the world that the medium represents" (34). Film and literary language are obviously different and have different expressive means. Film relies on mise-en-scène (actors, set, costume, lighting), mise-en-shot (camera position, movement, duration of the shot), editing (continuity, montage), and sound (voice-over, soundtrack). When we watch a mainstream Hollywood film (which has, as Bolter puts it, "been reluctant to remind the viewer of the multiple sources and constructed nature of the spectacle" ["Transference" 16]), we understand its language although we may not be aware of these techniques. As a result, we may instinctively identify with a character's emotions. Ellis's use of intermediality and his insistence on laying bare cinematic conventions work against the transparency of the medium, reveal the seams in the illusion, and inhibit the readers' immersion in *Glamorama*'s shallow world. For instance, as Victor has a fraught phone conversation with Lauren "the cameraman keeps circling the pay phone, distracting me into forgetting my lines, so I decide to improvise and surprisingly the director allows it" (197), and the makeup girl drops glycerin on his face to simulate tears (199). Rather than seeing a trapped Victor overwhelmed by the conversation, the reader witnesses the construction of an image; instead of tears of frustration, we see manufactured emotion. As cinematic effects are translated into a written medium, they cannot be genuinely reproduced. As a result, the filmic language changes its meaning and assumes a different role. Furthermore, Victor not only describes the making of a film but references the lives of the actors, changes in the script, budget cuts, and discarded scenes. The transparency of mainstream film conventions disappears; rather than identifying with Victor through the camera lens, we distance ourselves from him as events are defamiliarized.

The defamiliarization extends, crucially, to the terror attacks in the novel. Victor describes the preparation for a terrorist bombing as a series of dueling images:

> A shot of Scotch tape being applied with rubber gloves to a white metal gas canister [. . .] is undercut with one of me taking a shower, slowly soaping my chest, my legs, the camera gliding gratuitously up over my ass [. . .] Another shot of the thick metal canister sitting on a Hans Wegner ottoman. A quick montage of my character dressing. (362)

In a mainstream Hollywood film, this scene's mounting atmosphere of tension would be created by juxtaposing Victor's relaxed attitude while having a shower with the actual construction of the bomb. But translated to text, the opposite effect is produced making us aware of film techniques that we do not normally notice and underlining the constructed nature of the tension. Since as readers we lack a narrative frame we can trust as two different media (literary and filmic) seem to work against each other in a struggle to command the narrative voice, the result is not only narrative instability but an undoing of the seamless virtuality that the cinema/prose fiction interface veers toward and which culminates in the double of Victor who, in Part 5, usurps the narrative voice.

Even Part 5, which seems to assert the primacy of the virtual, offers clues that the double is not perfect. Though the "I" of the narration seems to be Victor's since he is still interested in brand names, designer labels, and music groups, this is a re-formed Victor with a new attitude toward life: "No more drinking binges, I've cut down on partying, law school's great, [. . .] I've stopped seriously deluding myself and I'm rereading Dostoyevsky" (509). But as the chapter progresses, we become aware that there may be something wrong with this new Victor. After Chloe's death in Paris, Alison Poole is Victor's new girlfriend but she senses there is something different in Victor (512). He is told to "check those photo books that were given to you" and "memorize the faces" (527). When he is attacked by two men, he kills them easily, punches some codes in his cell phone, gives his location, and identifies himself as "DAN" (523).

Baudrillard stresses that "the crime is never perfect" and attributes to artists the ability to combat it: "The artist," writes Baudrillard, "is always close to committing the perfect crime: saying nothing. But he turns away from it . . . The artist is, in Michaux's words, the one who, with all his might, resists the fundamental drive not to leave traces" (*The Perfect Crime* 1). Though *Glamorama*'s use of intermedial references and the cinema/prose fiction interface seem to commit Baudrillard's version of the perfect crime, the literary context—the fact that this is a novel, and that these references remain within the medium of a literary text—work against the transparency of virtuality and reassert the difference between the real and its illusion. Ellis's use of the cinematic/narrative interface enables him not only to expose the perfect crime—the subsumption of the real by the virtual, the total transparency offered by media—but to counteract the crime by situating its traces firmly within the literary text.

From the Literary Medium to the Internet: The Double Escapes the Text

But the novel, like Victor's double, seems to have an agenda of its own. It maintains a palpable presence beyond the bounds of the literary. "Glamorama Spies," a composition for flute, clarinet, violin, violoncello, and piano written in 1999 by Italian composer Lorenzo Ferrero, was inspired by the novel. Roger Avary (director of *Rules of Attraction*) attempted to adapt *Glamorama* to the screen, but the September 11, 2001, terrorist attacks hindered the project as the novel's topic became a sensitive matter. On Victor Ward's official site at geocities.com one can view Victor's portfolio (composed of photos of the actor cast as Victor in the planned adaptation), read a biography, and follow links to websites of real designers, models, and locations, the website of "The Impersonators" (Victor's band in *Glamorama*), and a 2002 journal describing Victor's travels in Europe. The disappearance of the real reached its peak in 2004 with the online edition of *YouthQuake Magazine*. In *Glamorama*, the achievement of which Victor was most proud was that his image had been featured on the cover of *YouthQuake*. The online *YouthQuake Magazine* features an interview by Christie Carnes with Victor Ward as well as an insightful essay on *Glamorama* by Joseph Suglia. Suglia accurately notes that for Victor the only significant things are those that recall a song lyric, television show, or film, and describes Victor as an empty vehicle of popular media.

Victor is also on MySpace, Facebook, and Twitter, to which he provides regular updates. Many of the songs that Victor quotes in *Glamorama* are available on his MySpace webpage, extending the intermedial references even further. These websites, the musical composition, and the film (if it had been made) all offer examples of what Rajewsky calls "media transposition" (51). The literary character is transformed into a digital one by using imaging technology and digital media. The digital simulates, appropriates, and refashions Victor's double both in the literary medium (by Bentley in the novel) and beyond that medium through profiles, websites, and social networks. Victor's double has moved from an image created "seamlessly" in *Glamorama*, to a narrative voice in Part 5 of the novel, to a digital construct that extends beyond the fictional literary world into the digital world of the internet. The double seems to overtake the real and escape the confines of the text.

The social networking websites invite the construction of fake personalities and even Bret Easton Ellis has several impersonators on Facebook. Attempting to open a Twitter account, Ellis found that both "BretEastonEllis" and "bretellis" were taken and he had to choose "eastonellis" (Goodyear); his present Twitter account is @BretEastonEllis. The first message he sent was "This is the real BEE," hardly a convincing claim online, but one that takes us back to *Glamorama*. In Part 6 of the novel, Victor attempts to convince his sister on the phone that he is, in fact, the real Victor: "It's me [. . .] It's Victor [. . .] Sally, it's really me" (540–41). The existence of Ellis impersonators indicates that the dangers of the digital that *Glamorama* suggested in 1998 were not far-fetched.

CHAPTER 6

"Merely Political": Glam Terrorism and Celebrity Politics in Bret Easton Ellis's *Glamorama*

Arthur Redding

"You make a mistake if you see what we do as merely political," reads the second epigraph to Bret Easton Ellis's 1998 novel *Glamorama*. The quotation is attributed to Adolf Hitler and implies that National Socialism involved more than a seizure of the government apparatus; it committed itself fully to a changed consciousness, one in which, as Walter Benjamin famously put it in "The Work of Art in the Age of Mechanical Reproduction," mankind "can experience its own destruction as an aesthetic pleasure" (242). In the same essay, Benjamin accords a central place to cinema, which brings new subjectivities into being by encouraging its audiences to cultivate the habit of "reception in a state of distraction" (240). *Glamorama*'s protagonist, who believes he is a character in the movies, is the very embodiment of distraction, and Ellis's concern, as in his more famously scandalous *American Psycho*, is again the aestheticization of violence. The novel depicts the ascendance of terrorist chic, where allure, distraction, and violence have all become radically democratized and circulate freely in a totalizing media sphere, disconnected from the political.

The decoupling of violent acts from any political or social consequence and the unlinking of media representations from reality initiate, in *Glamorama*, a series of detachments and fractures, with specific implications for consciousness, coherence, affect, and temporality. The novel's first epigraph, voiced by Krishna in the Bhagavad Gita (2.12), might prove illustrative: "There was no time when you nor I nor these kings did not exist" (Ellis n.p.). Here Krishna asserts that eternity underlies the temporal progression of earthly events. Typically, such progression secures the relationship between cause and effect, and in traditional novels the complex calibration of plot (what happens) with a narrative relying on the reader's capacity to connect the dots (our awareness of what happens) is what makes for a good read. In *Glamorama* neither of these conventional prerequisites is satisfied. Representations of events in the novel precede their occurrence just as the novel itself anticipates historical events like the terror attacks of September 11, 2001. The novel does away with the Kantian category of causality as the very link between cause and effect breaks down.

For Ellis, of course, the unraveling of causality and temporality says more about the nature of media than (as the Krishna quotation might suggest) any possibility of redemptive mysticism. And contra Benjamin's concluding hope that communism can counter fascism "by politicizing art" (242), *Glamorama* charts the evaporation of politics not only from artistic representations but from the public sphere. As the book progresses, it seems terrifyingly incapable of sustaining any links or relations whatsoever. As the plot veers toward incoherence, the reader's bafflement mimics the protracted confusion of the narrator who, careless and carefree in the opening pages, may, by the end of the book, no longer care that he does not care. Like the reader, he is merely aware of his own confusion.

Ellis's investigation—and my own in what follows—circles around the fate of consciousness under such conditions. The multiple uncouplings (of violent cause from political effect; of physical effect from affective response) that I describe in the first part of this chapter define the post-political world in which the novel is set. In such a world, the fate of literature (its potential for physical or emotional transformation) is very much in the balance; Victor Ward will, despite his best efforts to the contrary, wind up "disconnected" and, as early reviews suggested, the reader will no doubt abandon her or his efforts to navigate the labyrinthine plot of the book. The second part of this chapter interrogates the implications of this eclipse of the literary that accompanies the eclipse of the political. Such abandonment of affective engagement extends to the intersection of real violence with the cinematic spectacle of celebrity culture, as I discuss in part 3, and part 4 examines the fate of subjective affect—both real and simulated—in a political, literary, and cinematic arena informed by disconnection and fragmentation. If E.M. Forster's *Howards End* was driven by the dictate to "only connect the prose and the passion" and to "Live in fragments no longer" (186–87), *Glamorama* offers only one option: like Victor, we can "only *dis*connect."

Uncouplings: Politics, Affect, Violence

For a book so steeped in the zeitgeist, for a thriller that recounts a web of contemporary political conspiracies, *Glamorama* is curiously, even tendentiously, *apolitical*. There is conspiracy and violence aplenty in the novel, but readers learn next to nothing of the underlying motivations. "Everything's . . . connected . . . to the Japanese" reveals the most seemingly trustworthy character, Jamie Fields, in a dying confession that should, properly, bring a chunk of the truth to light: "Everything is bought with Japanese . . . money . . . from Japanese banks, and they . . . supply everything" (481). But Jamie's own reliability will very shortly be undermined with her final words: "I'm . . . not . . . Jamie Fields" (486). As in most spy novels, no one is ever who they pretend to be, and it is one of *Glamorama*'s more obvious postmodern conceits that the characters' "true" identities are never revealed.

There is, to be sure, a *Manchurian Candidate* thesis at work: like Raymond Shaw in the 1962 film, who is propelled without his knowledge into a central role in US politics in the midst of the Cold War, *Glamorama*'s Victor Ward (Victor Johnson, from *The Rules of Attraction*) finds himself drawn unwittingly into a plot to spread global terror, perhaps in order to induce a public climate of paranoia that will secure his father's nomination. We are presented with what Julian Murphet terms a "tunnel-vision" monologue (25), here delivered not by Patrick Bateman but by the vain, "semi-famous" (11) party-monster Victor who, like a pinball, is bounced around the streets and off the walls (literally, in some cases). Driving this comedy of errors is a new undetectable explosive called Remform, which various parties are trying to get their hands on. Followed, inexplicably, by film crews, Victor lurches uncomprehendingly about New York and Paris, downing Xanax and complaining about the cold, as the body count rises, the smell of shit gets stronger, and confetti decorates the scenery. At the same time, a faction opposed to his father threatens to blackmail the senator with videotaped evidence of Victor's misdeeds; the shadowy operative and puppet-master F. Fred Palakon is seemingly playing several parties against each other. Various deals are struck, agents are betrayed and murdered, and Victor finds himself a pawn in conspiracies that cycle out of control and beyond comprehension. Consequently, neither the book nor its characters—nor ultimately, its readers—*care* to fully apprehend or even comment upon the social struggles that produce such violence, its geopolitics, or its consequences. At heart, *Glamorama* is a rather brutal interrogation of our waning capacity to care.

In "Empires of the Senseless," Walter Benn Michaels persuasively contends that the genuine political acuity of Ellis's novel stems, paradoxically enough, from its depiction of a post-political landscape of generalized and deeply fascinating terror, wherein "terrorism cannot be linked to any particular political position" (105). *Glamorama*, Michaels argues, dramatizes a generalized detachment of violence from politics: "the acts of destruction its models/terrorists perform are unlinked to any particular political program" and the novel "can't work up any more interest in their religion or nationality than it can in their ideology" (105). The link between any *act* of political violence and its anticipated goal or outcome has been irreparably fractured; so too the connection between such acts and the ideological or national *cause* in whose name they are committed. "It's really about the will to accomplish this destruction," writes Ellis, "and not about the outcome, because that's just decoration" (337). Such an ideological decoupling of political cause from violent effect seems not only endemic to postmodern politics, but downright necessary for a novel that, as Per Serritslev Petersen indicates, anticipates the September 11, 2001, attacks on the World Trade Center and the Pentagon. But if, as Lee Harris argues, "in the case of 9/11, there was no rational political objective" (Peterson 135), US military response was equally *unhinged*: attacked by Saudis, the Bush administration responded by targeting Iraq; the rationale for the invasion (national security) was spurious; the supposed menace of weapons of mass destruction was fabricated. The media doublethink that made this response possible underscores Ellis's most salient lesson: genuine political struggles are reconstituted as manufactured image and militarism becomes spectacular and self-justifying; violence floats free of the gravitational tug of the social and is celebrated for its own sake. *Glamorama*'s shivering of causality applies not only to the attacks of 9/11 but to their aftermath—in both cases, the political falls out of the picture.

For Michaels, this generalized unlinking of violence from politics reflects a tendency on the postmodern left (most formidably represented in Michael Hardt and Antonio Negri's *Empire*) to theorize a politics that involves "a commitment to new subject positions instead of to more just societies" (110)—a feel-good politics, in short, that abandons the political project; a cultivation of affective intensity that sacrifices the organizational grunt-work necessary to secure justice. Ellis is less interested in the savagery of the contemporary social fabric than in the fate of privileged masculine subjectivity within it. He seldom makes any direct link between his characters' predicaments and the systemic inequities of unregulated privatization. But the dramatic tension in *Glamorama* arises from the protagonist's doomed effort to cultivate consciousness in the absence of ideological conviction: Victor struggles to cobble together something like awareness, something like a conscience, something like what he terms an attention span in a world in which nobody cares, nobody notices, nobody remembers, and nobody listens to anybody. At the start of the novel, Victor, the "It Boy of the moment" (159), cultivates a cool and studied indifference; over the course of the novel, I argue, his cool begins to wilt. But even as, confronted with yet another level of the conspiracy in which he is enmeshed, as he mutters "Oh shit oh shit oh shit," Victor is "beyond uneasiness": "You try to care. But you can't. Even if you wanted to, you can't" (459). A primary question in what follows is the very fate of affect; if Michaels is bemoaning the surrender of the political terrain, Ellis ponders an equally if not more troubling social horizon: the full eclipse of emphatic passion.

Affect, as Marco Abel and other critics contend, is not to be confused with emotion, but should properly be "configured as a *pre-subjective force*," and while "affect is always there, even in the works of . . . Bret Easton Ellis," it grips our bodies "before the moment of cognition kicks in" ("Intensifying"). For Abel there is what Deleuze has termed a "disjunctive synthesis" (*The Logic of Sense* 174) between affect and emotion. While I want to quibble with Abel's formula, which seems to want to sneak a causal model in through the back door of our emotional life, his point—that the forces that bear upon us are unlinked from both awareness and a capacity to care—is well-taken. If part of the interpretive problem of Ellis's notorious *American Psycho* hinged upon the reliability of the narrator—the question of whether the murders depicted really happened or simply took place in the mind of the deranged Patrick Bateman—*Glamorama* presents us with a more challenging hermeneutical knot, and so too a more invidious moral conundrum: it makes no difference whatsoever whether or not the events described really happened or not.

Writing and Terror in a Post-Political World

American Psycho at least provoked scandal, a politics of reception that looks quaintly antique from the point of view of *Glamorama*'s universe. For scandal too has by now become obsolete; it occasions titillation rather than outrage (though outrage is constantly simulated). This is the post-political condition to which, for Michaels, *Glamorama* offers a literary analogue: "the fantasy of the senseless—writing without meaning—has taken its place alongside the fantasy of empire—politics without believing—in or rather as the new discourse of terrorism" (113). For Michaels, any effort to exit this impasse would be merely nostalgic, hearkening back to a time (much softened in the glow of remembrance) when politics *did* matter. The contemporary jeremiads penned by political commentators across the blogosphere today all partake of this nostalgia and proceed rhetorically according to an intertwined logic: they excoriate hypocrisy, and, in the same gesture, aim to scold us into caring. But we never do care, Ellis implies, except fleetingly.

Now, the eclipse of politics might be an old story; *what people believe* has long ago ceased to be of as much import as how they *behave*, a recognition heartily shared by the discipline of sociology and endorsed by all of what we might call consumer culture, whose deprivations, deformations, and compulsive allure are at the core of Ellis's writerly concerns. In *Plotting Terror*, Margaret Scanlan describes "both writers and terrorists [. . .] as remnants of a romantic belief in the power of marginalized persons to transform history" (2). Scanlan argues that writers from Henry James and Joseph Conrad to Don DeLillo are fascinated, and frustrated, by the suspicion that, like terrorists, their capacity to shape public awareness has been eclipsed (primarily by the powers of journalism). "The terrorist novel," she concludes, "opens itself up to the more general question about the writer's ability to understand, respond to, and influence politics" (7).

In their 2003 study *Crimes of Art and Terror*, Frank Lentricchia and Jody McAuliffe lay out a curiously overlapping, if highly conservative, set of claims. Like Scanlan, Lentricchia and McAuliffe link writers to terrorists by dint of their shared romanticism, their impatient desire to rapidly remake the world at one blow. Oddly, though, they counsel writers to remain content in their marginal ineffectuality, "to rest with marginality and the understanding that the world will not be altered by artistic acts" (4). For Lentricchia and McAuliffe, the proper role of the writer would be to pry open and inhabit an ironic space, a space for nuanced critical reflection on the violence and superficiality of contemporary culture, the space, in short, of high modernist reflexivity. But such a call for cultural modesty is outmoded, to say the least. It evades any assessment of the field of contemporary cultural production. Patrick Bateman, for all his psychotic affectlessness, *reads*—he may be devoid of feeling, but he has an attention span. He is a voracious consumer of *GQ*, pornography, true-crime books, television shows, and he even styles himself a critic/commentator on pop music. We would be hard pressed, by contrast, to imagine Victor Ward *reading* anything, or paying much attention to publications that did not feature celebrities and, preferably, place his own visage on the cover. He too consumes pop music, though as we shall see, his mastery of the medium fails to make any difference in the chain of events. The question, to which Lentricchia and McAuliffe give short shrift in their discussion, but that Ellis places front and center, is whether culture is enough to make us—or anyone—care.

While Michaels laments culture's abandonment of politics after 9/11, such a withdrawal, Scanlan suggests, may well be inevitable in a thoroughly mediatized world: because terrorists represent "small groups alienated from the conventional ways of influencing the political process," she writes, they have seized upon the burgeoning visual mediascape as their theater of public relations (5). Thus, in *Glamorama* there are no authors (authorship implies a relatively self-conscious agency)—only scripts, film, fashion, and terrorism. Angela Woods adds that in *Glamorama* "terrorism is, like fashion, staged for the camera and dependent on the dissemination of the altered photographic image for its effect. These effects are registered only at the level of individual corporeality, they have no political outcome." Woods, with Jean Baudrillard, reads terrorism as symptomatic of rather than resistant to capitalism: "Victor's acts of violence in *Glamorama* are not those of an autonomous self-determining agent, but belong, Ellis seems to suggest, to a mode of subjectivity symptomatic of the decentered networks of power in the global economy" (Woods). Like Michaels, Woods is skeptical of such subjectivity's political potential.

But Ellis, I'll venture, is more radical in his claims. For Hardt and Negri, even if belief is no longer the issue, bodies and affects nonetheless continue to matter deeply. In *Glamorama*'s world, not only are there no political beliefs, there are no bodies (in any recognizable sense) anymore; if there is affect aplenty, as Abel argues, it does not register on the plane of coherent self-knowledge—there are simply short-lived, half-lingering sensations that propel characters whose subjectivity is under duress. Bodies have been absorbed into the cinematic sheen of current events—entertainment—and the once desperate effort to produce a vestige of sensation out of pornography, drugs, and violence (an effort already massively if vainly testified to in *American Psycho*) has succumbed to the relentless commoditization of these three in the fashion and entertainment industries. The themes of entertainment, terrorism, and the exhaustion of affect still resonate. As recently as the 2008 US Presidential elections, the public relations team of Republican John McCain's campaign endeavored to depict the Democratic nominee Barack Obama as both a celebrity *and* a terrorist! It should come as no surprise to studious readers of Ellis that such tactics failed. Nobody really cares.

Becoming Glamorous

As social satire, *Glamorama* assesses the narcissistic obsessions, addictiveness, and casual violence of 1990s New York club culture. One of the novel's more obvious references is the 1996 murder of Andre "Angel"

Melendez by "Club Kid" Michael Alig in a case that, as Deborah Orr notes, "reads like a story that has sprung from the mind of Bret Easton Ellis." The social menace represented by Victor is of movement without self-conscious agency, self-involved but stripped of critical self-awareness and coupled to a sense of entitlement. Ellis dishes up a satirical diagnosis of an overhyped life of privilege (college slacker-dom, yuppiedom, the burbs): his characters bask in the very eye of power, they are supremely entitled, but nonetheless insecure. If we as readers envy these characters, however, our capacity for empathy is strained. No reader of *American Psycho* will ever admit to "identifying" with Patrick Bateman. Few of us would admit to identifying with Victor; it is hard to dredge up a whole lot of sympathy for him. But in our everyday behaviors, we are, to a greater or lesser extent, compelled to emulate him. In fact, it is the requirement to identify with Victor conjoined to our necessary failure to empathize that seals the narrative deal. Victor is repeatedly told that he has "potential" (207, 210, 532); if this potential is never fully realized, this is not because Ellis's craft has failed him. Rather, to reiterate, the novel delineates something unique to postmodern empathy. As with the works of F. Scott Fitzgerald who, as many critics have observed, likewise lovingly satirized the social psychosis of wealth, we are put in the rather ticklish position of envying those whom we despise. In *The Great Gatsby*, Fitzgerald created the character of Nick Carraway in order to preserve a critically reflexive subjective distance from the allure and horror of his material. Ellis offers only the diminished consciousness of Victor Ward.

Ellis's rather brilliant gambit in his long book brings the world of celebrity culture into the orbit of international conspiracy politics, and thereby exposes the murderous hollowness of both. As Alex Blazer aptly comments, what unites the fashion and the terror industries is their shared reduction of body to spectacle: "the beautiful body of a Calvin Klein model is supplanted by a body blown to bits by a bomb. The body is a thing to be viewed, devoured, and destroyed, most notably for the spectacle of film" ("*Glamorama*" 183). Insofar as body becomes spectacle, Ellis apes and lampoons the media juxtaposition of celebrity gossip with the routine violence of current events: both are disembodied, glamorized, and effectively reduced to noisy ephemera. The model's superficiality and narcissism make him a prototype: the celebrity is Everyman. "Why me?" laments Victor, when he realizes the extent to which he is trapped, "I'm not . . . political." "Everyone is," Bobby replies. To Victor's plaint, "I'm an . . . American, y'know?" Bobby counters, "So am I" (358–59).

Victor does, eventually, figure a few things out—he is able to "decode" a false clue planted by the terrorists. The enigmatic communiqué reads

"WINGS. NOV 15. BAND ON THE RUN. 1985. 511" (497). Assuming the number "511" refers to the flight number of the plane targeted for bombing, CIA agents and French commandos storm the wrong plane. Victor's encyclopedic knowledge of pop music enables him to offer the "correct" reading of "511": he knows that the Paul McCartney and Wings song "1985" (from the album "Band on the Run") is exactly 5 minutes and 11 seconds long. But unlike Raymond Shaw in *The Manchurian Candidate*, who, at the last moment, identifies the perpetrators of the global terror plot, Victor's "correct" reading of 511 comes too late. In a four-page *tour-de-force* description of a 747 jetliner exploding mid-flight, we confront in painful detail an act of terrorism committed *for no reason whatsoever*: "'Why me?' someone wonders uselessly" among the blood, viscera, and dismembered limbs (501). There will be a few more assassinations before the novel ends, but the bombing of this unnamed flight is the culmination of mass violence and one of the few scenes in which Ellis does not remind us that some of the body parts, at least, are props. In one of *Glamorama*'s recurrent motifs, the bodies, as they land in the forest outside Paris, are covered with glitter, made glamorous: "since a cargo of party confetti and gold glitter—two tons of it—were being transported to America, millions of tiny dots of purple and green and pink and orange paper cascade over the carnage" (502). Even as the details of this scene are offered as if they are lifted from a screenplay ("A massive section of the fuselage lands [. . .] as a hail of glowing ash rains down. A long pause. The bodies lie clustered in clumps" [502]) the plot—and this is Ellis's point—unreels like a political Hollywood thriller that has lost its moral and epistemological bearings.

This scene is not narrated by Victor: a third-person omniscient narrative voice, which had begun to emerge in earlier scenes of wreckage and carnage, is here fully in control. This narrative voice is aligned with the point of view of a camera that "moves in on an airmail parcel bearing a Georgetown address, in which a Toshiba cassette player has been packed" (499), and the crash of the 747 is, in fact, the culmination of a process by which the reality of the violence increases as the novel distances itself from Victor's point of view. Earlier in the novel, a series of explosions along a street in London's Notting Hill had been initially presented in third-person as if they were really happening. When the narrative voice shifts back to Victor, who reports that "extras are letting makeup assistants wipe fake blood off their faces" (272), the effect is to reassure the reader that the carnage is purely staged. Subsequent explosions are followed and tracked by two film crews (Victor is followed from America by the cinematographer Felix and his entourage; Bobby's terrorists are tracked in Paris by a competing French film crew), and as the novel progresses, the real carnage intermingles with the filmed spectacle: "Shots of body parts—legs and arms and hands, most of them real—skidding across the platform. Shots of mutilated people lying in piles. Shots of faces blown off" (364). As the cinematic begins to infiltrate the real, the consequences become, quite literally, life and death: "because of a clue Bobby planted, an actor cast in the role of a young Algerian fugitive is shot to death outside a mosque" (364).

Against the Baudrillardian cliché that the real (could it ever be presumed to once have existed) has been submerged into simulacrum, the novel opposes a painfully real violence with violence as cinema or media spectacle. The question Ellis asks is not whether the two can be distinguished, but whether, as the distinction fades away, affect itself can be simulated. And if it can, what, if any, are the consequences? If *Glamorama* can be said to have a coherent psychological plot, such a plot would hinge on whether Victor's growing capacity to experience beyond himself culminates in a semblance of self-knowledge or empathy. But Victor's affective capacity has been numbed not only by the celebrity culture into which he has been swept up but by his own deliberate efforts to make himself glamorous: "Because I was dealing with the fact that we lived in a world where beauty was considered an accomplishment—I turned away and made a promise to myself: to be harder, to not care, to be cool" (545).

As David Punter notes, the symptomatic move in *Glamorama* involves "a constant sliding between worlds, between a sense of the real and a sense of the filmic" (68), and Victor's "goal . . . would not be to achieve an authentic freedom of action but rather to be slotted into a principal part in a drama which is 'his own' only in the sense that it is a story told about him." (70). But Victor is, at the very least, baffled when confronted with events that stray from the script, when he seems no longer to be the protagonist of the movie about him that is being filmed. While Ellis writes his novel just before the full advent of reality TV, blogs, Facebook, and Twitter, *Glamorama* anticipates the technological democratization of celebrity: a sensibility in which the act of being recorded secures proof of existence, a world in which everyone can potentially be a star of their own drama, in which their everyday actions—like Victor Ward working out at the gym—are news. So long as the spotlight is on him, Victor can be reassured of his own value. And like most of us, he can even countenance murderous violence unflinchingly, so long as he knows that it is only a movie. As Per Serritslev Petersen points out, when Victor witnesses the torture and murder of Sam Ho, the South Korean ambassador's son, he realizes to his dismay that "there is [. . .] no camera crew around" (323), and begins to hyperventilate and sob. Later, when his girlfriend Chloe Byrnes is murdered by Bobby Hughes, we anticipate Victor's breakdown, and look for a demonstration that he can feel such human sentiments as grief or regret. But this is not the case; instead, a film crew rushes into their hotel room immediately after Chloe's fatal hemorrhaging and abets Victor's revenge. As if he were the star of a Bruce Willis movie he rushes to the airport and, after a desperate struggle, is able to kill the villainous Bobby. Hollywood codes seem to overwrite the events of his life, sequestering him from the potential of affect.

Victor's various (cinematic) incarnations underscore how, as in *American Psycho*, identity in *Glamorama* is radically unstable. Characters are always confusing each other for someone else, calling people by others' names. Victor's own agent appears not to be aware of his existence, mistaking him over the telephone for someone named Dagby (30). Victor's life as a minor New York celebrity and his relationship with Chloe will both be undone by a photograph of him with Alison Poole, his boss's fiancée, and while Victor attempts to block publication of the photo, the image has taken on a life of its own. The metaphor becomes literal after he is dispatched, dejected, to Europe: while overseas, he hears rumors of Victor Ward's doings back in Manhattan. When he later reconnects with Chloe in Paris, he discovers that she is carrying the child of the *other* Victor (470). After he has been spirited off under armed guard to a hotel room in Milan, he calls his sister in DC and ends up in a one-sided phone conversation with his own double:

> "It'd be really cool if you stopped bothering my sister," the voice
>   says. "Okay?"
> Silence.
> "Goodbye," the voice says.
> A click.
> I'm disconnected. (541)

Victor has been rendered mute and, quite literally, disconnected. His image, Frankenstein-like, has become more human than he.

Ellis is quite explicit about the technical process by which images become real. While there were no film crews at hand during the torture and execution of Sam Ho, the event was videotaped. Victor will later come across Bentley digitally manipulating this recording to produce a counterfactual reality, a video of Victor fucking and then murdering Sam Ho. This image of Victor appears more capable of acting decisively in the world, exceeding what Victor is coming to recognize as his own unfilmed experience: the image jogs along the Seine and makes deals in Iran (408). The apolitical Victor does, at least, dredge up a condemnation—"I think you suck" he tells Bentley (408)—but it is far too late. Among the files on Bentley's computer is "'VICTOR' Washington DC w/Sally Johnson (sister)" (409), and it is this file come to life, presumably, who later will hang up on Victor, disconnecting him. Fittingly enough, it is Palakon who delivers the universal verdict:

> "So you're telling me we can't believe anything we're shown anymore?" I'm asking. "That *everything* is altered? That everything's a lie? That everyone will believe this?"
> "That's a fact," Palakon says.
> "So what's true, then?" I cry out.
> "Nothing, Victor," Palakon says. "There are different truths." (463)

The Transformation of Victor Ward

This "virtualization" of Victor Ward—his assumption of a fully filmic identity—has two consequences, both of which serve to disempower him. First, paradoxically enough, his own identity is being erased; as he becomes increasingly famous, he also becomes more anonymous. Second, the funneling of experience into representation, of biography into script, puts one's very existence at risk of being altered, to the point where a virtual or representational identity assumes a life of its own and acts in the world. In a case of art intimidating life, we might say, life itself can be photoshopped into material existence. But even as it emphasizes how "seamlessly" (407, 408) this process works, *Glamorama* makes us wonder how seamless this brave new world of images that have come to life can be and asks whether Victor can cultivate a capacity to read for evidence of doctoring, to learn how to see the indiscernible scars in this radical makeover of real life which, like his own body, has been to all appearances buffed to a flawless whole. The novel's refrain, "we'll slide down the surface of things," from the U2 song "Even Better Than the Real Thing," communicates at least two different messages, each of which might stand in for the epistemological options facing Victor. On the one hand, it suggests that he skate nimbly and comfortably along in a society that has become wholly superficial. Yet it also portends catastrophe: a hunk of shit hurled against a wall will also slide down its surface, which might be the most fitting image of Victor's story.

The opening sentence of *Glamorama*, as winning as all of Ellis's openings, offers yet another option. Victor, in the pay of minor Mafioso Damien Nutchs Ross, is overseeing the opening of a new nightclub, and is perturbed by what looks like specks on a wall panel: "Specks—specks all over the third panel, see?" he exclaims (5). Victor views the specks as flaws on the surface of things, an attitude that suggests a capacity to see the telltale cracks in the fabricated new world: "there they are," he insists, "*specks*, annoying tiny specks, and they don't look accidental, but like they were somehow done by a machine" (5). His assistants are indifferent to the specks, claiming either that they are not there, not visible, or that, like the confetti covering mutilated bodies which the specks foreshadow, they are decorative: "'Yes, save the specks,' Peyton says. 'Damien wants techno and those little fellows can definitely be construed as techno'" (11). The specks, as Blazer notes, "symbolize the abreaction of Victor's mind: the image-conscious narcissist is beginning to anxiously realize that his real life, his unconscious subjectivity, is being annihilated by acute vacuity" ("*Glamorama*" 182).

The specks on the panels also prefigure the image with which the novel will close, as Victor, in Milan, ponders a mural that depicts "a giant mountain":

> I'm falling forward, but also moving up toward the mountain, my
> shadow looming against its jagged peaks, and I'm surging
> forward, ascending, sailing through dark clouds, rising up, a
> fiery wind propelling me, and soon it's night and stars hang in
> the sky above the mountain, revolving as they burn.
> The stars are real.
> The future is that mountain. (546)

These stars, it seems, unlike the celebrities he once aspired to model himself after, are real. Or is Victor once again misapprehending the situation, confusing painted stars for genuine? Can he see the flaws in the surface of things? Or is he glossing over them? *Glamorama*, I will venture in closing, leaves the question entirely open. Indeed, the novel provides alternate endings—not in the sense that the two endings cannot be read sequentially and made sense of in terms of the plot, but rather that they leave us with competing versions of Victor Ward. On the one hand, he remains cool, aloof, benumbed, self-besotted, affect-less. Alternately, he has a percipient awareness of the depths of his own betrayal, and self-betrayal, which foreshadows at least an incipient capacity for resolution—he redeems genuine subjectivity. After the bombing of the 747, Victor, newly returned to New York, has presumably straightened up his act, enrolled in law school, and abandoned his partying ways. He has become a young man of substance, well-groomed, a made-over Prince Hal, befitting the son of a viable Presidential candidate. Victor publicly proclaims and performs his new found sense of having grown up, but his hard-earned maturity is marked by the cultivation of paranoia rather than self-awareness and signals a tempered solipsism rather than a renewed commitment to public citizenship. This new Victor, as superficial and media-manufactured an image as was his previous celebutante existence, differs from the former Victor by dint of being, simply but fleetingly, more successful: his agent, Bill, now recognizes who he is, and he has largely traded in his old circle of vacuous friends to mingle with such political glitterati as Chelsea Clinton and John F. Kennedy, Jr. He now makes the cover of *George* rather than *YouthQuake*: "THE TRANSFORMATION OF VICTOR WARD (UH, WE MEAN JOHNSON)" (450). But his father, who earlier "sent a car to 'insure [Victor's] presence' at lunch" (83), now feels no need to see him ("'We really don't need to see each other while you're here,' he says, 'I mean, do we?'" [515]), and Victor's fabricated world and self-image once again fall apart. He notices confetti in his new apartment, a sure sign of menace, and once again leaps into the leading-man role to become James Bond, handily dispatching two terrorist assassins.

And so he is spirited off to Milan in the novel's final part, to be kept safely inaccessible under armed guard while the photoshopped image assumes his public duties back in New York. It is this simulated Victor who eventually hangs up the phone, disconnecting him entirely from the public self. Does his abandonment signal the possibility of a new beginning? Victor claims as much—he is "surging," "ascending," and "rising up"—and Ellis hints at the same: unlike each preceding part, whose individual chapters had been numbered backwards in descending order, countdowns to catastrophe, the final part begins at zero and climbs skyward to the "real stars" (546).

PART III

Lunar Park

Introduction

On the surface, *Lunar Park* is the most traditional of Ellis's novels. Its protagonist is an introverted, self-destructive individual who reflects on his past, worries about his future, and interacts with other people who, for the most part, recognize and respond to him. It has a plot that not only generates suspense but, at least in part, resolves it. Its genre is readily identifiable as the ghost story—a continuation of an American tradition that extends from Washington Irving to Nathanial Hawthorne, Edgar Allan Poe, and Stephen King, to whom Ellis has described the novel as an homage. But like the suburban exterior of the house on Elsinore Lane that harbors frightful horrors, the strangeness of the novel emerges from and distorts the contours of the recognizable. Though it has a plot, that plot is blurred by multiple beginnings and endings; its protagonist overlaps, at times, with the author, whose writings are both the source of the hauntings in the house and the origin of the menace from outside it.

Reviews were, typically, mixed. *Lunar Park* was hailed as Ellis's best work, one that confirms its author's literary status and stylistic maturity, and dismissed as poorly executed genre fiction weakened by the self-absorption of a celebrity novelist. Ellis's presence in his own book was a sign of introspection, revealing depth, or of narcissism, confirming superficiality. In either case, *Lunar Park*'s gestures toward the autobiographical proved irresistible to reviewers, who treated the book as an opportunity to present a retrospective evaluation of Ellis's career and to declare the author of *Less Than Zero* damned or saved by his most recent product.

The chapters in this section offer the first sustained scholarly investigation of *Lunar Park*. While each touches on the presence of the author in his book, the scholars in this section set the eponymity and biographical coincidences within a spectrum of literary and critical traditions. In "'An awfully good impression': Truth and Testimony in *Lunar Park*," Jeff Karnicky affirms the philosophical seriousness of the novel by reading it through Jacques Derrida's work on testimony; for Karnicky, *Lunar Park*, like Maurice Blanchot's short piece "The instant of my death," comments on the nature of fiction by putting it in productive tension with fact. Henrik Skov Nielsen's "What's in a name? Double exposures in *Lunar Park*" takes the coincidences between biography and fiction in a different direction, establishing *Lunar Park* within the narrative mode of autofiction: a work of fiction that cannot be dissociated from autobiography (other examples of autofiction can be found in the work of contemporary French authors Michel Houellebecq and Frédéric Beigbeder, both of whom have cited Ellis as an influence). As autofiction, *Lunar Park* invites investigation of the biographical as well as the autobiographical. "Brand Ellis: celebrity authorship in *Lunar Park*," James Annesley's contribution to this volume, treats *Lunar Park*'s gestures toward autobiography as a source of insight into Ellis's recognition of himself as a commodity: marketable, reproducible, and recognizable. Annesley calls the book a mockubiography, a play on the "mockumentary" film genre of the 1984 cult classic *This is Spinal Tap* and, more recently, *Borat: Cultural Learnings of America for Make Benefit Glorious Nation of Kazakhstan* (2006).

As this section sets the stage for future scholarship on *Lunar Park*, the authors of the chapters expand the tradition of literary criticism that has emerged around Ellis and his work. For Karnicky, the ghosts in the novel and the figure of the writer that vies with Bret for narrative control over the events and their description offer a way into Ellis's complex approach to fiction, its relation to reality, and the primacy of reading and writing at the intersection of the two. Karnicky continues Clark's work on *American Psycho* in this volume by situating Ellis's work within a tradition of continental philosophy and treating it as a fulcrum for the relationship between words and world. The novel itself, of course, performs this investigation literally, as the narrator Bret is an unwilling detective whose pursuit of the truth of events uncovers the traces of his own literary misdeeds. For Karnicky, *Lunar Park* blurs the distinction between fiction and reality; like Schmid in his discussion of *Glamorama* in this volume, Karnicky argues that Ellis affirms the significance of this distinction even as the distinction itself is figured as, ultimately, inaccessible.

For Nielsen, *Lunar Park*'s problematization of fiction and fact applies to the relation between fathers and sons and authors and their works and extends beyond the text: back into the literary canon and out toward the world in which this canon figures and functions. Tracing the novel's explicit concern with paternity and its intertextual references to *Hamlet*, Nielsen identifies in the complexities of these relationships a recursive interaction of biography and fiction. This relation is imaged by the photographic term "double exposure" which, like the hauntings in the novel, problematizes the distinction between absence and presence and undoes assumptions of temporality and causality. Nielsen's focus on paternity and the *Hamlet* motif confirm Blazer's suggestion, in this volume, that these issues have dominated Ellis's fiction since *Less Than Zero*, and his reliance on terminology from photography reinforces Baelo-Allué's examination of intermediality in Ellis's work.

For Annesley, *Lunar Park* is an opportunity to outline a new methodology of reading, one that asks questions not just about the links between celebrity, consumption, and the author function, but about strategies for approaching contemporary literary and cultural production. Noting that Ellis's fiction has consistently defied many traditional critical grammars, particularly those that try to praise or blame, Annesley locates in the author's desire to play with his own self-image further evidence of his consistent attempts to toy with these categories. Annesley argues that Ellis does not attempt to resolve the vexed relation between reality and its representation but, rather, mobilizes and employs it as a critical tool with which to intervene in the debates around simulation, postmodernism, and commodification. Echoing Gomel, who situated *American Psycho* within, rather than against, the rigid syntaxes of fashion, and Redding, for whom *Glamorama*'s epistemic slipperiness articulated crucial aspects of contemporary desubjectivization, Annesley argues that Ellis's fiction needs to be read not as a commentary upon the modern mediascape but as work that is very much a part of it.

With *Lunar Park*, the novelist who vehemently dissociated himself from the narrator of *American Psycho* and who literally deconstructed the narrator of *Glamorama* reaffirms his commitment—voluntary or not—to his oeuvre only to problematize it further, blurring the boundaries between author and character and writer and work. The paradoxical effect is of foregrounding Ellis's stature as a serious author while making him disappear. In the elegiac final pages, Ellis resurrects *American Psycho*'s bleak reference to hermetic hell ("THIS IS NOT AN EXIT") with an image of ashes that efface and create the words of *Lunar Park*. The ashes are described as collapsing, bleeding, and, finally, "exiting the text" (308). This veiled reference to *American Psycho* leaves Ellis's readers with one last challenge: in the wake of this final exit, *Lunar Park* offers a declaration of love and a promise, by the author, to remain "right here, my arms held out and waiting" (308).

CHAPTER 7

"An Awfully Good Impression": Truth and Testimony in *Lunar Park*

Jeff Karnicky

Lunar Park begins with this statement: " 'You do an awfully good impression of yourself' " (3). This statement appears as a single paragraph, in quotation marks. Readers are then made aware, by the novel's second sentence, that "This is the first line of *Lunar Park*" (3). Why does Ellis state such an obvious thing? Anyone reading the novel must be aware that the first line of the novel is indeed the first line of the novel. For Ellis, the impression of redundancy offers an opportunity to reflect on his own writing. The second sentence of *Lunar Park* remarks of this statement that "in its brevity and simplicity it was supposed to be a return to form, an echo, of the opening line from my debut novel, *Less Than Zero*" (3). Over the next two pages, Ellis cites and analyzes the opening sentence of each of his novels. He notes their growing verbosity and concludes that "things were getting out of hand" (4). The terse opening sentence of *Lunar Park* marks a getting "back to basics" (4) in Ellis's fiction and also in his life. Chapter One of *Lunar Park*, appropriately titled "the beginnings," is meant to function as a new beginning for both Bret Easton Ellis the writer and Bret Easton Ellis the person, who are equivocally linked by the narrator who wonders "if fiction reveals a writer's inner life" (4).

The remainder of the opening chapter offers a detailed description of Ellis's life from the writing of *Less than Zero* to the book tour for *Glamorama*. In what follows I will argue that this description, like the novel itself, is a form of testimony—one that takes account of both Ellis's past as a writer (in the opening chapter) and Ellis's haunting by multiple ghosts and demons (in the remainder of the novel).

Testimony, as it is usually considered, is intrinsically related to the truth. Shoshana Felman and Dori Laub, in *Testimony: Crises of Witnessing in Literature, Psychoanalysis, and History*, define testimony as a "*vow to tell the truth*, to *promise* and *produce* one's own speech as material evidence for truth" (5). For Felman and Laub, testimony is best understood as a complex movement between text and context: "the empirical context needs not just to be *known*, but to be *read*; to be read in conjunction with, and as part of, the reading of the text" (xv). Such reading seems a perfect way to think about *Lunar Park*. Chapter One offers precisely those "political, historical, and biographical realities" to which Felman and Laub refer (xv). Ellis cites numerous sources—*The New York Post* (9), *Entertainment Tonight* (11), *The National Enquirer* (18)— as he describes the general debauchery of his life. Real people are mentioned—from George W. Bush (10) to Keanu Reeves (16)—as Ellis reflects on the social world that his novels gave him entry to. He cites reviews and analyses of his work from, among others, *Vanity Fair* (12) and *New York Magazine* (7), provides what he calls "the CliffsNotes version" (12) of events surrounding the publication of *American Psycho*, and admits that "there was something, well, evil" about that novel (13). But even as Ellis writes a seemingly factual account of his life, he gives readers reason to doubt his veracity. As I argue in more detail below, attempts to separate fiction from fact in *Lunar Park* are continually undermined; indeed, even separating the text from its context becomes difficult, if not impossible, as a large part of the novel's text is precisely about the context of Ellis's life. Yet it is still worthwhile to consider the novel as a form of testimony. Against Felman and Laub's definition, I posit Jacques Derrida's theory of testimony as a first person account of events in which the distinction between fiction and truth, though crucial, can never be definitively resolved.

Two Brets

Lunar Park clearly wants to blur the boundary between truth and fiction, a point made clear on the novelist's website at Random House. The site offers readers two versions of Bret Easton Ellis, illustrated by a head shot of the author split by a jagged line. The page has two columns; each provides biographical facts about and an interview with "Bret Easton Ellis." One column matches the facts of Ellis's life and one matches the information in *Lunar Park*. Both were born on March 7, 1964, and both are 6' tall. But one Ellis is 185 pounds and graduated from Bennington College in 1986, and one is 220 pounds and graduated from Camden College in 1986. The interviews, each of which purports to be an interview with Bret Easton Ellis, confuse matters further. In one, Ellis says "It's up to each reader to decide how much of *Lunar Park* actually occurred." In the other, he says "It's up to each reader to take a leap of faith and understand that everything in *Lunar Park* actually occurred" (Rabb). In short, the website demands that the reader take responsibility for his or her approach to *Lunar Park* by offering two competing versions of the novel's relation to the truth (appropriately, the web address is: www.2brets.com).

Right from the opening pages of *Lunar Park*, when the novelist describes being a student at Camden College in New Hampshire (5), one cannot help but wonder what Ellis is up to. Camden College is the fictional setting for *The Rules of Attraction* and is referred to (at least obliquely) in all of Ellis's other novels. It is often considered a fictional stand-in for Ellis's alma mater Bennington College. In interviews following the publication of *Lunar Park*, Ellis encouraged this confusion. "Do you believe me? Really? Even after reading my book?" he asks, leaving the interviewer with the impression that Ellis's "whole personality [is] just a game" (Grossman 66). Elsewhere he distances himself from it: "My worry is that people will want to know what's true and what's not . . . All these things that are in the book—my quote-unquote autobiography—I just don't want to answer any of those questions. I don't like demystifying the text" (Wyatt). This evasiveness is especially interesting because, in the midst of the controversy around *American Psycho*, Ellis emphasized the absolute difference between his own life and that of his serial-killer protagonist: "I can't say that [*American Psycho*] is autobiographical in any sense of the word," he states in an interview with *Rolling Stone*, "Patrick Bateman is a monster. I am not" (Love).

Nonetheless, critical responses to the novel assumed a strong connection between *Lunar Park* and the life of Bret Easton Ellis. Some critics noted the narcissistic elements of the novel, assuming that Ellis's main character is "a carbon copy of himself" ("Scrapings") or deplored the "me-me-me-ism . . . of his writing" (Duralde 82). Some sought to separate truth and fiction. "Where does reality end and fiction begin in *Lunar Park*?" (22), asked Holt and Abbot; to answer this question they "isolated the publishing history as reflected in the book and compared it to what really happened" (22). Most critics were not quite so literal minded. Scott writes of the difficulty of determining whether the novel's "awful happenings are taking place in the narrator's head, in the objective reality he inhabits or in some indeterminate zone between the two." For Scott, this indeterminacy has some potential, but Ellis fails to realize it: "I wish it were a more interesting question. That is, I wish Ellis had found the discipline necessary to pose it more cogently."

Other critics sought in the novel an element of autobiography, turning to the figure of Ellis's father in the novel as evidence. For Wyatt, the book's dedication to Ellis's father, Robert Martin Ellis, is "perhaps the biggest clue to Mr. Ellis." Grossman sees the relationship between Ellis and his father as a key to understanding "the real Ellis" (66). For many of the critics cited above, *Lunar Park*'s flirtation with autobiography is evidence of its failure. Janet Maslin describes the novel as an attempt "to reanimate his father [and] his own boyhood" and dismisses this attempt as gimmicky: Ellis "is over his head in these dark waters" (8). Reviewing the novel for *The New Statesman*, Rachel Aspden writes, "despite the atmosphere of heavy psychological revelation, it is difficult to unravel the significance of *Lunar Park*'s doppelgänger parade" (55). Rejecting this difficulty as a flaw, Aspden focuses on what she sees as the book's strength—Ellis's satiric voice: "Ellis has lost none of his talent for capturing the signs of the times with precision and wit" (55). *The Economist*'s reviewer also rejects the autobiographical in favor of social commentary: "the best of this novel lies in those rare interstices in which Mr. Ellis is not talking about Mr. Ellis. His descriptions of modern parenting and education are hilarious and mortally accurate" ("Scrapings").

While there is clearly no consensus in the critical reception of *Lunar Park*, most critics, as I note above, assume a strong connection between the content of *Lunar Park* and the world outside the novel. Whether they make this connection by fact-checking, by describing the narrator of *Lunar Park* as a narcissistic projection of the author, by noting the difficulty of separating the fictional from the real, or by identifying a kernel of autobiography in *Lunar Park*, each assumes that a clear distinction can be made between an author's life and the fictional world he creates. Treating *Lunar Park* as a satirical perspective on contemporary life also requires a clear distinction between fiction and reality so that fiction can be seen as an exaggerated version of the real world. Ellis, of course, invites these connections throughout the book. But he also undermines them.

Lunar Park is not the first novel to blur the lines between fiction and reality. Literary critics have grappled with these sorts of novels as they have tried to understand how such fiction works. Brian McHale examines the kinds of worlds created by fiction as he seeks what he calls an "ontology" of postmodern novels: fiction uses language to describe a possible world that may or may not have a relation to the real world. Dorrit Cohn defines fiction as "nonreferential" and notes that fiction's "reference to the world outside the text are not bound to accuracy" (15). For Cohn, "ambiguous texts" such as novels that appear to be accounts of real lives (*Lunar Park* is an example) are still clearly distinguishable as fictional or factual: "we read [them] in one key or the other . . . [it] is not a matter of degree but of kind" (35). McHale echoes Cohn on this point: the author as character is always "as fictional as any other character. The ontological barrier between an author and the interior of his fictional world is absolute, impenetrable" (215). While fiction is always in some relation to reality, and may even trouble it (for McHale, postmodern fiction in particular "systematically disturbs the air of reality" [221]) the two are nonetheless distinct. Postmodern fiction mirrors the complexities of the world in which it is written (McHale 39), a formulation that depends on a clear line between fiction and reality: the mirror-world of fiction must be distinguishable from what it reflects. For these theorists of fiction, the borders between fiction and fact may be unclear but the difference between the two remains firm. But the Bret Easton Ellis who does an "awfully good impression" of himself, I claim, eludes the boundaries—however blurry—between the two. Perhaps another way of reading *Lunar Park* is possible, a way that does not, to use Ellis's words, "want to know what's true and what's not."

"I'm everyone"

If the critical responses to *Lunar Park* in particular, and postmodern fiction in general, have maintained the distinction between the "historical and biographical realities" and the text that Felman and Laub posit as the foundation of testimony, Jacques Derrida's work on testimony and Maurice Blanchot's work on writing offer an alternate approach to the novel. Derrida's *Demeure*, which takes the form of an extended reading of Maurice Blanchot's short story "The Instant of My Death"—a text that both is and is not autobiographical—grounds its definition of testimony in writing and in reading. There is, Derrida argues, no failsafe way to differentiate testimony from literature; rather than relying on the distinction between fiction and truth, testimony invites this distinction but ultimately eludes it.

"The Instant of My Death" tells the story of a young Frenchman's brush with death during WWII. He is taken from his home and set in front of a firing squad. At the last moment, the soldiers are distracted by the sound of a nearby battle and move away. The narrator reflects on the man's mental state, noting as he does so that such insight is impossible: "I know, I imagine that this unanalyzable feeling changed what there remained for him of existence. As if the death outside of him could only henceforth collide with the death in him. 'I am alive. No, you are dead'" (9). This copresence of two orders of being ("I am alive. No, you are dead"), so similar to the world of *Lunar Park* (in which Bret refers to himself numerous times as "the ghost" and in which the realistic subur-ban life he lives with his family is permeated by paranormal events) is one of the reasons Derrida finds it impossible to categorize Blanchot's text. "I do not know," he writes, "whether this text belongs . . . to the space of literature, whether it is a fiction or a testimony" (*Demeure* 26). In the long close reading of Blanchot that follows, Derrida does not attempt to separate fiction from testimony; rather, he argues that fiction and testimony are inextricably linked.

For Derrida, the very act of testimony, of bearing witness to some-thing, implies the "possibility of fiction" (*Demeure* 29). Testimony is not proof; because of this, one can never be certain that a testimony refers exactly to events as they happened. Derrida's argument should not be dismissed as simply a fall into relativism where fiction and testimony, and thus truth and lies, become equally valid. Rather, the inextricable link between fiction and testimony enables Derrida to call both catego-ries into question. He writes that "the possibility of literary fiction *haunts* so-called truthful, responsible, serious, real testimony as its proper possibility" (*Demeure* 72 my emphasis). Here it is important to remember that *Lunar Park* is, essentially, a ghost story; Derrida's formulation enables us to read the paranormal events in the novel—events that the narrator claims are true but which are dismissed or disbelieved by other characters—as a statement about the relation between literary fiction and truthful testimony. The repetition of the word "possibility" is key here: testimony cannot exist without the pos-sibility of fiction; fiction cannot exist without the possibility that it refers to real events. The multiple "beginnings" and "endings" of the novel point to the role of possibility in *Lunar Park* and further situate it on "the border between literature and its other" which, writes Derrida, "becomes undecidable" (*Demeure* 92). Rather than doing away with truth, this undecidability is the condition of possibility for truth: from its "chaos," "a right reference to truth emerges or arises" (*Demeure* 92). A reader of *Lunar Park*, for instance, could believe that Bret Easton Ellis's testimony is false—after all, Ellis cannot have attended the fictional Camden College. Another reader could believe the narrator who asserts that "every word is true." Both would be missing the point. Undecidability is the underlying structure of *Lunar Park*. Any reference to truth that the novel may make reinforces the fulcrum of truth and fiction on which it rests. This, and not its power to reflect or establish empirical fact, is what makes the novel a testimony.

According to Derrida, testimony must be in the first person: "one must oneself be present, raise one's hand, speak in the first person" (*Demeure* 33). *Lunar Park*, of course, is a first person novel, but the "I" who speaks (and writes) throughout the novel complicates the distinction between the "one" who speaks and the "oneself" who is present. There seems to be more than one Ellis in the novel: there is an Ellis who tells the story as narrator of events, an Ellis who is a character in the novel, and an Ellis who is the author of the novels attributed to Bret Easton Ellis. There is also "the writer" who emerges in the course of the novel and who may or may not be Bret Easton Ellis. As this chapter develops, I will note the different iterations of Ellis's "I"; ultimately, though, I will argue that all of these "I"s become indistinguishable within *Lunar Park*'s testimonial space.

In other words, *Lunar Park* complicates both the truth of testimony and the "I" who speaks or writes it, but such complications only enhance its testimonial quality. Derrida asks readers to "take the example of two perfectly identical discourses" (*Demeure* 37). If one discourse identifies itself as fiction by, for example, being published and sold as a novel (*Demeure* 37), it need bear no responsibility to the truth, even if it claims, as the narrator of *Lunar Park* does, that "every word is true" (30). In other words, the structure of testimony can be fictionalized because it can be repeated: iterated and reiterated. *Lunar Park* is precisely such a repetition—Ellis describes the novel as a "retelling" (30). This iterability is a quality that testimony shares with writing: in "Signature Event Context," Derrida notes the "essential iterablity" (20) of anything written. This quality of iterablity signals, for Derrida, "the possibility of fiction *and* lie" and establishes "the right to literature" (*Demeure* 42). The opening sentence of *Lunar Park* marks a number of iterations. It is reported speech (it appears in quotation marks); it is writing (a fact pointed to in the following sentence, "This is the first line of *Lunar Park*"); and it refers to replication, to a doubling of—to return to Derrida's terms—the "one" who speaks and the "oneself" who gives testimony. From its very first line, *Lunar Park* establishes itself as testimony in Derrida's sense of the term: it blurs the boundary between fiction and fact, identifies itself with writing, and claims the right to literature.

Things get more complicated in Chapter Two, the first sentence of which is a repetition of the first sentence of Chapter One. The sentence is spoken to Ellis by his wife, Jayne Dennis, after Ellis tells her that he is going as himself to the Halloween party he is throwing. This repetition adds another beginning to those of the first chapter, and extends the self-reflexive autobiographical statements of that chapter to the remainder of the novel. The sentence also seems to denote two different Ellises. In Chapter One, the narrating "I" refers to Bret Easton Ellis who writes and quotes his writing as he reflects on his role as an author. In Chapter Two, "I" refers to the narrator and identifies that narrator as a character in the novel—the protagonist. " 'You do an awfully good impression of yourself'" (31), suggests that not only the narrator but the protagonist of *Lunar Park* is an awfully good impression of the author.

"[A] testimony," writes Derrida, "is always autobiographical: it tells, in the first person, the sharable and unsharable secret of what happened to me, to me, to me alone, the absolute secret of what I was in a position to live, see, hear, touch, sense, and feel" (*Demeure* 43). Bret Easton Ellis gives first person testimony throughout *Lunar Park*. As Ellis shifts from writing about his fiction to writing about the haunting of his house, he tells the reader just how isolated he was: he alone can tell this story. He writes that many people "dispute the horror of the events that took place," including his ex-wife and his mother (30). He complains that he is not allowed to quote from the files the FBI has kept on him since the prepublication of *American Psycho*. He goes so far as to say that "the thing that haunted me the most" was precisely that isolation: "[s]ince no one knew what was happening in that house, no one was scared for us" (30). Both the opening pages and the reference to "the last two words of the book" which should, he writes, "be self-explanatory *to the reader*" (30 emphasis mine) mark *Lunar Park* as writing, as iteration: the secret has always already been repeated.

The multiple Ellises that narrate *Lunar Park* further complicate testimony's autobiographical quality. The replications of Bret Easton Ellis in the course of the novel inscribe the author as himself a function of repetition. Ellis dresses as the "full-on Bret" (31) for the Halloween party. He later describes himself as "the ghost" (52). Ellis sees himself in both his son and his dead father. The Terby doll that comes alive is another repetition, as Ellis reverses the spelling of its name "y-bret" as a question, "why Bret?" The student, Clayton, who first appears at the Halloween party dressed as Patrick Bateman, replicates Ellis throughout the novel and he eventually tells Ellis, "I'm everything. I'm everyone. I'm even you" (227).

If, as Derrida argues, the possibility of fiction "haunts" testimony, this haunting points to the centrality of writing: "This haunting is perhaps the passion itself, the passionate place of literary writing" (*Demeure* 72). *Lunar Park's* hauntings emerge from precisely that place. Ellis is haunted by literary writing: his published and unpublished works, including some that no one but himself has read. Donald Kimball, the detective who interviews Ellis about a series of murders that seem to be based on *American Psycho*, is himself a character from that novel. The detective asks, "you're not a fictional character, are you, Mr. Ellis?" (124). A few days later, after Aimee Light is murdered in a way that does not follow the plot of *American Psycho*, the detective then dismisses any connection between Ellis and the murders. But Ellis is not completely convinced. He returns to his childhood home in Los Angeles and to the first draft of *American Psycho*, an early version of the novel "that no one but me had ever read" (279), and finds a deleted chapter that matches the latest murder. Only a writer can be haunted in the way that Ellis is. The addition of Ellis as writer to Ellis as author marks yet another iteration.

This iteration is literalized with the emergence of the writer, who appears as Ellis reflects on the border between his writing and his life: "I was good at making up things and detailing them meticulously, giving them the necessary spin and shine" (146). Here Ellis seems to be thinking of himself as a successful author. But as he continues to reflect, he notes that "A writer's physical life is basically one of stasis, and to combat this constraint, an opposite world and another self have to be constructed daily" (146–47). This binary, though, is not stable, and Ellis comes to realize that the categories cannot be reliably distinguished: "Lying often leaked from my writing life [. . .] into the part of me that was tactile and alive [. . .] I was at a point at which I believed the two had merged and I could not tell one from the other" (147). Confronted with "the reality," Ellis instructs himself to "invent a new chapter heading: 'The Night that Never Happened'" (147). This attempt to render reality fictional is encouraged by the writer, who "convinced me that everything was normal" (148). From this point on, the writer gains in power and becomes a prominent voice in the novel. The writer begins to think on his own; he asks Ellis questions and he whispers in Ellis's ear (206–07); he forms "his own theories" (210) about how and why Ellis is haunted. In short, "the writer" begins to wrestle with Ellis for control over *Lunar Park*. Ellis and the writer represent "two opposing strategies for dealing with the current situation." Ellis yearns for "answers," "clarity," and "control"; the writer is aligned more explicitly with fiction: "the writer craved myth and legend and coincidence and flames. The writer wanted Patrick Bateman back in our lives" (212). And the writer, Ellis confesses, "was winning" (212). The writer reshapes reality. He says to Ellis, "*look how black the sky is* [. . .] *I made it that way*" (216).

The grounds for contestation between Ellis and the writer appear to be the very difference between fiction and fact that approaches to fiction and to testimony presume. In a statement that seems to echo Felman and Laub's definition of testimony, Ellis states: "There is really no other way of describing the events that took place in 307 Elsinore Lane during the early morning of November 6 other than simply relating the facts" (232). This is one argument he wins with the writer, convincing him the events in question did not require "the embellishments the writer would have insisted on" (232). But in the course of this account (titled "the darkness"), writing is revealed to be the source of the hauntings. Writing asserts its power over both testimony ("facts") and fiction ("embellishments"). As Ellis realizes that the murder of

Aimee Light replicates the deleted scene from *American Psycho* that he had written but never published, he finds "The Toy Bret," "an illustrated book I had written when I was seven" (282) in which "I saw the Terby replicated a hundred times" (283). The creature that had attacked Ellis and his son is also revealed to be a fictional creation of Ellis's from "The Tomb," a story he had written when he was twelve (251). Ellis is haunted by what he calls "physical manifestations of [. . .] fictional creations" (256). The "facts" that Ellis had insisted on recounting (even though the writer "wanted this job" [232]) reflect the inextricability of fiction and reality.

Derrida writes that testimony must "allow itself to be haunted" by the possibility that it is untrue: by "the *possibility*, at least, of literature" (*Demeure* 30). In *Lunar Park*, Ellis testifies that all writing is haunted in just this way. His fictional characters literally haunt his material existence. However important it is to distinguish between fiction and reality (after all, the monster of his childhood writing leaves Ellis in fear of his and his children's lives and drives them from their home) the two can never be extricated. Ellis wonders, "how can a fictional thing become real?" (250), but he never answers that question. He realizes that he will "never find explanations" (282), a conclusion echoed by the writer who whispers, "*that's because explanations are boring*" (282). At this point Ellis realizes that he will never make sense of what has been happening. Neither he nor the writer has the power to make everything clear. "Everything would remain disguised and remote. I would struggle to piece things together, and the writer would ultimately deride me for attempting this task. There were too many questions. This would always happen" (282). What Derrida says of Blanchot's "Instant" seems equally true of *Lunar Park*: "The text testifies to this strange event in a way that is abyssal, elliptical, paradoxical, and for that matter, undecidable" (*Demeure* 53).

"We're a lot of people"

The intersection of repetition, writing, and haunting that flows through Ellis's testimony can perhaps be understood in terms of Blanchot's own work on writing, specifically, Blanchot's understanding of writing as a haunted return. The first sentence of *Lunar Park*—"a return to form, an echo" of the first sentence of *Less Than Zero* (3)—identifies Ellis as a writer in Blanchot's sense of the term. For Blanchot, the writer is the one who constantly returns to earlier writings:

> The obsession which ties him to a privileged theme, which obliges him to say over again what he has already said . . . illustrates the

necessity, which apparently determines his efforts, that he always come back to the same point, pass over again the same paths. (*The Space of Literature* 24)

For Ellis, the return is necessary because he wishes to erase the excesses of his life and literature. For Blanchot, the necessity is slightly different: the writer returns to the work because "the writer never knows whether the work is done. What he has finished in one book, he starts over or destroys in another" (*The Space* 21). The writer, for Blanchot, cannot simply stop writing—not because he seeks perfection, or because she wants to produce a great work, but writing itself is "the interminable, the incessant" (*The Space* 26). The writer becomes the one who cannot cease writing, and thus must return again and again to what he or she has written. *Lunar Park* shows that Ellis cannot escape his earlier writings: he is haunted by their return.

The reader, too, experiences Ellis's writing as a return. The last attack of the Terby (through Ellis's dog, Victor, which the Terby possesses) is a repetition in origin and in effect. The dog's name repeats that of Victor Ward from *Glamorama*, who is himself a recurrence of the Victor from *The Rules of Attraction*. As Ellis describes in gory detail the dog's attack (290–93), readers are returned to an earlier, more terse description of events in Ellis's illustrated story that included pictures of "the Terby attacking a dog" and of "the Terby entering the dog and making it fly" (283). The words "disappear here" (288) which Ellis sees scrawled against a poster in his son's room and hears whispered by the writer and by Clayton (295) have also echoed throughout Ellis's work (it is accorded a significant place in both *Less Than Zero* and in *Glamorama*). Ellis cannot help but return to and repeat interminably what he has already written.

Ellis begins the short final part of *Lunar Park* with the sentence "There was one last story to write" (305), a sentence that not only recalls the role of writing throughout the novel, but which combines the first person testimony in Derrida's sense with the task of writing that Blanchot describes in *The Writing of the Disaster*: "to write (of) oneself is to cease to be, in order to confide in a guest—the other, the reader— entrusting yourself to him who will henceforth have as an obligation, and indeed as a life, nothing but your inexistence" (*The Writing* 64). In a phone conversation with a disembodied voice that might be Clayton or Patrick Bateman, Ellis is told, "I want you to face the disaster that is Bret Easton Ellis" (230). He and his iterated selves have come to populate every space of the novel. When Ellis asks the voice on the phone "Is this . . . Patrick?" the voice replies "We're a lot of people" (228). Later, Ellis attempts to end the hauntings by writing a story in which Patrick Bateman dies. But as he writes the story, he realizes that this attempted erasure will not work. "Even as he is consumed by flames he says 'I am everywhere'" (283). Ellis's son disappears but this disappearance, too, underscores Ellis's perpetual replication: the writer tells him, "*the boy was you*" (299). Ellis realizes that he and Clayton—whose name recalls Clay, the narrator of *Less Than Zero*—"were always the same person" (295). There is no escape from the disaster of Bret Easton Ellis: Ellis the narrator, Ellis the author, Ellis's characters, and the writer become indistinguishable. At novel's end, a reader cannot find a "real" Bret Easton Ellis and a reader cannot distinguish between fiction and fact. Even as Ellis writes himself and his work into what Blanchot calls "inexistence," he "disappears here"—into his own writing. The novel concludes with the promise that Ellis is and will be forever in this writing: "in the pages, behind the covers, at the end of *Lunar Park*" (307).

In his reading of Blanchot's "Instant," Derrida writes of "the testimonial message that passes into the blood of reality through the epidermis of fiction" (*Demeure* 60). Derrida never states just what this testimonial message might be, just as he never resolves the undecidability of Blanchot's narrative. Ellis never tells us what "Lunar Park" means, or names the word that marked the absence of his father or his son (306). The novel's opening pages include this instruction to the reader: "Regardless of how horrible the events described here may seem, there's one thing you must remember as you hold this book in your hands: all of it really happened" (30). But as the novel progresses, Ellis relinquishes this injunction: again, addressing the reader, he states, "I am not going to try to make you believe anything. You can choose to believe me, or you can turn away" (272). But a reader does not, or perhaps cannot, make such a choice because Ellis has *written over* the line between fiction and truth. The distinction remains, but the reader is left with no assurance as to where it lies. Rather than attempting to erase this writing, to distinguish truth from lies, we should read it as a mark of the power of writing and of *Lunar Park*'s written testimony. Ellis's "awfully good impression" is not just an impersonation, it is an imprint. In the final pages of the novel Ellis scatters his father's ashes which whisper to him, "*I want to show you something*" (306). As the ashes cover everything, this is what they reveal: "an awfully good impression" on both fiction and on truth.

CHAPTER 8

What's in a Name? Double Exposures in *Lunar Park*

Henrik Skov Nielsen

In Bret Easton Ellis's *Lunar Park* a crucial plot turn revolves around a question about a name. Toward the end of the book a "paranormal investigator," Robert Miller, demonstrates to the character Bret Easton Ellis that the name of the murderous Terby doll forms a question about Ellis's own first name. When read backwards the name of the doll is YBRET: "Why Bret?" This means, the investigator says, that Bret Easton Ellis is the source of the haunting of the house on Elsinore Lane where he lives with his family (264). This question about the name of the character as well as the author connects to a whole series of questions in the text: about fiction and nonfiction, and about characters, narrators, and authors. This chapter examines these questions and problems in *Lunar Park* through the literary genre that has come to be known as "autofiction."

But "Bret" is not the only name that raises questions. The novel also contains many references to Shakespeare's play *Hamlet*. The references seem exaggerated and superficial, and on many levels *Hamlet* and *Lunar Park* are very different. But rather than dismissing these references as superfluous ornaments, we should ask ourselves, with reference to yet another Shakespeare play, "what's in a name?" (*Romeo and Juliet* 2.2.43). The question is not only "Why Bret?" but also "Why Hamlet?" With the help of terms and concepts offered by the genre of autofiction, I approach *Lunar Park*'s relationship to its author and to Shakespeare and *Hamlet* as a double exposure: a term from photography that refers to the superimposition of one image over another. Double exposure has often been used as a technique to visually portray ghosts and haunting. In *Lunar Park* double exposure works on a narrative level: fiction is superimposed on nonfiction and characters are superimposed on authors. Consequentially, the concept of double exposure offers a way to understand the many ghosts that haunt the novel.

Autofiction

Hardly anything could be more familiar to literary scholars than talking about "fictional narratives." But even this simple expression contains a slight tension between the *invention* associated with fiction and its root in the Latin "fictio" and the *knowing* associated with narration and its root in the Latin "gnarus." How can you invent what you know or know what you invent? In all standard conceptions of narrative theory, answering this question has required splitting the tasks and distinguishing between the narrator who *knows* and the author who *invents. Lunar Park* problematizes the division between narrator and author and between fiction and nonfiction, and points to some of the problems that plague this division.

One of these problems is a question of classification. How do we distinguish between fiction and autobiography? In his much-discussed *On Autobiography*, Philippe Lejeune says that in most cases we need only look at the cover and compare the name of the author to the name of the protagonist: "*Name of the protagonist = name of the author.* This fact alone excludes the possibility of fiction," states Lejeune (17). But Lejeune then asks:

> Can the hero of a novel declared as such have the same name as the author? Nothing would prevent such a thing from existing, and it is perhaps an internal contradiction from which some interesting effects could be drawn. But, in practice, no example of such a study comes to mind. (18)

Just 2 years after the publication of *On Autobiography* (the original title is *Le pacte autobiographique*) in 1975, the author Serge Doubrovsky provided just such an example with his novel *Fils* (1977). In *Fils*, the protagonist, author, and narrator all share the same name, but the novel does not, in Lejeune's terms, enter into an autobiographical contract: it does not present itself to the reader, or demand to be read unequivocally, as autobiography. On the back cover of *Fils*, Doubrovsky suggested the term "autofiction" for books such as his, in which the protagonist, author, and narrator share the same name. Later, narrative theorist Gérard Genette (without even mentioning Doubrovsky) expanded the term "autofiction" to denote any long or short fictional narrative in which the author and one of the characters have the same name

(*Fiction & Diction* 68–84). The discussions about autofiction continue: Philippe Gasparini, Claudia Gronemann, and Vincent Colonna, as well as Lejeune and Genette, have published important texts on the subject. In the course of this critical discussion, it has come clear that autofictions—especially in Genette's broader definition—are hardly rare (even before 1975). *Lunar Park*, of course, is an autofiction both in the narrow sense established by Doubrovsky and in Genette's broader sense of the term: it is a novel labeled as fiction in which one of the characters (in this case, the protagonist) has the same name as the author.

Autofiction troubles the tradition of classical narratology and structuralism in which the relationship between narrator and author has traditionally been a cornerstone in the distinction between fiction and nonfiction. In nonfiction written narratives, communication is taken to proceed from author to reader; in fictional ones, communication is assumed to proceed from a narrator to a narratee. This distinction is problematic for several reasons. First, it assumes an absolute division between fictional and nonfictional narratives; second, it seems to encounter difficulties when facing a range of limit cases where the extent of the text's fictionality is difficult to decide. On the surface, autofiction may seem to do away with the distinction between fiction and nonfiction, fueling theories of "panfictionality"—the view that all discourse is fictional (Ryan 177). But as Marie-Laure Ryan notes, this view, too, is problematic: "[t]he possibility of hybridization does not necessarily mean that the two categories are inherently indeterminate: the many shades of gray on the spectrum from black to white do not turn black and white into the same color" (165).

While it is not enough, then, to dismiss the difference between fiction and nonfiction, the relation between the two assumes different forms. We can distinguish texts that present themselves as *neither* fiction *nor* nonfiction (I call these texts "underdetermined") from texts that present themselves—in some cases at different times, in others, at the same time—as *both* fiction *and* nonfiction (and hence can be called "overdetermined"). Autofictions are key examples of the latter type. I wish here to analyze *Lunar Park* as an example of an overdetermined text: an autofiction that sends mixed or mutually exclusive messages about its status as fiction or as nonfiction. But first, some words about the author.

The Author

Ellis's descriptions of himself, both within his novels and outside them, are almost always conflicting, if not flagrantly contradictory. In his books as well as in interviews, Ellis makes frequent references to himself, his time at college, his drug abuse, and so on. This tendency of Ellis's is included in *Lunar Park*, as the narrator reflects on his life and reputation:

> a lot of people thought I was gay . . . . The gay thing being the outcome of a drunken British interview . . . I had told countless interviewers about sexually experimenting with men—and went into explicit detail about the collegiate threesomes I had at Camden in a *Rolling Stone* profile. (18)

Though the narrator of *Lunar Park* denies he is gay, and in the novel itself is ensconced in a heterosexual relationship in which he has fathered a child, *Lunar Park* is dedicated not only to Ellis's father but to his partner of six years, Michael Wade Kaplan. In interviews, Ellis has maintained that his sexuality is "undeclared," arguing that to identify himself as gay, straight, or bisexual "would limit and direct the interpretation of what he has written, in a way he wouldn't like" (Heath). Many critics have assumed that the dedication to Kaplan, as well as Ellis's references to their relationship in interviews surrounding the publication of *Lunar Park*, settle the issue of Ellis's sexuality. But rather than unambiguously categorizing Ellis, one should note how he—both within his literary work and outside it—seems to deliberately apply a strategy of doubling, of elusiveness, and of mutually exclusive characterizations. Furthermore, as Heath notes, Ellis directly links his identity as an author to the interpretation of his work.

Since the publication of his first novel *Less Than Zero*, whose narrator Clay resembles Ellis in many ways, Ellis has been associated with his characters, and long before the publication of *Lunar Park* Ellis contributed to this association, alternately describing himself as engaging in the same self-destructive behavior as his characters and as living the boring life of a thinking and reading author (Kay). In the *Rolling Stone* profile mentioned in *Lunar Park*, Ellis describes his two first sexual experiences which took place within a week and were with a man and a woman respectively, recounts becoming involved with a male classmate while dating a girl in his class, and recalls participating in "an inordinate number of threesomes while I was at college . . . I liked the idea a lot" (Heath). The interviewer adds that "The threesomes were always made up of him as the third person with a male-female couple" (Heath). The significance of this account lies in Ellis's embrace of an undetermined position: both literally and categorically, he is "always" between a man and a woman.

In a conversation excerpted in *Harvard Crimson Magazine*, Ellis again eludes categorization, describing himself as "a total postmodernist . . . into post-postmodernism . . . but edging towards naturalism at the same time" (Kay). His interlocutors conclude by comparing Ellis not only to his characters, but to his books:

> Really, it's not very complicated. Ellis is obsessed with models, drugs, sex, magazines and violence and that's what he writes about. . . . A virtuoso of quotable quotes and absurd silliness, Ellis lives cocktail party chitchat. He's a master of persuasion and listeners become believers even though he says nothing. . . . Like the novels he writes, Ellis-the-person has a fluffy, immediate appeal. He delivers cheap and intoxicating amusement but, when it's all over, leaves absolutely nothing behind. (Kay)

As the above assessment demonstrates, Ellis eludes easy categorization to such a degree that he seems to disappear. He is a made out of "persuasion" and "quotes," and he is like "the novels he writes." In his commitment to elusiveness and ambiguity—emblematized by his accounts of his sexual history—Ellis established his similarity to a literary text long before the publication of *Lunar Park*.

This version of Ellis, established in his interviews and in his previous novels, offers a key to understanding the figure of the author in *Lunar Park*. The fact that Bret Easton Ellis appears by his own name in a work clearly designated "fiction" on the back cover confirms *Lunar Park* as an autofiction in the sense established by Doubrovsky and Genette. But in addition to this paratextual matter there is no doubt that much of what is said about Bret the protagonist holds true for Ellis the author as well. The book is narrated in the first person and begins with a description of Bret Easton Ellis's career as a writer, blended with short analyses of the changes in his own prose and the differences between the opening lines of his earlier works such as *Less than Zero* and *The Rules of Attraction*.

In the opening pages of *Lunar Park* Bret describes his promotional tours, his relationship with his publisher, the scandal following *American Psycho*, and his friendship with Jay McInerney—all information that is well known to any reader who has been following Bret Easton Ellis's career and reading his books. But there are also elements that are not in accordance with Ellis's biography. Bret claims to have attended Camden College (5) and to be married to a woman called Jayne Dennis (a fictional character who nonetheless has her own easily Googleable website). As the book progresses, its more overtly fictional elements increase: ghosts, the living doll, mysterious disappearances, houses changing shape, and much more. It culminates in bloody scenes where Bret is almost swallowed by a monster. The fictional character Patrick Bateman appears and begins (maybe as a copycat killer incarnation) to re-enact the murders from *American Psycho*.

Clearly, in *Lunar Park* there is a genuine clash of fictional and nonfictional spheres. While the novel is very far from embellished nonfiction (since the fictional parts are so obviously fictional) it also contains many pieces of true and supposedly true personal information about the author's life. It therefore seems rather reductive to ignore this information and classify the book as fiction. In the contractual language of Lejeune (a point occluded by the translation of *Le pacte autobio-graphique* as *On Autobiography*) the reader of *Lunar Park* enters into two mutually exclusive pacts: One asking her to use the material in the novel in a search for the truth about what really happened *and* another telling her to treat the material in the novel as creating a nonreferential fictional world that makes all search for truths outside the work itself useless. The reader is expected to do both at the same time.

Susan Lanser has argued that this paradoxical position is not unusual: readers, she states, often draw a connection between the author and the first-person narrator; even in fiction, these connections are much stronger than narrative theory has hitherto allowed. In both ambiguously designated works (like autofictions) and in narratives clearly identified as fictions, writes Lanser, "readers *routinely* 'vacillate' and 'oscillate' and even double the speaking voice against the logic of both structure and stricture" (207). She adds: "readers may ignore the technical boundaries of fictional voice, in effect *doubling* the 'I' so that the narrator's words sometimes belong to the author *as well as* to the narrating character and sometimes do not" (216). In both cases, Lanser uses the word "double/doubling" for the activity of the reader.

Overdetermined autofictions overtly invite such doubling, urging readers to read them as at once fictional and nonfictional. In *Lunar Park* reading with a double vision—as proposed by Lanser—is not only possible, it is necessary. Any reading that approaches the book solely as referential or solely as nonreferential will miss something. The narrative cannot be read as pure fiction—the similarities between the narrator and the author, especially in the first chapter, are striking, and go far beyond the fact that they share the same name. Nor can the narrative be read purely as nonfiction. Instead, the reader must assume that there is an equivocal relation between the first-person narrator and the author. Keeping this ambiguity in mind, the narrative can be read as a partly true communication from author to reader about the author's life (relating important facts about this life even as it flagrantly deviates from biographical truth) *as well as* a partly fictional communication from author to reader about the life of a haunted, drinking author. The real author shares his name and the pronoun "I" with this abuser, but surely not all of his experiences.

Double Exposures

Lunar Park, then, is rife with doubles and doublings. There is a doubling of voices (the "I" ambiguously referring to the author and/or the character) and there is a doubling of the readers' reading strategies (reading the book as at once fictional and nonfictional). Within the text, doubles abound (Clayton, for example, functions as one of Bret's doppelgängers; the house on Elsinore Lane is a double of the house in Sherman Oaks where Bret, and Ellis, grew up). The figure of the author is also doubled when the writer makes his appearance.

Like the gradually appearing film crews in *Glamorama* that accentuate the uncertainty of Victor's position (is he a character in a book or an actor in a film?), the writer emerges in *Lunar Park* from page 148 onwards. Whereas "I" predominantly refers to Bret as a character-narrator whose knowledge is limited, "the writer" seems to function as a literalization, within the work, of the author. The writer has information that Bret lacks ("The writer told me that two of the officers had masturbated to sex scenes in *American Psycho*" [249]), interrogates him ("*Do you really believe that, Bret?*" [218]), and occasionally corrects him ("*Wrong, Bret. Robby imagined escape*" [220]).

The writer, in this sense, is Bret's double. But the presence of the writer in *Lunar Park* also invites us to read the novel as metafiction. The metafictional elements of *Lunar Park* are very prominent, from the first line about playing, acting, and being ("You do an awfully good impression of yourself" [3]) and throughout the first chapter as the opening lines of Ellis's earlier works are quoted and commented on. When Bret tells his wife that he is coming to the Halloween party dressed up as himself ("'I've decided against wearing masks,' I said proudly. 'I want to be real, honey'" [31]) the metafictional aspects of the narrative are commented upon on a meta-metafictional level. The question, obviously, is how real can you be when you are dressed up for Halloween, or how dressed up can you be if you are coming as yourself—a mise en abyme, or mirroring effect, that resonates with the overall structure of the book. In the course of the novel, the metafictional elements reach an almost parodic level: "I found myself in Patrick Bateman's shoes: I felt like an unreliable narrator, even though I knew I wasn't. Yet then I thought: Well, had he?" (122). In addition to these obvious metafictional elements, as I will demonstrate, the novel combines the autofictional and the metafictional by adding a particularly biographical reading of *Hamlet* to the pronounced use of Bret Easton Ellis's autobiographical material.

In essence, any autofiction is itself a doubling, by virtue of its combination of fictional and nonfictional strategies and techniques. In *Lunar Park* the doublings form both a method and an objective—both a means and an end. To describe this effect I wish to borrow a term normally reserved for visual media: "double exposure." The *OED* defines the term as "(*a*) an accidental exposure of the same plate or film twice; (*b*) the deliberate superimposition of a second image on an exposure already made" ("Double," def. 8). Historically, this technique has been used to create photographic images of ghosts or to add people or objects not originally present at the scene.

Autofictions are counterparts, in the textual medium, to the double exposure in the visual medium. If, in a double exposed image we see each of the two exposures (perhaps without knowing which is which) and the image they create together, autofictions superimpose an image of the real author over an image of characters in a fictional world. In the case of *Lunar Park*, it is especially significant that, historically, this technique has proved especially apt for creating images of ghosts and objects that were not originally there. The photographic technique of "double exposure" brings together temporally or spatially distinct figures. Consequentially, the two images (whether in the visual or the written medium) then tend to recursively haunt each other. In the textual form of double exposure, the reader's knowledge about the author (from interviews, biographies, the media, and so on) contributes to his or her view of the author in the literary work and vice versa: exaggerations, fictional inventions, narrative fantasies in the work contribute to rumors and fantasies about the author. In any autofiction, then, the reader sees the sum of two pictures or two narratives superimposed over each other and haunting each other. One is the ghost of the other.

In *Lunar Park* these general conditions of double exposure and recursive haunting are rendered visible and literalized in several different ways. First, and most immediately, the fictional Bret living in the suburbs is literally haunted by ghosts. Second, these ghosts have to do with the real father and the real writings of the real author. Third, the fact that the author is himself a part of the work is emphasized and literalized with the appearance of the writer. Finally, Ellis mobilizes *Hamlet* as another narrative about ghosts, fiction and fact, and sons and fathers to add to the double exposures in *Lunar Park*.

Haunting Shakespeare

There are an overwhelming number of references to *Hamlet* in *Lunar Park*. Not only does Bret live with his family on Elsinore Lane (30), they visit Fortinbras Mall (106), drive down Ophelia Boulevard (110), and Claudius Street (176), and a girl is supposedly murdered at the Orsic [sic] motel (194). The emails that Bret receives in the middle of the night from the Bank of America in Sherman Oaks where his father's ashes are kept are reminiscent of the first act of *Hamlet* when the ghost of Hamlet's father approaches him.

However, attempts to read *Lunar Park* as a retelling of *Hamlet* are doomed to fail. Though the plot contains superficial similarities, these are greatly outweighed by the differences. Some of the key plot elements of *Hamlet* involve fratricide, the potential of incest, the ghost's wish to be avenged by the son, and the avenger's protracted hesitation to fulfill that wish. It is probably uncontroversial to say that these elements are constitutive for any telling of the story of *Hamlet*. In *Lunar Park*, however, not one of these plot elements is present. Neither Bret nor Robby nor any other character has anything to avenge and there is no incestuous relationship (although Robby finds it hard to acknowledge Bret as his "Dad"). However, *Lunar Park* shares with *Hamlet* some formal, structural similarities. Both are about sons and fathers and about ghosts and haunting. The ghosts of the father show up at around the same time in each text ("spirits who show themselves between night and dawn want something," says the paranormal investigator Bret hires [261]). And just as Hamlet is in doubt as to whether the nightly apparition is to be trusted ("The spirit that I have seen / May be a devil" [2.2.598–99]), two possible co-extensive forces are haunting Bret:

> Miller [the paranormal investigator] tried to explain a situation to me.
> It involved a ghost who wanted to tell me something.
> It involved a demon who did not want this information imparted to me.
> There were actually two forces opposing each other within the house. (273)

Nonetheless, these references and similarities are quite superficial and contribute little to understanding the plot or to the reading experience. If the references to *Hamlet* do not seem to add up to anything like the full picture it is because other parts of the picture consist of bio-graphical information about the author. The point is that *Lunar Park* is not so much, or not just, drawing upon *Hamlet* as it is drawing upon the relationship between the play, its characters, and its author. *Lunar Park* is quite emphatic about the prominence of the biographical, as the novel's opening chapter is, essentially, the biography of its author. The diegetic realm of the novel (*Lunar Park*) is not only fissured by its extradiegetic elements (the author's life), it mirrors another diegetic realm (*Hamlet*) and that realm's extradiegetic elements (Shakespeare's biography).

Shakespeare was known for playing the role of the ghost in early stagings of *Hamlet*. This biographical fact has found its way into the literary canon. For example, it is dramatized in James Joyce's *Ulysses*:

> The play begins. A player comes on under the shadow, made up in the castoff mail of a court buck, a wellset man with a bass voice. It is the ghost, the king, a king and no king, and the player is Shakespeare who has studied *Hamlet* all the years of his life which were not vanity in order to play the part of the spectre. (181)

In "The Death of Hamnet and the Making of Hamlet," Stephen Greenblatt suggests that during the composition of *Hamlet*, Shakespeare was thinking both of his dead son and of the fact that his father was either dead or dying. *Lunar Park* draws on this structure in that the author is repeatedly described as a ghost (52, 53, 298). Both Ellis and Shakespeare appear as ghosts in their own fictional creations, and each may be haunted by his own father. In the same essay, Greenblatt also suggests that Shakespeare was haunted by his vanished son:

> By the time the father reached Stratford the boy—whom, apart from brief visits, Shakespeare had in effect abandoned in his infancy—may already have died. On August 11, 1596, Hamnet was buried at Holy Trinity Church: the clerk duly noted in the burial register, "Hamnet filius William Shakspere." ("The Death")

Lunar Park borrows this theme of abandonment in the form of Bret's reluctance to acknowledge Robby as his biological son (16) and his leaving his son behind at home to go on tour. The 11-year-old Robby disappears, mirroring the death of Hamnet at the same age. Furthermore, the resonance of the name Hamlet (a name shared by the deceased king and the melancholy prince) with Shakespeare's son echoes the resonance between Ellis's father Robert and Bret's fictional son Robby (Bret describes this coincidence of names as the "catalyst" for the events in *Lunar Park* [16]). Thus, by virtue of the authors' biographies, both Hamlet/Hamnet and Robby/Robert resonate beyond the confines of a fictional text. Finally, the closing lines of *Lunar Park*, in which Bret visits the safe-deposit box that contains the ashes of his father, reveal that "The box containing what remained of my father had burst apart and the ashes now lined the sides of the oblong safe" (306). The box that "burst" parallels Hamlet's impression of his own father's refusal to be contained by death: "Let me not *burst* in ignorance; but tell/ Why thy canonized bones, hearsed in death,/Have *burst* their cerements" (1.4. 46–51 emphasis mine). Clearly, parallels between the two texts are in operation, and they are central to the hauntings in *Lunar Park*.

Because *Lunar Park* demands to be read simultaneously as fiction and as nonfiction, the novel can be viewed as a double exposure: the (nonfictional) story about the author is superimposed on the (fictional) story about the character. This technique is then re-doubled in the references to Shakespeare and his play *Hamlet* that invite the reader to read this relationship as paralleled by the relationship between Ellis and *Lunar Park*. The consequence of this double superimposition or double double exposure in *Lunar Park* is that Bret takes up several subject positions at once in the book. Ellis jokingly hints at the complexities of these levels in an interview:

"And yes for as much as the Bret Ellis character does have certain autobiographical aspects, I am the Robby character watching that marriage disintegrate but then that also means there's a whole oedipal connection that if I'm Bret, I'm married to my mother," he laughs. ("Behind Bret's Mask")

Bret is the haunted son as well as the haunting ghost. In relation to the ghost of his father he is Hamlet; in relation to his son Robby he is the ghost. The simultaneity of these multiple subject positions recalls the image of Shakespeare playing the ghost of the father in *Hamlet*, the title of which cannot but recall the name of his lost son. In *Lunar Park*, Bret is referred to as "the ghost" not only when he has an extreme hangover (52, 53) but in the wake of the hauntings of the house on Elsinore Lane and after Robby's disappearance—significantly, with a shift to the second person pronoun: "*Because—in the end, Bret—you were the ghost*" (298). This makes for a peculiar circular structure in which the relationship between Robby and Bret becomes equivalent to the relationship between Bret and his father Robert. Bret, recalling how Robby took his hand at a wedding party in Nashville, "dreamt that Robby's forward motion was carrying me with him, just as I had dreamt the same hand of my father's when I had guided him [. . .] to show him the same lizard Robby had tried to show me" (148). Eventually, Bret states the matter explicitly: "I was now my father. Robby was now me" (160). Given that Robby (a diminutive of Robert) is, Bret is convinced, named after his father Robert (15–16), the circular structure suggests an eternal recurrence of hauntings from fathers to sons. Bret is caught in a circle of hauntings, haunted by the past and by the future, and by fiction as well as fact.

Haunting as Revision and Transference

As I stated above, *Lunar Park* can be described as a double double exposure in the sense that biographical fact and fiction co-exist in the text *and* in the sense that the many references to Shakespeare and *Hamlet* invite the reader to consider the parallels between the relationship of fact to fiction in both texts. This is not to say that *Hamlet* is autofiction, but that the relation between Shakespeare's biography and the play adds a dimension to the relation between Ellis's biography and the novel, offering the reader two specific keys to understanding the hauntings in the novel: the centrality of revision and the function of transference.

In *Shakespeare: The Invention of the Human*, Harold Bloom reads *Hamlet* as, essentially, a work of revision: *Hamlet* is a play that stages and reflects hauntings from earlier versions of the play. "The mystery of Hamlet, and of *Hamlet*," writes Bloom, "turns upon mourning as a mode of revisionism, and possibly upon revision itself as a kind of mourning for Shakespeare's own earlier self" (400). Such a revision of the earlier self is not the only revision at play in *Hamlet*, since Bloom also views *Hamlet* as a revision of an earlier, now missing version of the play (the *Ur-Hamlet*). Significantly, Bloom images this revision in terms of doubling: "Indeed, we might say that there is a peculiar doubling: Hamlet contends not only with the Ghost but with the ghost of the first Ghost as well, and with the ghost of the first Hamlet" (402).

In *Hamlet in Purgatory*, Greenblatt reads *Hamlet* in terms of transference, according to which ghostliness is transferred from father to son. Discussing the phrase "Adieu, adieu, remember me" which the ghost speaks and which Hamlet repeats (1.5.91, 111) he observes that this repetition gives the impression that Hamlet "wants to ventriloquize the Ghost's words by making them his 'word'" (*Hamlet in Purgatory* 228). Greenblatt also notes the odd phrase "I am dead" which Hamlet twice speaks in the final scene of the play (5.2.275, 280) and concludes that this phrase "has an odd resonance: these are words that are most appropriately spoken by a ghost. It is as if the spirit of Hamlet's father has not disappeared; it has been incorporated by his son" (*Hamlet in Purgatory* 228–29).

Both revision and transference are at work in *Lunar Park* even before the novel begins. The epigraph from *Hamlet* that precedes the first chapter combines the themes of revision (of earlier versions) and of transference (from father to son): "from the table of my memory/ I'll wipe away all trivial fond records,/ All saws of books, all forms, all pressures past/ That youth and observation copied there" (*Lunar Park* n.p.). As Adam Phillips rightly remarks, *Lunar Park*'s epigraph offers "only half of the sentence" (19) from *Hamlet* and omits the following lines: "And thy commandement all alone shall live/ Within the book and volume of my brain/ Unmix'd with baser matter" (*Hamlet* 1.5.102–04). The "commandement" is the ghost's injunction "Remember me" which, Greenblatt notes, Hamlet repeats. Given the image of the mind as a "book" in the omitted lines, we can imagine that Hamlet is revising his life and the content of his brain just as Ellis revises his life and reflects on his writing in *Lunar Park* and, as Bloom suggests, as Shakespeare revised and reflected on the *Ur-Hamlet*. For Bret, for Ellis, for Hamlet, and for Shakespeare, the father lives on as a result of this revision—as Greenblatt puts it, the spirit of the father has been "incorporated."

Conclusion

From its opening pages, *Lunar Park* is staged as an attempt at revision: both of the author's lifestyle (from a tumultuous, urban, drug-dependant existence to the supposed peace and security of family life in the suburbs) and of his writing style which has become "overly complicated and ornate" (3). Both attempts are thoroughly unsuccessful since life on Elsinore Lane, like life at the castle in Elsinore, is anything but quiet and peaceful. Though Bret treats the opening sentence of *Lunar Park* as a revision of his writing style and a reversion to his earlier work—in terms that presage the hauntings in the novel, he describes this sentence as a "return" and an "echo" (3)—this sentence is anything but uncomplicated. Rather than exorcising the demons that had tormented Bret and propelled him toward revision, haunting proves to be eternal and circular: it is inherited from fiction to fiction and from father to son not in spite of attempts at revision but because of them. Describing his life and his writing career (specifically, the publication of *Less Than Zero* to which he aims, stylistically, to return), Bret states as the "most important" result: "I escaped my father" (5). "The thing I resented most about my father," writes Bret, "was that the pain he inflicted on me—verbal and physical—was the reason I became a writer" (6). But as *Lunar Park* makes clear, revisions to exorcise demons necessarily only lead to redoubled hauntings, and Bret is revealed, by the reversion of the spelling of TERBY, to be their source (264). Bret is the source of the hauntings in two senses. First, in the sense that he—and not the house—is haunted; second, because the haunting emanates from him: he is the creator of Patrick Bateman, Terby, "the thing" and the other fictions that plague him and his family. As the reversion reveals, any revision—of life or of work—brings ghosts with it.

Just as, in Bloom's words, Hamlet "contends not only with the Ghost but with the ghost of the first Ghost as well, and with the ghost of the first Hamlet," Bret contends not only with the ghost of his father but with the ghosts of this ghost in its earlier forms—his fictions. Bret is haunted by versions of himself and of his father (both fictional and real) and, furthermore, by his (and Ellis's) real father and by his (and Ellis's) real writings (including their fictional versions of the father). As an overdetermined autofiction, *Lunar Park* presents fact and fiction as haunting each other in a very literal way. Reading the novel in terms of a double exposure reveals further hauntings: the novel is haunted by another literary text about the ghost of a father, a text in which fact and fiction haunt each other. The epigraph to *Lunar Park* duplicates the transference of ghostliness from author to character and from father to son that Greenblatt described in *Hamlet*; the novel itself reduplicates this transference. By superimposing this double exposure of *Hamlet* and its author on to Ellis's text, *Lunar Park* becomes, in effect, a double double exposure in which the recursive hauntings of *Hamlet* and of Shakespeare haunt the recursive hauntings of Ellis and his writing, his father and his son. The hauntings are intratextual, intertextual, and extratextual. The question, "Why Bret?" points to the question, "Why Hamlet?": the two reflect each other and duplicate each other, a double double exposure that extends beyond the text of *Lunar Park* into the literary canon and the author's own life.

CHAPTER 9

Brand Ellis: Celebrity Authorship in *Lunar Park*

James Annesley

When, in "Just Look Like One," a 1999 episode of *Law and Order: Special Victims Unit*, Detective Munch (Richard Belzer) hears the name of Hampton Trill mentioned in connection with the murder of two teenage fashion models, he seizes the chance to hold court in the squad room by offering an acerbic précis of the writer's career. Describing Trill as "a Brat-packy little poseur, was published when he was 19, thinks he's the Emile Zola of premillennial Manhattan," Munch not only demonstrates his erudition and his familiarity with the book pages of *The New York Times* but also manages to articulate his contempt for the author of *Manhattan Sonata* and *Bennington Requiem*.

The unflattering portrait develops when Munch and his partner, Detective Cassidy (Dean Winters), interview Trill (Damian Young) at his home on the Upper East Side. Knowing that the dead models had attended a party there on the night of the murders and suspecting that the pair may have been buying prescription drugs from a dealer living in the same building, the detectives are keen to question the writer about both his neighbors and his guests. The interview takes place on Trill's terrace, with the Manhattan skyline spread out behind. Trill, still in his dressing gown, adds to the decadent mood by remaining seated on a sun-lounger throughout and sipping a cocktail, while answering their questions with a supercilious languor. The presence of a pair of bikini-clad women on the roof terrace supplements the louche atmosphere and as the scene develops the audience is encouraged to flirt with the possibility that Trill may be more than just a witness. Sharing this intuition and suspicious of the author's arrogant indifference, Munch is keen to put him under pressure. To do so, he leaves off probing the novelist's version of events to focus instead on what he sees as Trill's crimes against literary taste. Asking "how so many reviewers failed to notice your blatant theft of Joan Didion?" and going on to describe Trill's most recent novel as a "snoozefest," he manages to unsettle Trill, not by contradicting his account of the fatal party, but by attacking his literary talents. As the detectives leave, Trill looks crestfallen and perturbed. He is, the audience suspects, more troubled that his literary talents are in doubt, than because he is caught up in a double murder.

With all of these details established and regardless of the disclaimer that reads, "this story is a work of fiction. No actual person or event is depicted," the literate viewer does not need Munch's powers of deductive logic to be able to identify the well-known American novelist who serves as the template for Hampton Trill. Connect the nod to his precocious career with the Brat Pack, Joan Didion and Bennington College and there really is only one suspect. It is not quite an anagram, but it is close enough: for Hampton Trill read Bret Easton Ellis.

The question, as far as readers of Ellis are concerned, is why this portrait of him should feature in a popular American crime drama? An easy answer lies within the show's own frames of reference. As far as *Law and Order* is concerned, Trill serves a clear function in terms of clarifying and defining Detective Munch's character. A well-liked figure on American TV, Munch has had a long career and made his own intertextual journey. Originally a detective in *Homicide: Life on the Streets*, the character from the Baltimore murder squad took a new post with the Special Victims Unit, bringing his laconic wit and wisdom to New York. More a low-rent Sherlock Holmes than a posturing Vic Mackey, Munch's sparring with Trill works to play with familiar ideas of the detective as reader and gives him the opportunity to reaffirm his position as the intellectual cop, a man able to bring wry insight to every case file.

Even though this account of Trill's function in "Just Look Like One" makes sense, key questions about the wider dynamics of this portrait remain, particularly with regard to Ellis. The most obvious point is that when compared to instantly recognizable celebrities like Madonna, Tom Cruise, or Michael Jackson, Ellis is, in truth, a little anonymous. The fact that only a relatively small number of audience members would actually recognize him in the fictional Hampton Trill makes his appearance here particularly puzzling. Despite his relative lack of fame, however, the scriptwriters did not choose to describe Trill in generic terms as *any* young writer, but decided instead to make it absolutely clear that he was a cipher for Ellis. Part of the rationale for this has to lie with a reading of Ellis as a public figure. He may not shine as brightly as many much more luminous stars, but he is a well-known author (oxymoronic as that may be). What is interesting, then, about the portrait of Hampton Trill in *Law and Order* is the ways it offers an insight into the hostility Ellis arouses and his status as a writer and as a brand.

The substance of Munch's critique of Trill and, by implication, Ellis can be broken down as follows. He is unoriginal (evidenced in the unflattering comparison with Didion), he is overly concerned with the superficial (Munch calls him a "trendoid"), and he is boring (his recent novel is a "snoozefest"). He is all style and no substance, a point reinforced by the show's depiction of his laziness (still in his dressing gown during office hours), his wealth (the large upscale apartment), and his sleaziness (the association with drugs, models, and partying).

In this regard, both Munch and "Just Look Like One" align themselves with some fairly well-worn criticisms of Ellis's work. For John Aldridge, Ellis is a technician, not a talent, a writer more concerned with "literary chic" than literature. For Gerald Howard his "mediagenic" profile is the main priority (366). Steve Almond, writing in *The Boston Globe*, puts it more simply, calling him the author of the "worst novel I've ever read." Even those who praise him often do so in damningly faint ways. When Rosa Eberly writes about *American Psycho* in *Citizen Critics*, her lukewarm conclusion is that Ellis's only real value lies in his ability to provoke debate (130). More significantly, the most strident criticisms come from those who see Ellis as promoting and propagating violence against women and as the author of a novel that offers both encouragement to and instructions for those looking to do it themselves. In this context, *Law and Order*'s willingness, for a brief while at least, to float the suggestion that Trill/Ellis may in fact be responsible for the murder of two models literalizes these allegations, playing with the possibility that the author of *American Psycho* may not just have written about murder, but may in fact actually be a murderer. This is not quite what Roger Rosenblatt had in mind when he reviewed *American Psycho* under the heading "Snuff This Book! Will Bret Easton Ellis Get Away With Murder?" but it certainly adds resonance to some well-established arguments.

Added together, all of these implications signal the very particular ways in which Ellis's work has been read and received. Celebrated for his precocity, mocked for his commercialism, attacked for his violent imagery, and subject to a whole range of confused and confusing readings of the links between the author and his characters, his life, and his subject matter, Ellis's brand is a many and varied thing.

What makes "Just Look Like One" significant is that the desire to fictionalize Ellis, to implicate him in murders that in some way reflect the plot of his most famous novel (the women are killed in what looks like a sadistic sexual assault) pre-empts the themes that Ellis himself takes up in *Lunar Park*. Indeed, a plotline that involved a fictional version of Ellis implicated in fictional murders on a TV show would have sat well among all of the other complex and self-reflexive strands that make up *Lunar Park*.

Suburban Ambush

Though for *The New York Times* it offers a "lurching ride to nowhere" (Scott), *Lunar Park* has a legitimate claim to be Ellis's best work since *Less Than Zero*. At its heart lies a complex mockubiographical design. Beginning as a novel about a writer called Bret Easton Ellis that mixes established fact with implausible fiction, the novel shifts registers and develops into a suburban horror story that owes much to films like *Halloween* and *Nightmare on Elm Street* and the fiction of Stephen King. *Lunar Park* starts with the fictional Ellis trying to reorient himself after years of excess and literary celebrity. The novel begins with the narrator (now married to Jayne Dennis, a movie actress with a fame to equal Julia Roberts's) leaving Manhattan behind for a dysfunctional family life in the suburbs. The plan is to rehabilitate his life, his relationship with his wife and his son, and his career.

Unsurprisingly, this project is soon in trouble. The fictional Ellis, like the author himself we suspect, is uniquely unsuited for ordinary life in Midland County, a point made with great comic effect in scenes that show him visiting a petting zoo, struggling to interact with his neighbors, and trying (and failing) to behave like a responsible citizen while teaching creative writing at the local college. Predictably, it is not long before the backsliding Ellis, overwhelmed by SUVs and parents' evenings, finds himself drawn back to the darkness, his movements dogged by increasingly malignant toys and unexplained murders. With his mind plagued by echoes of the violence conjured in his novels and his steps haunted by the ghost of his dead father, the narrator's world rapidly unravels. Before long he is lost inside his own mind, trapped in a lonely lunar park of artificiality, sorry memories, and nightmares.

At the core of the novel is an intense self-consciousness about the nature of Ellis's own status as a writer. *Lunar Park* opens with the observation, "You do an awfully good impression of yourself" (3), a thought that is developed in later pages with the statement "my life—*my name*—had been rendered a repetitive, unfunny punch line and I was sick of eating it" (25). Taken together, these two remarks work to define the novel's focus on Ellis's identity, his celebrity, and his brand.

In simple terms, this self-consciousness becomes the source of *Lunar Park*'s knowing humor. In one scene, for example, Ellis has the narrator see the family dog, Victor (not Ward in this instance, but the suggestion is there nonetheless), lying on the grass outside their home:

> When he gave me a cursory look, I gave one back and then picked up a Frisbee and threw it at the dog. It landed near where he was lying. He glanced at me contemptuously, then lifted his head and looked over at me as if I were a fool before nudging the orange disc away with his snout. (87)

Even the dog is unconvinced by the narrator's attempt to act like a normal suburban guy and regards him not just as a "fool" but as a fraud. What is significant here is that the comedy does not just come from the animal's contempt, but from the very image of Ellis (fictional or otherwise) trying to interact with a dog at all. So laden is the author's brand with the values of metropolitan chic that the very idea of him playing Frisbee with a pet seems as improbable as it is farcical. Ellis knows, this scene implies, that precisely because his readers only ever imagine him in the bar of some Paul Schraeger hotel, they will find it absurdly difficult to picture him on a suburban lawn. Understanding his own brand gives him the freedom to play with the disjunction these expectations create in terms that drive the humor not just of this scene, but of the novel as a whole. Brand Ellis, in these terms, offers creative possibilities for the author and provides a source for much of what goes on in *Lunar Park*.

While acknowledging the comic potential offered by this play on authorial identity, it is important to understand that the novel's reflections on the status of the author open up a range of other more complex insights into both the reading of Ellis's fiction and the nature of literary celebrity itself. *Lunar Park* is certainly a very funny novel, but it is a dark and disturbing one too. Indeed, the spiraling nightmare described in *Lunar Park*, in which the fictional Ellis finds his steps plagued by a growing collapse of the distinctions between his personal life and the imagined world of his novels, seems to suggest a self in crisis. Stalked by a man who may or may not be Clay and another who may or may not be Patrick Bateman, investigated by a detective called Donald Kimball (the name of the investigator who interviews Patrick in *American Psycho*) and troubled by a growing inability to differentiate between his facts and his fictions, the narrator seems overwhelmed by his creations. The implication is that Ellis is aware that his name circulates widely, creating meanings and values over which he has no control. To interpret these movements, a more detailed understanding of selfhood and literary celebrity is required.

Star Authors

There is no sense that literary celebrity is a specific feature of late twentieth-century life. Leo Braudy's *The Frenzy of Renown*, for example, discusses Lord Byron's fame alongside that of George Washington and Napoleon Bonaparte, noting that Byron was, like other famous men,

> celebrated not for his position or his poetic ability so much as for the literary display of "himself"—a swirling whirlpool of almost sexual allure in which his audience might glimpse an image not of their public selves so much as those desires and aspirations that had seemed socially unfit or irrelevant, now writ large and grand. (401)

In this regard, Byron meets Daniel Boorstin's definition of a celebrity. He is, in Boorstin's terms, a "person who is well-known for their well-knownness" (58). At heart, Boorstin's reading of celebrity functions in relation to a wider account of inauthenticity. The existence of celebrities who are known not for their achievements, but by virtue of the self-perpetuating mechanisms of their own pre-eminence, is, for Boorstin, the marker of a society increasingly lost to the power of the culture industry's chicanery. Celebrity, in his account, is part of an affirmative culture, complicit with the mass deceptions of consumer society.

This sense that the rise of celebrity signals a culture in decline is, as Joe Moran observes in *Star Authors*, even more keenly felt in relation to the emergence of literary celebrity because literature (like other high-cultural forms) is commonly seen to stand in opposition to the vulgarization of mass culture. In this context, the fact that the values of celebrity can infect the world of books would seem to indicate that these superficial concerns are becoming increasingly powerful and pernicious. The activities of Ernest Hemingway, signing up to advertise Ballantine's Ale and Pan American Airlines, for example, are thus read as *prima facia* evidence of an increasingly crass and commercialized culture, a culture that has grown strong enough to colonize and co-opt even the most elevated and sanctified of cultural terrains.

The effectiveness of Moran's account lies in its willingness to interrogate this reading of the processes at work by stepping away from narrow accounts of literature's high culture status and, against simple condemnations of star authorship, to offer instead a reading that recognizes the specificity of the author's role and the context in which celebrity authors emerge:

> Literary celebrity . . . is not simply an adjunct of mainstream celebrity . . . but an elaborate system of representations in its own right, produced and circulated across a wide variety of media. Rather than being a straightforward effect of the commodification of culture, it raises significant questions about the relationship between literature and the marketplace. (4)

This position connects with more general accounts of celebrity that recognize that fame is not "a property of specific individuals. Rather it is constituted discursively by the way in which the individual is represented" (Turner et al. 11). Celebrity does not operate from the top down, but through the interaction of writers and readers, stars and audiences, producers and consumers. In this respect, its function mimics the function of a commodity. For some, as might be expected, the shift from star to brand is another alarming sign of the imperial power of globalizing consumer society. Andrew Wernick's *Promotional Culture*, for example, reads celebrity in purely instrumental terms as a mechanism designed to facilitate selling; Naomi Klein, in a similar vein, sees the *Forbes Celebrity 100* as yet more evidence of branding's increasing hegemony. Their views need, however, to be set against an understanding of the communicative operation of, in P. David Marshall's terms, stardom as a "discursive regime" and understood as more than just the sign of vulgarization and cultural decline.

Ellis's novels have, of course, asked questions like this before, particularly with regard to the status of consumption. As I argued in *Blank Fictions, Less Than Zero* describes both the deadening influence of consumer culture at the same time as it recognizes the possibilities, offered by MTV, *The Face*, and popular music, of shaping a sense of self, a relationship with others, and a particular kind of contemporary aesthetic. In *Lunar Park* it seems that Ellis is complicating his already intricate understanding of the forces at work by linking his brand identity as an author to his established account of consumer culture. The difference is that in *Less Than Zero* he could discuss consumption, products, and franchises without really having to think about his own direct complicity. *Lunar Park* shows Ellis recognizing that his own name has now become a brand and circulates alongside the other commodities in his text. In these terms the increasingly self-reflexive quality of the fiction Ellis has published since *American Psycho* can be explained by understanding that Ellis is a writer who cannot now write about branding and consumption without writing about himself as well.

This position opens up a way of interpreting what is, at first glance, the most alienating feature of *Lunar Park*. The decision to base a novel on the interrogation of the status of the author seems like a tedious premise and legitimate questions can be asked about a book that promises familiar reflections on fictionality as it dwells on the troubles of a millionaire novelist. It is the emphasis on brand Ellis that makes it possible to read *Lunar Park* as more than just another reworking of 40-year-old essays by Roland Barthes and Michel Foucault, which argue that the author is effectively "dead" and has no control over his text, in terms that shadow the gameful (and perhaps even gamey) ploys of Paul Auster and, more recently, Dave Eggers or the immensely popular films scripted by Charlie Kaufman for directors Spike Jonze (*Adaptation*) and Michel Gondry (*Eternal Sunshine of the Spotless Mind*). Such looping, self-reflexive texts are concerned with foregrounding the self-evidently fictional status of their narratives and problematizing the power relations locked within the DNA of authorship. Ellis is using his imagined version of himself to articulate a sense of the writer as a commodity. In *Lunar Park* he writes about himself so that his brand may be understood in discursive relation to contemporary culture's constellation of commercial signs.

In this respect Ellis's novel works more as an analysis of the status of the celebrity author than as a critique or satire of his own authority. When he has his narrator tell us that the novel he is currently writing will be "all about the hard sell (the million-dollar advance guaranteed that)" as well as "poignant and quietly devastating," he is toying with the readers' sense of his own cynicism (70). When he has Donald Kimball sit in the fictional Ellis's office in the house on Elsinore Lane and ask him questions about a series of murders that resemble those described in *American Psycho*, he is outlining a response to what he sees as the extensive misreadings of his own novels: "I thought the idea was laughable," the narrator says, "there was no one as insane and vicious as this fictional character [. . .] This was the book's thesis. It was about society and manners and mores, and not about cutting up women" (122). Detective Kimball's observation, "the author of the book isn't in the book," only serves to underline Ellis's point (124).

Ellis might in these moments simply be playing the prankster, offering a series of self-referential jokes that set out to disassemble both general ideas of celebrity authorship and his own self image. Certainly the account of the extravagant book tour offered in the novel's first chapter, weighed down with implausible anecdotes, signals a willingness to add to the many apocryphal stories already in circulation about Ellis's life. The problem is that the process of interrogating celebrity seems a little narrow. Ellis does expose fame as a "pseudo event" (Boorstin's term), work to untangle the contradictions and falsifications that constitute celebrity, and mock the confusions that surround the tensions between the person and the mediatized narratives that surround the star, but nothing about this is really new. True, Ellis is writing from the inside, but even so, to read his novel as a straightforward critique of celebrity is limited. For one thing, celebrity manages to successfully deconstruct itself. So implausible and so self-evidently fictional are the mythologies that surround celebrity, there is scarcely any need for Ellis to add anything to the debate.

More particularly, if *Lunar Park*'s ambition is simply to expose the illusions that surround literary celebrity, questions must be asked about how it differs from other recent mockubiographies and literary fakes. The novels of J.T. LeRoy, for example, were marketed alongside a careful presentation of LeRoy as a teenage genius, a feral child, who was drawing on experiences of hustling, petty criminality, and sexual abuse. The revelation that the LeRoy persona was in fact the creation of Laura Albert, a 40-year-old woman from Brooklyn, only served to illustrate the extent to which readers are invested in the blurring of the author's story and the fictions in the text. Similarly, when James Frey made his name with *A Million Little Pieces* (2003), readers were drawn to the apparent authenticity of his tale of drug addiction and redemptive rehabilitation. The discovery that Frey had fabricated important parts of his hugely successful memoir led to a court case and a public confrontation with his former champion Oprah Winfrey. Apparently less complex and contrived than the fakery of J.T. LeRoy, Frey was willing, upon discovery, to confess his deceptions and make public statements of contrition. While Albert's desire to portray her fakery as self-conscious pranksterism might seem a little self serving, particularly after the fact, the elaborate nature of the LeRoy story and the way Albert used celebrity supporters (Shirley Manson and Dennis Cooper among them) to establish the renown of her own creation does evidence the complex layers of fabrication at work. Leaving these differences aside, the general point is that both mockubiographies rearticulated familiar questions about the tension between authenticity and inauthenticity and the nature of literary celebrity in terms that parallel the vision of the fictional Ellis offered in *Lunar Park*. That Ellis's description of *A Million Little Pieces* as "a heartbreaking memoir . . . inspirational and essential" should have been used as a strapline on the cover of early editions of Frey's memoir only serves to strengthen this sense of the connections.

The obvious difference between Ellis on the one hand and Frey and LeRoy/Albert on the other, however, is that while Frey and LeRoy/Albert sought to deceive, Ellis did not. In the end, neither Frey nor LeRoy/Albert had any control over the controversies they provoked, a situation very different from Ellis's. It is hard not to reflect upon the almost perfect fit that exists between the hyperbolic tenor of *American*

Psycho, its vision of mediatized frenzy and unreality, and the controversy that blew up around the novel both before and after its publication. Ellis fuels these suggestion when, in *Lunar Park,* his narrator discusses the novel in jaded tones. He offers "the CliffsNotes version" for "those who weren't in the room at the time" and sums up the novel as "pornographic and extremely violent" (12).

Though the sentiments offered here are unquestionably disingenuous and accordingly hard to weigh and measure, what can be tracked with certainty is a return to *Lunar Park's* self-conscious focus on the Ellis brand. Ellis is not working as a prankster looking to expose preconceptions. He is instead looking to reflect upon the operation of such pranksterism and to interpret the confusion it engenders. Neither an attempt to exonerate his reputation, nor an attempt to protect it by raising ironic screens, Ellis's use of his fictional alter ego enables him to analyze his own brand, and it is the clarity with which he does so that stands out.

This approach is not limited to his fictional account of the writing of *American Psycho* but applies throughout the novel and is established early on in "the beginnings," the long opening chapter of *Lunar Park* in which the narrator offers a series of astute and knowing observations on Ellis's career. Describing *Less Than Zero* as a novel that offers an "indictment [. . .] of the Reagan eighties and, more indirectly, of Western civilization in the present moment" (5), dismissing the Brat Pack as "a media-made package: all fake flesh and punk and menace" (8), and acknowledging that the controversy around *American Psycho* is so well-documented that he feels "no need to go into great detail about it here" (13), the narrator not only provides an elegant summary of the arguments that have informed critical responses to Ellis's fiction, but works to short circuit many established reading of Ellis's work (my own *Blank Fictions* included) in terms that imply that these insights are more than a little tiresome and predictable. Worse than that, they also suggest that these critical responses were anticipated in the novels themselves. The implication is that when critics make these moves, they reinforce Ellis's aesthetic strategies, rather than interrogate them. These short-circuiting processes can be illustrated best by returning once more to consider the critique of Ellis offered by "Just Look Like One" and connecting it with the way *Lunar Park* conceives brand Ellis.

Shiny Booklike Objects

Detective Munch's criticisms of Trill/Ellis rely upon a version of what might be called the depth model. For Munch, Trill/Ellis's fiction is false and deceptive, a corruption of real literature that, he implies, should offer depth rather than surface. Valued truths hidden underneath valued visions of artistry are opposed to Trill/Ellis's superficiality in terms that represent his fiction as light, trashy, and disposable. In this version, literature and commerce are antithetical and Trill/Ellis's willing engagement with consumer society becomes the sign of his incorporation.

As might be expected, *Lunar Park* does nothing to counter these allegations. Instead the narrator seems intent on inciting further charges by making a range of inflammatory observations that include his admission that since the 1980s "it was almost as if the novel itself didn't matter anymore—publishing a shiny booklike object was simply an excuse for parties and glamour" (9). Offering a clear rebuke to romantic conceptions of authorship and challenging the foundations upon which such conceptions rest, *Lunar Park* rejects the depth model out of hand and exposes the inadequacies articulated in the episode of *Law and Order*.

"Just Look Like One" works through what is in effect a form of ideological critique. At the center of the show's narrative are four principal suspects. Alongside Hampton Trill are a sleazy English photographer Carlo Parisi (Ritchie Coster), his business partner and former lover Deborah Latrell (Catherine Dent), and Nene Lazlo (Bebe Neuwirth), the head of a modeling agency. As the show progresses, the detectives interview all four of these characters, and the investigation gives them an opportunity to reflect upon the ugliness of the beauty industry and, by implication, the media as a whole. Drugs, eating disorders, the malign influence of predatory men on young women, and the tyranny of the image all feature in terms that will be familiar to anyone who has read Naomi Wolf's *The Beauty Myth* (1991). As Latrell puts it, "Beauty is power—until you lose it and then you got nothing."

As if to reinforce this message, the episode adds two subplots. The first shows Detective Stabler at home, worried about his 14-year-old daughter's eating habits. The second sees Detective Jefferies (Michelle Hurd) in court, giving evidence in a case against the father of a teenage rapist. The father is accused of conspiracy because he allowed his son to be exposed to the Rapeman series of comics. The argument is that the parent is complicit because he failed to prevent his child from reading these magazines and by omission made it likely that the boy would act out what he saw on the page. The case is thus set up as an attempt to establish a legal demonstration of the power of media influence.

In all of these ways, "Just Look Like One" offers a fairly standard critique of the media. Following conventional logic, it argues that advertising and the fashion industry subject all of us, and young women in particular, to intense pressures, pressures that are, in an extreme way, made flesh in the violent sexual murders investigated by the Special Victims Unit. In these terms, "Just Look Like One" does a good job of joining the dots and clearly identifies the fashion industry's commodification of the female body with forms of sexual violence. Like the fashion business, advertising, and pornography, Ellis is, in the show's estimation, implicitly part of a kind of degenerate continuum that contributes to sexual violence. When Trill is first mentioned, Munch is not surprised to hear his name "in the middle of all this," and his caustic approach to Trill suggests that he sees the author, and by implication Ellis himself, as, if not a murderer, then at the very least a general moral threat (as it turns out, Trill is innocent).

In this way, the show offers a straightforward ideological critique of the fashion industry and the media and, by implication, the fiction of Bret Easton Ellis. The problem is, however, that having established its position in this way, *Law and Order* opens itself up to a whole host of counter-arguments. First is the irony of a television show offering an account of the malign influence of a work of literary fiction. This is a role reversal that Dwight MacDonald would have struggled to have imagined when he first discussed the emergence of middlebrow culture in 1962. Second, this argument is made by a TV show in which all of the primary female detectives are slim, well-dressed, under 40, and tackle dirty police business in carefully styled hair and full makeup. The simple point is that because *Law and Order* is itself part of the celebrity–media–commodity matrix it cannot offer an effective critique of other parts of that same matrix without having its critical position compromised by its own complicity.

More damning still is the fact that if the show is concerned that Ellis is both overrated and overexposed, then, despite its own intentions, it does nothing but add to his profile. As *Lunar Park* makes clear, Ellis is very aware that his brand values include notoriety, superficiality, decadence, sleaziness, and a kind of anti-authoritarian cool. This is what the reader gets from a Bret Easton Ellis product. The consequence is that, because all of these values are articulated so perfectly in this mainstream TV show, *Law and Order* ultimately serves a promotional function, unintentionally celebrating and selling what it looks to condemn. That this episode of *Law and Order* should use a plot and a milieu that mirrors so many of the stories and settings employed by Ellis in his novels makes the circuit complete. Like his most famous novel, the show has a place in the mediascape that not only blunts its critique, but makes it complicit. As Ellis's narrator in *Lunar Park* explains, in his discussion of the "year of being hated" that followed the publication of *American Psycho*:

> I was taken seriously. I was a joke. I was avant-garde. I was a traditionalist. I was underrated. I was overrated. I was innocent.

I was partly guilty. I had orchestrated the controversy. I was
incapable of orchestrating anything. I was considered the most
misogynist writer in existence. I was a victim of the burgeoning
culture of the politically correct. (12)

In this passage that exposes the paucity of the depth model and the
limitations of the reliance on binaries, Ellis not only articulates the
ways in which his fiction defies easy mechanisms of praise or blame, but
indicates that this defiance is an essential part of the Ellis brand.

Brand Ellis

All of these questions about the author's brand, the status of Ellis in
contemporary fiction, and the discourse within which his fiction operates connect to the novel's other principal theme—paternity. Concerned
not just with how his novels are parented (by a wide range of figures
that include the author himself, his literary friends, his publisher, his
agent, his reader, and the media), Ellis is also preoccupied with his own
father.

At first glance, the references to Fortinbras Mall, Claudius Street,
and Elsinore Lane look like another pastiche that plays once more on
the clash between high and low culture. It is almost as if Ellis could
not resist teasing his readers with the possibility that America's most
self-consciously trashy author might dare to rewrite *Hamlet*. On closer
inspection, however, and once the *Hamlet* allusions are connected
with the grim presence of the fictional Ellis's fictional father, the
Shakespearian thematics start to come into focus, a focus that can
be made clearer by noting that Ellis dedicates *Lunar Park* to his
own father, Robert Martin Ellis. A wealthy property analyst, Robert
Ellis is remembered by his son as "violent, emotionally abusive and very
difficult to live with" (Gerard 14) and the pair were largely estranged
throughout Ellis's life. This biographical detail is given increased
importance as the relationship between Patrick Bateman and Ellis's
father is established: "You based this fictional character, this Patrick
Bateman, on your father" (261). The novel thus links the haunting
of Elsinore Lane by Ellis's fictional characters with the emails he is
receiving from the Bank of America in Sherman Oaks, a bank that
holds the narrator's father's ashes in its vault. More layers are added to
this network of associations through the fictional Ellis's relationship
with his fictional son, also called Robert.

The ash imagery that pervades *Lunar Park* further complicates this
network of relationships. The trail of ashes functions as an image that
links writing to guilt and responsibility. When, at the end of the novel,
the narrator finally looks in the safety deposit box and sees that his

father's burnt remains have burst the bag that held them, he notices a word traced in the ash. We do not learn what this word is, but we do know that it is the same word he saw when he examined the drawing of the lunar landscape in his own son's bedroom. Mirroring the dusty landscape of the moon depicted in his grandson's drawing, Robert Ellis has made his own lunar park from his own mortal remains. Ash becomes a sort of broken medium for communication. The author's text, *his* lunar park, is linked to the body of the father and the empty spaces of his disappeared son—this intricate pattern of relationships is marked in the delicate tracery of ash. Indeed, the final pages of *Lunar Park* imagine ash falling over everything, sweeping across the whole of the narrator's life both past and present in ways that shadow the function of snow at the ending of James Joyce's "The Dead":

> You watched as the ashes kept rising and danced across a multitude of images from the past, dipping down and then flying back into the air [. . .] They shifted over the graves of his parents and finally entered the cold lit world of the dead where they wept across the children standing in the cemetery and then somewhere out at the end of the Pacific [. . .] they began exiting the text, losing themselves somewhere beyond my reach, and then vanished [. . . .] (306–08)

The ash is all-consuming, covering everything, creating a mournful sense of confederacy between the living and the dead in a way that is both potently elegiac and personal. This quality is sustained in the novel's final sentences:

> So, if you should see my son, tell him I say hello, be good, that I am thinking of him and that I know he's watching over me somewhere and not to worry: that he can always find me here, whenever he wants, right here, my arms held out and waiting, in the pages, behind the covers, at the end of *Lunar Park*. (308)

Clearly, this is more than the fictional Ellis talking to his imagined son. It is, instead, Ellis imagining that in his own fiction he both hears his real father's voice and sees his face, a face that for all the confusion and unhappiness of his life, seems to articulate, not just through the dark pages of *Lunar Park* but through all of the novels Ellis has written, a message of love.

Perhaps surprisingly, considering its seemingly contrived and artificial conceit, *Lunar Park* has, in conclusion, a much more poignant quality to it than any of Ellis's previous novels and carries with it a personal insight and intimacy that is undimmed by the narrative structure. When a ghostly voice making an anonymous call explains to the narrator, "I want you to realize some things about yourself. I want you to reflect on your life. I want you to be aware of all the terrible things you have done. I want you to face the disaster that is Bret Easton Ellis" (230), the novel is almost asking to be read in confessional terms as a rather bleak response to the complexities of the brand that Ellis has in part created for himself and in part had created for him.

More focused than *Glamorama* and more complex and ambiguous than *American Psycho*, *Lunar Park* is not trapped in safe questions about the relationships between the smoke and the mirror that are the traditional domain of self-reflexive novels but is, in contrast, enabled by them. His chamber of horrors, his poetic dovetailing of personal fact and media fiction, his reliance on an iconography drawn from the sign systems of celebrity and popular culture, all combine in a novel that defies the attempt to privilege depth over surface and resists the desire to resolve the tension between Ellis as the writer of satires and Ellis as one who helps create the conditions he is looking to satirize. In *Lunar Park* Ellis finds a strategy for looking into the heart of contemporary life and uses it to construct a vision of the colonialism of consumption and the media in terms that are subtle and challengingly ambiguous. This is not invective, but analysis. Ellis is no more against celebrity, branding, or media society than he is against electricity or the wheel. Instead he examines the world created by this confluence of forces and asks his readers to think about how they are going to live in it. *Lunar Park's* provocative conclusion is that answers can only be found by skating on the surface, not by diving into the depths.

Works Cited

Abel, Marco. *Violent Affect: Literature, Cinema, and Critique After Representation.* Lincoln: University of Nebraska Press, 2007.

——. "Intensifying Affect." *Electronic Book Review.* EBR Public. 24 Oct 2008. Web. 21 Sept 2009.

Adams, Hazard, ed. *Critical Theory Since Plato.* 1971. Rev. ed. New York: Harcourt Brace Jovanovich, 1992.

Adaptation. Dir. Spike Jonze. Screenplay by Charlie Kaufman. Columbia, 2002. Film.

Aldridge, John W. *Talents and Technicians: Literary Chic and the New Assembly-Line Fiction.* New York: Scribner, 1992.

Allen, Graham. *Intertextuality.* London: Routledge, 2000.

Almond, Steve. "Ellis masquerades as Ellis, and it is not a pretty sight." *Boston.com.* The Boston Globe. 14 August 2005. Web. 30 July 2009.

American Psycho. Dir. Mary Harron. Lions Gate, 2000. Film.

Amerika, Mark and Alexander Laurence. "Interview with Bret Easton Ellis." *The Write Stuff.* http://www.altx.com/interviews/. AltX. 1994. Web. 28 June 2009.

Annesley, James. *Blank Fictions: Consumerism, Culture and the Contemporary American Novel.* London: Pluto, 1998.

——. *Fictions of Globalization.* London: Continuum, 2006.

Aspden, Rachel. "Why, Bret?" *The New Statesman.* 10 Oct 2005: 54–55.

Ayers, Sheli. "*Glamorama* Vanitas: Bret Easton Ellis's Postmodern Allegory." *Postmodern Culture* 11.1 (2000): N. pag. Web. 26 July 2009.

Badiou, Alain. *The Century.* 2005. Trans. Albert Toscano. Oxford: Polity, 2005.

Baelo-Allué, Sonia. "Serial Murder, Serial Consumerism: Bret Easton Ellis's *American Psycho* (1991)." *Miscelánea: a journal of english and american studies* 26 (2002): 71–90.

Bakhtin, Mikhail. *Problems of Dostoyevsky's Poetics.* Ed. and trans. Caryl Emerson. Minneapolis: University of Minnesota Press, 1984.

——. *Rabelais and His World.* Trans. Helene Iswolsky. Bloomington: Indiana University Press, 1984.

Baldwin, Kristen. "Psychodrama." *Entertainment Weekly.* 14 April 2000: 34–38.

Barthes, Roland. *S/Z*. Éditions du Seuil: Paris, 1970.

——. *Camera Lucida*. Éditions du Seuil: Paris, 1980.

Baudrillard, Jean. "The Precession of Simulacra." Natoli and Hutcheon 342–76.

——. *The Perfect Crime*. London and New York: Verso, 1996.

——. *The Spirit of Terrorism*. London and New York: Verso, 2002.

Baxter, Tara, and Nikki Craft. "There Are Better Ways of Taking Care of Bret Easton Ellis Than Just Censoring Him." Russell 245–53.

Begley, Adam. "Lights! Camera! Bombs? How to Flub a Fine Satire." *The New York Observer*. The New York Observer. 10 Jan. 1999. Web. 10 Oct. 2005.

Benjamin, Walter. "The Work of Art in the Age of Mechanical Reproduction." 1936. *Illuminations*. Trans. Harry Zone. Ed. Hannah Arendt. New York: Schocken, 1969. 217–51.

——. *Charles Baudelaire: A Lyric Poet in the Era of High Capitalism*. 1973. Trans. Harry Zohn. London: Verso, 1997.

Black, Joel. *The Aesthetics of Murder: A Study in Romantic Literature and Contemporary Culture*. Baltimore: The Johns Hopkins University Press, 1991.

Blanchot, Maurice. *The Space of Literature*. 1955. Trans. Ann Smock. Lincoln: University of Nebraska Press, 1982.

——. *The Writing of The Disaster*. 1980. Trans. Anne Smock. Lincoln: University of Nebraska Press, 1995.

——. "The Instant of My Death." 1994. Trans. Elizabeth Rottenberg. Stanford: Stanford University Press, 2000.

Blazer, Alex E. "Chasms of Reality, Aberrations of Identity: Defining the Postmodern through Bret Easton Ellis's *American Psycho*." *Americana* 1 (2002): N. pag. Web. 9 June 2009.

——. "*Glamorama, Fight Club*, and the Terror of Narcissistic Abjection." Prosser 177–89.

Bloom, Harold. *Shakespeare: The Invention of the Human*. New York: Riverhead, 1998.

Blume, Harvey. "Portrait of the Artist as a Social Satirist." *Atlantic Online*. The Atlantic. 10 Feb 1999. Web. 8 Dec. 2004.

Bolter, Jay David and Richard Grusin. *Remediation: Understanding New Media*. 1999. Massachusetts: MIT Press, 2000.

Bolter, Jay David. "Transference and Transparency: Digital Technology and the Remediation of Cinema." *Intermédialités* 6 (2005): 13–26.

Boorstin, Daniel. *The Image: A Guide to Pseudo-Events in America*. New York: Atheneum, 1973.

Borat: Cultural Learnings of America for Make Benefit Glorious Nation of Kazakhstan. Dir. Larry Charles. Perf. Sacha Baron Cohen. 20th Century Fox, 2006. Film.

Brannon, Robert."Torturing Women as Fine Art: Why Some Women and Men Are Boycotting Knopf." Russell 239–44.

Braudy, Leo. *The Frenzy of Renown: Fame and its History*. New York: Oxford University Press, 1986.

Buchanan, Ian and John Marks, eds. *Deleuze and Literature*. Edinburgh: Edinburgh University Press, 2000.

Burke, Kenneth. *A Rhetoric of Motives.* 1950. Berkeley: University of California Press, 1969.

Carnes, Christie. "He's it, baby: A talk with Victor Ward." *Youthquake Magazine. www.youthquakemagazine.com.* Web. 9 Sept 2009.

Chapple, Freda and Chiel Kattenbelt, eds. *Intermediality in Theatre and Performance.* Amsterdam: Rodopi, 2006.

Clarke, Jamie. "Interview with Bret Easton Ellis." *Mississippi Review* 27.3 (1999): 61–102.

Cohn, Dorrit. *The Distinction of Fiction.* Baltimore: Johns Hopkins University Press, 1998.

Cojocaru, Daniel. "*Confessions* of an *American Psycho*: James Hogg's and Bret Easton Ellis's Anti-Heroes' Journey from Vulnerability to Violence." COV&R Annual Conference on *Vulnerability and Tolerance.* Amsterdam Free University, Netherlands. 2007. *Colloquium On Violence & Religion (COV&R).* Universität Innsbruck, 2007. Web. 29 Oct 2009.

Colebrook, Claire. "Inhuman Irony: The Event of the Postmodern." Buchanan and Marks 100–33.

Corliss, Richard. "A Yuppie's Killer Instinct." *Time* 155.15 (2000): 78.

Corneille, Pierre. "Discours des trois unités, d'action, de jour et de lieu." 1660. *Oeuvres de P. Corneille.* Ed. M. Ch. Marty-Laveaux. Vol. 1. Paris: Hachette, 1862. 98–122.

Dean, Jodi. *Aliens in America: Conspiracy Cultures from Outerspace to Cyberspace.* Ithaca: Cornell UP, 1998.

Debord, Guy. *The Society of the Spectacle.* 1967. Trans. Donald Nicholson-Smith. New York: Zone Books, 1995.

Deleuze, Gilles. *The Logic of Sense.* 1969. Trans. Mark Lester with Charles Stivale. New York: Columbia University Press, 1990.

——. "Coldness and Cruelty." *Masochism*: "Coldness and Cruelty," Gilles Deleuze; "Venus in Furs," Leopold von Sacher-Masoch. Trans. Jean McNeil. New York: Zone, 1989. 9–138. Trans. of *Présentation de Sacher-Masoch: le froid et le cruel avec le texte intégral de* La Vénus à la fourrure. Trans. Aude Willm. Paris: Minuit, 1967. 15–115.

Delvaux, Martine."The Exit of a Generation: the 'Whatever' Philosophy." *The Midwest Quarterly* 40.2 (1999): 171–86.

Derrida, Jacques. "Signature Event Context." *Limited Inc.* Ed. Gerald Graff. Trans. Samuel Weber and Jeffrey Mehlman. Evanston, Illinois: Northwestern University Press, 1988. 1–24.

——. *Demeure: Fiction and Testimony.* 1998. Trans. Elizabeth Rottenberg. Stanford: Stanford University Press, 2000.

Dostoyevsky, Fyodor. *Crime and Punishment.* 1866. New York: Penguin, 1968.

"Double." Def. 8. *The Oxford English Dictionary.* 2nd edn 1989. Web. 15 Sept 2009.

Doubrovsky, Serge. *Fils.* Paris: Éditions Galilées, 1977.

Dryden, John. "An Essay of Dramatick Poesie." 1668. *The Works of John Dryden: Prose 1668–1691.* Ed. Samuel Holt Monk. Vol. 17. Berkeley: University of California Press, 1971. 3–81.

Duralde, Alonso. "The Real Me." *Advocate.* 8 Aug (2005): 81–82.

Durand, Alain-Philippe and Naomi Mandel, eds. *Novels of the Contemporary Extreme.* London: Continuum, 2006.

Eberly, Rosa. *Citizen Critics: Literary Public Spheres.* Urbana: University of Illinois Press, 2000.

Ellis, Bret Easton. *Less than Zero.* New York: Simon and Schuster, 1985.

——. *The Rules of Attraction.* New York: Penguin, 1987.

——. "Note to Amanda Urban." 15 July 1987. www.randomhouse.com/kvpa/ eastonellis. Random House. Web. 29 June 2009.

——. *American Psycho.* New York: Vintage, 1991.

——. *The Informers.* New York: Knopf, 1994.

——. *Glamorama.* 1998. New York: Vintage Contemporaries, 2000.

——. Interview. www.randomhouse.com. Web. April 15, 2003. http://www. randomhouse.com/boldtype/0199/ellis/interview.html

——. "Behind Bret's Mask." Interview. *Manchester Evening News.* 10 Oct. 2005. Web. 20 Aug 2009.

——. *Lunar Park.* New York: Alfred A. Knopf, 2005.

Eternal Sunshine of the Spotless Mind. Dir. Michael Gondry. Screenplay by Charlie Kaufman. Focus Features, 2004. Film.

Felman, Shoshana and Dori Laub. *Testimony: Crises of Witnessing in Literature, Psychoanalysis, and History.* New York: Routledge, 1991.

Fillin-Yeh, Susan, ed. *Dandies: Fashion and Finesse in Art and Culture.* New York University Press, 2001.

Fitzgerald, F. Scott. *The Great Gatsby.* New York: Scribner's, 1925.

Forster, E.M. *Howards End.* 1910. New York: Vintage Books, 1961.

Freccero, Carla. "Historical Violence, Censorship, and the Serial Killer: The Case of *American Psycho.*" *Diacritics* 27.2 (1997): 44–58.

Freese, Peter. "Bret Easton Ellis, *Less Than Zero*: Entropy in the 'MTV Novel'?" *Modes of Narrative.* Königshausen: Naumann, 1990. 68–87. *Contemporary Literary Criticism.* Gale. N. pag. Web. 18 Feb. 2007.

Freud, Sigmund. *The Interpretation of Dreams.* 1900. Trans. James Strachey. New York: Avon/Basic, 1965.

Frey, James. *A Million Little Pieces.* New York: Random House, 2003.

Garelick, Rhonda K. *Rising Star: Dandyism, Gender, and Performance in the Fin de Siècle.* Princeton University Press, 1998.

——. "The Layered Look: Coco Chanel and Contagious Celebrity." Fillin-Yeh 35–59.

Genette, Gérard. *Fiction & Diction.* 1991. Trans. Catherine Porter. Ithaca: Cornell University Press, 1993.

Gerard, Nicci. "Bret and the beast in the Corner." *The Observer Life* 16 Oct 1994: 14. *LexusNexus.* Web. 21 Sept 2009.

Gomel, Elana. *Bloodscripts: Writing the Violent Subject.* Columbus: Ohio State University Press, 2003.

Goodyear, Dana. "The Real Bret Easton Ellis." *The New Yorker* 27 April 2009: 19–20.

Greenblatt, Stephen. *Hamlet in Purgatory.* Princeton: Princeton University Press, 2001.

——. "The Death of Hamnet and the Making of *Hamlet.*" *The New York Review of Books* 51.16 (2004): N. pag. *Nybooks.com.* Web. 20 Aug 2009.

Grossman, Lev. "Less Than a Hero." *Time* 166.8 (2005): 66.

Halloween. Dir. John Carpenter. Compass International, 1978. Film.

Hardt, Michael and Antonio Negri. *Empire.* Cambridge: Harvard University Press, 2000.

Heath, Chris. "Bret Easton Ellis." *Rolling Stone* 802/803 (1998–1999). Web. 20 Aug. 2009.

Helyer, Ruth. "Parodied to Death: The Postmodern Gothic of *American Psycho*." *Modern Fiction Studies* 46.3 (2000): 725–46.

Highsmith, Patricia. *The Talented Mr. Ripley.* New York: Coward-McCann, Inc., 1955.

Holt, Karen and Charlotte Abbott. "*Lunar Park*: The Novel." *Publishers Weekly* 252.27 (2005): 22–23.

Horace. *Ars Poetica.* Composed c. 20 B.C. *Horace's Satires and Epistles.* Tr. Jacob Fuchs. New York: W. W. Norton, 1977.

Houen, Alex. "Novel spaces and taking place(s) in the wake of September 11." *Studies in the Novel* 36.3 (2004): 419–37.

Howard, Gerald. "Mistah Perkins – He Dead: Publishing Today." *American Scholar* 58.3 (1989): 56–72.

Hume, Kathryn. *American Dream American Nightmare: Fiction Since 1960.* Chicago: University of Illinois Press, 2000.

Hutchings, Peter. "Violence, Censorship and the Law." *Cardozo Studies in Law and Literature* 6.2 (1994): 203–24.

Irving, John. "Pornography and the New Puritans." *New York Times Book Review* 29 Mar 1992. *ProQuest Historical Newspapers.* Web. 29 June 2009.

James, Henry. "The Turn of the Screw." 1898. Mineola, NY: Dover, 1991.

——. *The Ambassadors.* New York: Methuen, 1903.

Joyce, James. *Dubliners.* 1914. New York: Oxford University Press, 1967.

——. *Ulysses.* 1922. Oxford: Oxford University Press, 1993.

"Just Look Like One." *Law and Order: Special Victims Unit: The First Year.* 4 Oct 1999. Universal, 2005. DVD.

Kattenbelt, Chiel. "Theatre as the Art of the Performer and the Stage of Intermediality." Chapple and Kattenbelt 29–39.

Kauffman, Linda S. *Bad Girls and Sick Boys: Fantasies in Contemporary Art and Culture.* London: University of California Press, 1998.

Kay, Shara R. and Jonathan S. Paul. "Don't Be an Asshole." *The Harvard Crimson Magazine* 18 Feb 1999. Web. 20 Aug. 2009.

Kellner, Douglas. "*The X-Files* and Conspiracy: A Diagnostic Critique." Knight, *Conspiracy Nation* 205–32.

Klein, Naomi. *No Logo: Taking Aim at the Brand Bullies.* London: HarperCollins, 1999.

Knight, Peter, ed. *Conspiracy Culture: From Kennedy to the X-Files.* London: Routledge, 2000.

——. *Conspiracy Nation: The Politics of Paranoia in Postwar America.* New York: NYU Press, 2002.

Kristeva, Julia. *Desire in Language: A Semiotic Approach to Literature and Art.* Ed. Leon S Roudiez. New York: Columbia UP, 1980.

Lacan, Jacques. *The Seminar of Jacques Lacan, Book III: The Psychoses, 1955–1956.* 1981. Ed. Jacques-Alain Miller. Trans. Russell Grigg. New York: Norton, 1993.

——. "L'instance de la lettre dans l'inconscient ou la raison depuis Freud." *La psychanalyse* 3 (1957): 47–81. Rpt. *Écrits*. Le Champ Freudien. Series directed by Jacques Lacan. Paris: Éditions de Seuil, 1966. 493–528.

——. "Subversion du sujet et dialectique du désir dans l'inconscient freudien." Congrès de Royaumont, Les Colloques philosophiques internationaux, 19–23 Sept 1960. *Écrits*. Le Champ Freudien. Series directed by Jacques Lacan. Paris: Éditions de Seuil, 1966. 793–827.

——. *Écrits: A Selection*. 1966. Trans. Bruce Fink. New York: Norton, 2006. 31–106.

Lanser, Susan. "The 'I' of the Beholder: Equivocal Attachments and the Limits of Structuralist Narratology." Phelan and Rabinowitz 206–19.

Lehmann-Haupt, Chistopher. "'Psycho': Whither Death Without Life?" *New York Times* 11 March 1991. ProQuest Historical Newspapers. Web. 29 June 2009.

Lejeune, Phillippe. *On Autobiography*. Trans. Catherine Leary. Minnesota: University of Minnesota Press, 1989. Trans. of *Le pacte autobiographique*. Paris: Seuil, 1975.

Lentricchia, Frank and Jody McAuliffe. *Crimes of Art and Terror*. Chicago: University of Chicago Press, 2003.

LeRoy, J. T. *The Heart is Deceitful Above All Things*. New York: Bloomsbury, 2001.

Love, Robert. "Psycho analysis." *Rolling Stone* 601 (4 April 1991): 45–46, 49–51.

Lyotard, Jean-François. *The Postmodern Condition: A Report on Knowledge*. Trans. Geoff Bennington and Brian Massumi. Theory and History of Literature, Vol. 10. Minneapolis: University of Minnesota Press, 1984. Trans. of *La condition post-moderne: rapport sur le savoir*. Paris: Éditions de Minuit, 1979.

Lyotard, Jean-François, and Jean-Loup Thébaud. *Just Gaming*. Trans. Wlad Godzich. Theory and History of Literature, Vol. 20. Minneapolis: University of Minnesota Press, 1985. Trans. of *Au juste*. Paris: Christian Bourgois, 1979.

MacDonald, Dwight. *Against the American Grain: Essays on the Effects of Mass Culture*. New York: Random House, 1962.

Mailer, Norman. "Children of the Pied Piper." *Vanity Fair* 54.4 (March 1991) 154–59, 220–21.

The Manchurian Candidate. Dir. John Frankenheimer. United Artists, 1962. Film.

Mandel, Naomi. "'Right Here in Nowheres': *American Psycho* and Violence's Critique." Durand and Mandel 9–19.

Marshall, P. David. *Celebrity and Power: Fame and Contemporary Culture*. Minneapolis: University of Minnesota Press, 1997.

Maslin, Janet. "Books Of The Times: Coaxed Down the Rabbit Hole With Bret or 'Bret'." *New York Times* 8 Aug (2005): 8.

McHale, Brian. *Postmodernist Fiction*. Routledge: London and New York, 1987.

Mendelsohn, Daniel. "Lesser Than Zero." *New York Times Book Review* 24 Jan (1999): 8.

Messier, Vartan. "Violence, Pornography, and Voyeurism as Transgression in Bret Easton Ellis' *American Psycho*." *Atenea* 24.1 (2004–06): 73–93.

Michaels, Walter Benn. "Empires of the Senseless: (The Response to) Terror and (the End of) History." *Radical History Review* 85 (2003): 105–13.

"Mission Statement." http://www.details.com. Condé Nast. 16 Dec 2008. Web. 3 Dec 2010.

Moran, Joe. *Star Authors: Literary Celebrity in America.* London: Pluto, 2000.

Murphet, Julian. *Bret Easton Ellis's* American Psycho: *A Reader's Guide.* New York: Continuum, 2002.

National Organization for Women. Resolution. *Library Journal* 2.91 (1991): 114.

Natoli, Joseph and Linda Hutcheon, eds. *A Postmodern Reader.* New York: SUNY Press, 1993.

Nielsen, Henrik Skov. "The Impersonal Voice in First-Person Narrative Fiction." *Narrative* 12.2 (2004): 133–50.

——. "Telling Doubles and Literal-Minded Reading in Bret Easton Ellis's *Glamorama.*" Durand and Mandel 20–30.

A Nightmare on Elm Street. Dir. Wes Craven. New Line Cinema, 1984. Film.

Orr, Deborah. "Comment: We Once Applauded This." www.independent.co.uk. The Independent. 23 April 1999. Web. 3 August 2009.

Pennachia Punzi, Maddalena. *Literary Intermediality: The Transit of Literature through the Media Circuit.* Bern: Peter Lang, 2007.

Petersen, Per Serritslev. "9/11 and the 'Problem of Imagination': *Fight Club* and *Glamorama* as Terrorist Pretexts." *Orbis Litterarum* 60 (2005): 133–44.

Phelan, James and Peter Rabinowitz. *A Companion to Narrative Theory.* Malden: Blackwell, 2005.

Phillips, Adam. "Remember Me." *London Review of Books* 1 Dec (2005): 19–20.

Poe, Edgar Allan. "The Tell-Tale Heart." 1843. *The Best of Poe: The Tell-Tale Heart, The Raven, The Cask of Amontillado, and 30 Others.* Delaware: Prestwick, 2006.

Prosser, Jay. *American Fiction of the 1990s: Reflections of History and Culture.* London: Routledge, 2008.

Punter, David. "e-textuality: Authenticity after the Postmodern." *Critical Quarterly* 43. 2 (2001): 68–91.

Pyrhonen, Heta. *Mayhem and Murder: Narrative and Moral Problems in the Detective Story.* University of Toronto Press, 1999.

Rabb, Jefferson. "Bret Easton Ellis: Official website." *2brets.com.* Random House. Web. 2 July 2009. <http://www.randomhouse.com/kvpa/eastonellis/>

Rajewsky, Irina O. "Intermediality, Intertextuality and Remediation: A Literary Perspective on Intermediality." *Intermédialités* 6 (2005): 43–64.

Ratcliff, Carter. "Dandyism and Abstraction in a Universe Defined by Newton." Fillin-Yeh, *Dandies* 101–27.

Rein, Irving, Philip Kotler, Michael Hamlin, and Martin Stoller. *High Visibility: Transforming Your Personal and Professional Brand.* 3rd edn. New York: McGraw Hill, 2006.

Rimmon-Kenan, Shlomith. *Narrative Fiction: Contemporary Poetics.* London: Methuen, 1983.

Rosenblatt, Roger. "Snuff This Book! Will Bret Easton Ellis Get Away With Murder?" *New York Times Book Review* 16 Dec 1990: 3, 16.

Rushkoff, Douglas. *The GenX Reader*. New York: Ballantine, 1994.

Russell, Dana E. H., Ed. *Making Violence Sexy: Feminist Views on Pornography*. New York: Teachers College Press, 1993.

Ryan, Marie-Laure. "Postmodernism and the Doctrine of Panfictionality." *Narrative* 5.2 (1997): 165–87.

Sacks, Peter. *Generation X Goes to College: An Eye-Opening Account of Teaching In Postmodern America*. Chicago: Carus, 1996.

Sahlin, Nicki. " 'But This Road Doesn't Go Anywhere': The Existential Dilemma in *Less Than Zero*." *Critique* 33.1 (1991): 23–42.

Salinger, J.D. *The Catcher in the Rye*. 1951. New York: Bantam, 1979.

Scanlan, Margaret. *Plotting Terror: Novelists and Terrorists in Contemporary Fiction*. Charlottesville: University of Virginia Press, 2001.

Scarry, Elaine. *The Body in Pain: The Making and Unmaking of the World*. Oxford: Oxford University Press, 1985.

Schmid, David. *Natural-Born Celebrities: Serial Killing in American Culture*. Chicago: University of Chicago Press, 2005.

Schoene, Berthold. "Serial Masculinity: Psychopathology and Oedipal Violence in Bret Easton Ellis's *American Psycho*." *Modern Fiction Studies* 54.2 (2008): 378–97.

Schneider, Steven Jay. " 'I guess I'm a pretty sick guy': Reconciling Remorse in *Thérèse Raquin* and *American Psycho*." *Excavatio* 17.1–2 (2002): 421–32.

Scott, A. O. "*Lunar Park*: Hero and Heroin." *Nytimes.com*. The New York Times 14 Aug 2005. Web. 30 July 2009.

"Scrapings." *The Economist* 6 Aug 2005: 69.

Seltzer, Mark. *True Crime: Observations on Violence and Modernity*. New York: Routledge, 2007.

Shakespeare, William. *All's Well that Ends Well*. *The Riverside Shakespeare*. G. Blakemore Evans, ed. Boston: Houghton Mifflin Co., 1974.

——. *Hamlet*. *The Riverside Shakespeare*. G. Blakemore Evans, ed. Boston: Houghton Mifflin Co., 1974.

——. *Romeo and Juliet*. *The Riverside Shakespeare*. G. Blakemore Evans, ed. Boston: Houghton Mifflin Co., 1974.

Shaviro, Steven. *Connected, or What It Means to Live in the Network Society*. Minneapolis: University of Minnesota Press, 2003.

——. "Lunar Park." *The Pinocchio Theory*. http://www.shaviro.com. 29 Aug 2005. Web. 29 June 2009.

Shklovsky, Victor. "Art as Technique." 1917. Trans. Lee T. Lemon and Marion J. Reis. Adams 751–59.

Sidney, Sir Philip. *An Apology for Poetry* or *The Defence of Poesy*. 1595. *An Apology for Poetry*. Ed. Geoffrey Shepherd. Manchester: Manchester University Press, 1965. 3rd edn. rev. and ed. R. W. Maslen. Manchester: Manchester University Press, 2002.

Siegle, Robert. *Suburban Ambush: Downtown Writing and the Fiction of Insurgency*. Baltimore: Johns Hopkins University Press, 1989.

The Silence of the Lambs. Dir. Jonathan Demme. Orion, 1991. Film.

Sophocles. *Oedipus Rex*. c. 429 B.C. Sir George Young, trans. Mineola, NY: Dover, 1991.

Stephenson, William. "'A Terrorism of the Rich': Symbolic Violence in Bret Easton Ellis's *Glamorama* and J. G. Ballard's *Super-Cannes*." *Critique* 48.3 (2007): 278–93.

Story, Mark. "'And as things fall apart': The Crisis of Postmodern Masculinity in Bret Easton Ellis's *American Psycho* and Dennis Cooper's *Frisk*." *Critique* 47.1 (2005): 57–72.

Suglia, Joseph. "Bret Easton Ellis: Escape from Utopia." *YouthQuake Magazine* 27 May 2004. N. pag. Web. 26 July 2009.

Tanner, Laura E. *Intimate Violence: Reading Rape and Torture in Twentieth-Century Fiction*. Bloomington: Indiana University Press, 1994.

This is Spinal Tap. Dir. Rob Reiner. Embassy Pictures, 1984. Film.

Tighe, Carl. *Writing and Responsibility*. New York: Routledge, 2005.

Tinberg, Scott. "Reassessments; The Gen X poster boy's endless ennui." *Los Angeles Times*. Los Angeles Times 23 March 2008. Web. 18 May 2008.

Toal, Drew. "Uh, excuse me. I was informed that there would be vampires in this film." *Time Out New York* 708 Apr 23–29 (2009). *Newyork.timeout.com*. New York Time Out. Web. 13 Sept 2009.

Todorov, Tzvetan. *The Fantastic: A Structural Approach to a Literary Genre*. 1970. Trans. Richard Howard. New York: Cornell University Press, 1990.

Turner, Graeme, Frances Bonner, and P. David Marshall. *Fame Games: the Production of Celebrity in Australia*. Melbourne: Cambridge University Press, 2000.

Tyrnauer, Matthew. "Who's afraid of Bret Easton Ellis?" *Vanity Fair* 57.8 (1994): 70–73, 100–01.

"Ward, Victor." *victorwardmodel*. www.geocities.com. Yahoo! N.d. Web. 9 Sept 2009.

——. victorward. www.myspace.com. N.d. Web. 9 Sept 2009.

Wernick, Andrew. *Promotional Culture: Advertising Ideology and Symbolic Expression*. London: Sage, 1991.

Wilde, Oscar. *The Picture of Dorian Gray*. 1890. New York: Random House, 1998.

Wolf, Naomi. *The Beauty Myth*. New York: W. Morrow, 1991.

Woods, Angela. "'I *am* the Fucking Reaper': *Glamorama*, Schizophrenia, Terrorism." *Colloquy: Text, Theory, Critique* 8 (2004): N. pag. Monash University. May 2004. Web. 21 Sept 2009.

Wyatt, Edward. "The Man in the Mirror. *Nytimes.com*. The New York Times 7 Aug 2005. Web. 21 Sept 2009.

The X-Files. Created by Chris Carter. Fox Broadcasting Company. Sept 1993–May 2002. Television.

Young, Elizabeth and Graham Caveney. *Shopping in Space: Essays on America's Blank Generation Fiction*. London: Serpent's Tail, 1992.

Žižek, Slavoj. *The Sublime Object of Ideology*. London: Verso, 1995.

——. "Welcome to the Desert of the Real!" *The South Atlantic Quarterly* 101.2 (2002): 385–89.

——. *Welcome to the Desert of the Real!: Five Essays on September 11 and Related Dates*. New York: Verso, 2002.

——. *Violence: Six Sideways Reflections*. London: Profile Books, 2008.

Further Reading

Works on Ellis

The following essays offer a range of critical approaches to the novels discussed in this volume. Their inclusion in this section reflects the central role each has played in subsequent critical work on Ellis in general and on each novel in particular. Freccero offers a nuanced reflection on the cultural context *American Psycho* entered into and the nature of the novel's engagement with it, and Young's reading of the novel has proved seminal for scholars. Mandel's essay offers an example of how both the novel and the controversy provide fruitful ground for critical and philosophical investigation. The essays on *Glamorama* reflect that novel's triparte relevance to studies of media (Ayers), terrorism (Woods), and narrative (Nielsen). *Lunar Park* has not yet been the subject of much scholarly work, but Shaviro's and Phillips's essays have set the stage for critical reflection on the novel.

Ayers, Sheli. "*Glamorama* Vanitas: Bret Easton Ellis's Postmodern Allegory." *Postmodern Culture* 11.1 (2000): N. pag. Web. 26 July 2009.

Freccero, Carla. "Historical Violence, Censorship, and the Serial Killer: The Case of *American Psycho*." *Diacritics* 27.2 (1997): 44–58.

Mandel, Naomi. "'Right Here in Nowheres': *American Psycho* and Violence's Critique." *Novels of the Contemporary Extreme*. Ed. Alain-Philippe Durand and Naomi Mandel. London: Continuum, 2006. 9–19.

Nielsen, Henrik Skov. "Telling Doubles and Literal-Minded Reading in Bret Easton Ellis's *Glamorama*." Durand and Mandel 20–30.

Phillips, Adam. "Remember Me." *London Review of Books* 1 Dec (2005): 19–20.

Shaviro, Steven. "Lunar Park." *The Pinocchio Theory*. http://www.shaviro.com. 29 Aug 2005. Web. 29 June 2009.

Woods, Angela. "'I *am* the Fucking Reaper': *Glamorama*, Schizophrenia, Terrorism." *Colloquy: Text, Theory, Critique* 8 (2004). Monash University. May 2004. Web. 21 Sept. 2009.

Young, Elizabeth. "The Beast in the Jungle, the Figure in the Carpet." Young and Caveney, eds. *Shopping in Space*. Boston: Atlantic Monthly Press, 1992. 85–129.

The *American Psycho* Controversy

The controversy around the publication of *American Psycho* has proved crucial for subsequent work on Ellis, and readers who wish to focus on the controversy in particular may be guided by the texts in this section. Murphet provides an extensive account of the events surrounding the publication of *American Psycho* and mounts a spirited defense of that novel. Eberly outlines the parameters of the debate and usefully situates the controversy within a historical and literary context. Love offers a lively description of the controversy and interviews Ellis on its aftermath.

Eberly, Rosa. *Citizen Critics: Literary Public Spheres*. Urbana: University of Illinois Press, 2000.
Love, Robert. "Psycho analysis." *Rolling Stone* 601 (4 April 1991): 45–6, 49–51.
Murphet, Julian. *Bret Easton Ellis's* American Psycho: *A Reader's Guide*. New York: Continuum, 2002.

Works on the Period

The following books offer an overview of the literary and cultural context in which Ellis's novels appear. Annesley and Young and Caveney set Ellis's work in dialogue with that of other US writers of the period and within the tradition of "Blank Fiction." "U.S. Literature: Blank Fiction," an online bibliography, is a valuable source of scholarship on Blank Fiction, including that of Ellis. Delvaux, Rushkoff, and Ellis's own essay articulate the ethos of Ellis's generation. Chamberlain and Grassian address Generation X specifically, from both a cultural and a literary perspective. Durand and Mandel situate Ellis's work in a broader international context, as a manifestation of the phenomenon of contemporary extreme literature.

Annesley, James. *Blank Fictions: Consumerism, Culture and the Contemporary American Novel*. London: Pluto, 1998.
Chamberlain, Lisa. *Slackonomics: Generation X in the Age of Creative Destruction*. Cambridge, MA: Da Capo Press, 2008.
Contemporary Narrative in English Research Group. "U.S. Literature: Blank Fiction." http://cne.literatureresearch.net/. University of Zaragosa. N.d. Web. 28 Sept. 2009.
Delvaux, Martine. "The Exit of a Generation: the 'Whatever' Philosophy." *The Midwest Quarterly* 40.2 (1999): 171–86.

Durand, Alain-Philippe Durand and Naomi Mandel, eds. *Novels of the Contemporary Extreme*. London: Continuum, 2006.

Ellis, Bret Easton. "The Twenty-somethings: Adrift in a Pop Landscape." *The New York Times* 2 Dec (2001): H1, 37.

Grassian Daniel. *Hybrid fictions: American literature and Generation X*. Jefferson: McFarland & Company, 2003.

Rushkoff, Douglas. *The GenX Reader*. New York: Ballantine. 1994.

Young, Elizabeth and Graham Caveney. *Shopping in Space: Essays on America's Blank Generation Fiction*. London: Serpent's Tail, 1992.

Other Resources

Film Adaptations of Ellis's Novels

Though reception of film adaptations of Ellis's novels has been generally lukewarm (with the possible exception of Mary Harron's *American Psycho*), film adaptations remain a useful resource for students and scholars of the author. An adaptation constitutes both a reading of a novel and a visual version of the world in which it is set.

Less Than Zero. Dir. Marek Kavievska. Twentieth Century-Fox, 1987. DVD.

American Psycho. Dir. Mary Harron. Lions Gate, 2000. DVD.

Rules of Attraction. Dir. Roger Avary. Lions Gate, 2002. DVD.

The Informers. Dir. Gregor Jordan. Senator Entertainment, 2009. DVD.

Documentaries

This is not an Exit: The Fictional World of Bret Easton Ellis. Dir. Gerald Fox. FRF, 1999. VHS.

Other Novels

The works included in this section were chosen because of a link between the author and Ellis, be that one of association or of influence. Readers are encouraged to consider them as supplemental to the primary texts referenced in the volumes included in "Works on the Period" (above).

Beigbeder, Frédéric. *£9.99*. Trans. of *99 francs*. 2000. Trans. Adriana Hunter. London: Picador, 2002

Coupland, Douglas. *Generation X: Tales for an Accelerated Culture*. New York: St. Martin's Press, 1991.

Houellebecq, Michel. *Whatever*. Trans. of *Extension du domain de la lutte*. 1994. Trans. Paul Hammond. London: Serpent's Tail, 1999.

McInerney, Jay. *Bright Lights, Big City*. New York: Vintage Books, 1984.

Palahniuk, Chuck. *Fight Club: A Novel*. New York: Henry Holt, 1997.

Tartt, Donna. *The Secret History*. New York: Knopf, 1992.

Wallace, David Foster. *Brief Interviews with Hideous Men*. Boston: Little Brown, 1999.

Notes on Contributors

James Annesley is Senior Lecturer in American Literature at Newcastle University (UK), and the author of *Blank Fictions* (1998) and *Fictions of Globalization* (2007).

Sonia Baelo-Allué is Assistant Professor of English at the Department of English and German Philology of the University of Zaragoza (Spain). She completed her Ph.D. dissertation on Bret Easton Ellis in 2007. Her publications include articles on "blank fiction" writers, intermediality, and the representation of violence in literature. Her current research centers on trauma and literature and she is coediting a volume on the subject. She is also preparing a monograph on Bret Easton Ellis. The research carried out for the writing of her chapter in this volume has been financed by the Spanish Ministry of Science and Technology (MCYT) and the European Regional Development Fund (FEDER), in collaboration with the Aragonese Government (no. HUM2007–61035/FILO).

Alex E. Blazer is Assistant Professor of English at Georgia College & State University (US) where he teaches twentieth- and twenty-first-century American literature and critical theory. He has published articles on Barrett Watten, *The Matrix* Trilogy, Bret Easton Ellis, and Chuck Palahniuk as well as a book, *"I Am Otherwise": The Relationship between Poetry and Theory after the Death of the Subject* (Dalkey Press, 2007). He is currently working on a book-length, existential and psychoanalytical study of contemporary American novels by William H. Gass, Paul Auster, Bret Easton Ellis, Chuck Palahniuk, and Mark Z. Danielewski.

Michael P. Clark is Professor of English and Vice Provost for Academic Planning at the University of California, Irvine (US). His most recent book is an edition of *The Eliot Tracts*, a collection of religious books and pamphlets written by and about colonial Puritan missionaries and their work with Native

Americans in seventeenth- and eighteenth-century New England. His other publications include articles on early American literature, witchcraft, and millennialism; books on Jacques Lacan and Michel Foucault and articles on literary theory; and articles on Vietnam and the representation of war in contemporary US society.

Elana Gomel is Senior Lecturer at the Department of English and American Studies, Tel-Aviv University (Israel). She has been a visiting scholar at Princeton, Stanford, and the University of Hong Kong. She is the author of three books: *Bloodscripts: Writing the Violent Subject* (Ohio State University Press, 2003); *We and You: Being a Russian in Israel* (Kineret, 2006); *The Pilgrim Soul* (Cambria, 2009), and many articles, on topics ranging from science fiction to narrative theory, from the poetics of evolution to the Victorian novel. Her new book, *Postmodern Science Fiction and the Temporal Imagination*, is forthcoming from Continuum.

Jeff Karnicky is Assistant Professor of English at Drake University (US). He is the author of *Contemporary Fiction and the Ethics of Modern Culture* (Palgrave-Macmillan, 2007), which argues for the ethical relevance of contemporary fiction by writers such as David Foster Wallace and Richard Powers. He has also published articles on Don DeLillo, Irvine Welsh, and on birds in contemporary America. His current research focuses on human interactions with birds, from both a cognitive and environmental perspective. He thanks the following: the Center for the Humanities at Drake University who provided a grant to help complete this essay; Megan Brown, Marco Abel, and Jeff Nealon for discussions of Bret Easton Ellis; Naomi Mandel for her excellent editing.

Naomi Mandel is Associate Professor of English and Comparative Literature at University of Rhode Island (US). She is the author of *Against the Unspeakable: Complicity, the Holocaust, and Slavery in America* (University of Virginia Press, 2006) and coeditor, with Alain-Philippe Durand, of *Novels of the Contemporary Extreme* (Continuum, 2006). She is currently working on a book-length project that explores the relation between violence and reality in contemporary fiction.

Henrik Skov Nielsen is Associate Professor and Director of Studies at Scandinavian Institute, University of Aarhus (Denmark). He is the author of articles and books in Danish on narratology and literary theory, including his dissertation on digression and first-person narrative fiction, *Tertium datur— on literature or on what is not*. His publications in English include articles on psychoanalysis, Edgar Allan Poe, Extreme Narration and an article on first-person narrative fiction, "The Impersonal Voice in First-Person Narrative Fiction" in *Narrative* 12. 2 (2004). A recent article, "Colonised Thinking," on the US influence on the humanities in Europe was published in *Oxford Literary Review*, 2008. He is the editor of a series of anthologies on literary theory, and is currently working on a narratological research project on the relationship between authors and narrators, with an article, "Natural Authors, Unnatural

Narration," forthcoming in Alber and Fludernik, *Postclassical Narratology*. He wishes to thank Naomi Mandel for her comments on earlier drafts of this paper and her many inspiring suggestions.

Arthur Redding is Associate Professor and Chair of the English Department at York University in Toronto (Canada). He has written about various American literary and cultural figures, from Emma Goldman to Kathy Acker. *Turncoats, Traitors, and Fellow Travelers: Culture and Politics of the Early Cold War* (Mississippi) appeared in 2008 and *Raids on Human Consciousness: Writing, Anarchism, and Violence* (South Carolina) in 1998. He is currently completing two manuscripts: one on ghosts and the gothic in contemporary US literature and a second on American public intellectuals. He thanks Jared Morrow for research assistance and Naomi Mandel for her generous editorial guidance.

David Schmid is Associate Professor in the Department of English at the University at Buffalo (US), where he teaches courses in British and American fiction, cultural studies, and popular culture. He has published on a variety of subjects, including the nonfiction novel, celebrity, film adaptation, *Dracula*, and crime fiction and he is the author of *Natural Born Celebrities: Serial Killers in American Culture*, published by the University of Chicago Press in 2005. He is currently working on two book-length projects: *From the Locked Room to the Globe: Space in Crime Fiction* and *Murder Culture: Why Americans are Obsessed by Homicide*.

Index